Distribution Revolution

Distribution Revolution

*Conversations about the Digital Future
of Film and Television*

Edited by

MICHAEL CURTIN, JENNIFER HOLT,
AND KEVIN SANSON

With a Foreword by Kurt Sutter

University of California Press

University of California Press, one of the most distinguished university presses in the United States, enriches lives around the world by advancing scholarship in the humanities, social sciences, and natural sciences. Its activities are supported by the UC Press Foundation and by philanthropic contributions from individuals and institutions. For more information, visit www.ucpress.edu.

University of California Press
Oakland, California

CWC
CARSEY-WOLF CENTER
UNIVERSITY OF CALIFORNIA, SANTA BARBARA

Library of Congress Cataloging-in-Publication Data

Distribution revolution : conversations about the digital future of film and television / edited by Michael Curtin, Jennifer Holt, and Kevin Sanson ; foreword by Kurt Sutter.
    pages cm
  ISBN 978-0-520-28324-4 (hardback)
  ISBN 978-0-520-28325-1 (paperback)
  1. Motion pictures—Marketing   2. Motion pictures—Distribution.   3. Television programs—Marketing.   4. Television broadcasting.   5. Digital media—Influence.   6. Chief executive officers—United States—Interviews.   7. Motion picture producers and directors—United States—Interviews.   8. Television producers and directors—United States—Interviews.   I. Curtin, Michael, editor of compilation.   II. Holt, Jennifer, 1968–editor of compilation.   III. Sanson, Kevin, editor of compilation.
  PN1995.9.M29D58 2014
  384'.84—dc23

                                                     2014003241

Manufactured in the United States of America

23 22 21 20 19 18 17 16 15 14
10 9 8 7 6 5 4 3 2 1

In keeping with a commitment to support environmentally responsible and sustainable printing practices, UC Press has printed this book on Natures Natural, a fiber that contains 30% post-consumer waste and meets the minimum requirements of ANSI/NISO Z39.48-1992 (R 1997) (Permanence of Paper).

Contents

Foreword

 kurt sutter ✔
@sutterink
Digital delivery of film and television, like most hasty births, has been clumsy, painful, and at times bloody.

 kurt sutter ✔
@sutterink
But once the schmutz is wiped off, the cord cut, and the baby's mouth wrapped around a teat, one can appreciate and marvel at the new life.

 kurt sutter ✔
@sutterink
I know being a male and a failed gentile, I have no right using child-birth as a metaphor or the word "schmutz" in a sentence.

 kurt sutter ✔
@sutterink
But curbing impulses—not necessarily my strong suit. Like the digital new age, I can be entertaining, unpredictable, and a bit scary.

 kurt sutter ✔
@sutterink
I believe DD is the future of film/TV. In the not-too-distant yet-to-come, there won't be programming, just content & distribution. And porn.

kurt sutter ✅
@sutterink

And like all things that change an industry, with great power comes the need for thoughtful reflection, fiscal and ethical responsibility.

 kurt sutter ✅
@sutterink

But this is Hollywood, so with great power usually just comes a better table at Toscana. Responsibility and ethics are for the S&P folks.

 kurt sutter ✅
@sutterink

Perhaps that's a bit jaded. But the truth is, fear is always the first response to change. No one knows how DD will look in 2, 5, 10 years.

 kurt sutter ✅
@sutterink

We speculate, create, react, adjust. That's the equation at play now: forecasts + $$$ = startups + consumer whims + regulation = confusion.

 kurt sutter ✅
@sutterink

"Distribution Revolution" helps make sense of the mayhem. All we can do is keep the discussion going. That's what these professionals do.

 kurt sutter ✅
@sutterink

From the studio to the lab, this book takes a thorough look at the incestuous and inevitable relationship between tech and entertainment.

 kurt sutter ✅
@sutterink

So, buy the book and read it, bitches.

Acknowledgments

First and foremost, we thank the Carsey-Wolf Center at the University of California, Santa Barbara for the institutional support that helped make the interviews in this book possible. A number of individuals deserve special recognition, most notably Constance Penley, Ronald E. Rice, Richard Hutton, and Nicole Klanfer. Members of the Carsey-Wolf Center Advisory Board facilitated introductions and access. We are grateful for the enthusiasm they all have demonstrated for the interview initiative and our other research endeavors at the Media Industries Project (MIP).

Joshua Green provided keen leadership in this project's earliest stages. Ethan Tussey and John Vanderhoef aided us with indispensable research assistance. Likewise, we thank Rebecca Epstein and Erin Lennon for their copyediting skills and Lorena Thompkins for her transcription services. Isabelle Carasso deserves credit for the initial concept behind our cover design.

At the University of California Press, Mary C. Francis and Kim Hogeland masterfully guided this book through the publishing process (and did so, we might add, at breakneck speed). We thank them for their stewardship.

Last, but certainly not least, we are indebted to the industry personnel who spoke to us at length about the digital future of film and television. We hope they find this book a testament to the productive potential of such critical conversations between media professionals and academic researchers. Such collaboration has been a hallmark of Marcy Carsey's and Dick Wolf's vision for MIP since its inception in 2009. We thank them sincerely for their enthusiastic and unstinting support.

Introduction

Making of a Revolution

Michael Curtin, Jennifer Holt, and Kevin Sanson

In the past five years, the scramble to manage the digital future of film and television has sparked both turmoil and transformation, forcing industry leaders to reconsider established maxims about how screen media are created, circulated, and consumed. We see it almost every day in the headlines of trade papers and the mainstream press. For example, the 2007 Writers Guild strike hinged on payments and residuals for network and cable television content being streamed online. After a long and bitter conflict, the writers finally settled when the studios agreed to pay them more for digitally distributed work. Although the strike was costly for all concerned, the writers seemed to understand that a new era was dawning. Not only were digital platforms recycling content from other media, they also were becoming original creative forces in the entertainment industry.

Netflix is perhaps the most obvious example. In 2013, the leading subscription video-on-demand (SVOD) service surprised its cable and network counterparts with prominent Emmy nominations for original productions such as *Arrested Development* and *House of Cards*. Netflix says more original content is on the way. Meanwhile, Amazon and Hulu are rolling out their own programming. For now, these new shows look much like their broadcast and cable peers, but the programmers at the major SVOD services say that they don't need to play the ratings game and that they're aiming to break the mold with new approaches. Inflated rhetoric perhaps, but they have already proven that they are willing to leave tradition behind by releasing an entire season's worth of original episodes all at once, which has film and television companies abuzz with speculation about further innovations on the horizon.

Of course the major media conglomerates have their own plans for the digital future. That became clear when Kevin Tsujihara was tapped to take charge of Warner Bros.' legendary Burbank studios, marking the first time a studio head was chosen from the home entertainment division, a unit that is now laser-focused on digital innovations. Remarkably, Jeff Bewkes, Time Warner's CEO, passed over his film and TV studio chiefs for the post, raising eyebrows throughout the Hollywood community and likely signaling that he no longer considers digital delivery simply an ancillary aftermarket.

When looking to understand the current tumult in the media landscape, it is therefore clear that distribution networks and technologies are where the seeds of transformation have been sown. Indeed, screen media distribution has undergone a veritable revolution in the twenty-first century, overthrowing institutional relationships, cultural hierarchies, and conventional business models. These transformations are largely due to the fact that the distribution business has long been the linchpin of Hollywood's creative strategies and financial success. Since the early days of the major studios, distributors have relied on a sequential release pattern, or "windowing," to fully exploit the value of the content they control. By making content available in different markets for discreet periods of time, distributors have been able to wring the most revenue out of each market without sales from one window (e.g., digital video disc [DVD] sales) "cannibalizing" the profits from another (e.g., domestic theatrical exhibition). Yet widespread technological innovations have made traditional strategies look obsolete and betray the urgent need to refine the complicated calculus of windowing in the digital era. As content proliferates across screens of all sizes, the expansion of digital delivery platforms and cloud-based storage technologies has transformed when, where, and how consumers engage with entertainment. Armed with high bandwidth and a bevy of connected gadgets, audiences expect "anytime, anywhere" access, even if it requires them to turn to unauthorized means, such as peer-to-peer (P2P) file-sharing networks, to get it. Ultimately, the conversations in this book map a wide range of concerns about the digital ecosystem but nevertheless draw similar conclusions: major film and television companies must radically realign their business models around fresh modes of delivery or risk losing their audiences to a host of new rivals in the digital space.

Currently, the most innovative and successful competitors include Amazon, Apple, and Netflix, all of whom exist somewhere between the dream factories of Hollywood and the high-tech entrepreneurialism of Silicon Valley. These companies are formidable contenders for the time and attention of audiences, yet their increasing popularity has prompted content providers to view them as uneasy allies. Likewise, many third-party app developers—whose business models rest on their abilities to deliver programming to tablets and mobile devices—continue to feed the rapacious appetite for screen media wherever and whenever consumers want it. As a result, audiences are more fragmented than ever, and some even express frustration with what seems like too many choices from too many platforms and services. Still, digital alternatives are gaining steam and are widely seen as the most important drivers of economic growth. This poses a key challenge for the major Hollywood studios: How do they monetize the digital space without jeopardizing long-standing (and quite lucrative) relationships with exhibitors, advertisers, and cable operators?

Despite all of the "disruptive" innovations, most of the money being made today in film and television is still being made the old-fashioned way: in theaters, from ads on linear television, or from syndication deals. As such, some eyeballs are simply more important than others. For example, broadcast and cable television viewers continue to command exponentially higher advertising rates than those who view content on computers and mobile screens. At the same time, profound changes are taking place as taste-based algorithms and other emergent audience metrics are beginning to challenge traditional measurement techniques and undermine the premium prices charged for conventional TV advertising. Audience engagement, rather than size, is the current zeitgeist, but no one knows for sure how to quantify it. In this context, social media has emerged as an extremely important marketing and promotional tool, particularly because of the way it builds online communities around particular content brands. This, in turn, has attracted the attention of content providers, advertisers, and creators. Yet the digital brand experience for online audiences still has a long way to go, and producers feel pressed to tinker endlessly with new techniques for generating buzz via social media. Unfortunately, this means that the creative workforce—especially writers and directors—often bears the brunt of this additional labor. Producing content for websites, social media pages, and other interactive ventures rarely replaces traditional workplace routines; instead, it has become the "second shift" of the digital era, putting extra demands on the time and energy of creative talent without offering additional compensation.

In light of these developments, there has been some experimentation by mainstream media, but studios, cable companies, and broadcast networks nevertheless hesitate to transform their existing business models in any substantial way. Cloud-based "TV Everywhere" services such as Comcast's Xfinity or HBO Go are prime examples, as they seem to address common desires for anytime, anywhere access to television content on laptops and other mobile devices. But they do so only on the industry's terms—that is, anytime, anywhere access is no substitute for a cable subscription; rather, it requires one. Similarly, studio-based content providers are developing their own digital platforms, such as Crackle or NBC.com, and also cooperating on collaborative ventures such as the digital storage locker UltraViolet. Yet consumers seem to perceive these branded destinations as walled gardens, and therefore none of these initiatives has generated the same degree of enthusiasm as the new breed of "upstarts," such as Netflix or Voddler.

Furthermore, the major studios and networks remain unsure about which pricing structures and payment systems are most appropriate in the digital space. Movie studio experiments with premium video-on-demand (VOD) releases have provoked negative reactions from theater owners who worry that this practice eats into ticket sales. Similarly, the never-ending cry from consumer advocates for à la carte cable TV pricing options has done little to break up bundled channel packages. These examples suggest a fundamental confusion over how best to value content and audiences in the digital era. And yet the ultimate determination of those values affects everything from licensing fees and global trade to compensation for below-the-line labor and the nature of competition.

Taken together, this revolution is defined by debates over the value of content, the behavior of audiences, and the creation of frictionless, user-friendly access. Each of these issues is tied to questions of agency and power. Who will be the ultimate winners? That will partially depend on the sustainability of legacy business models and the adaptability of industry leaders. Further consideration must be given to independent distribution platforms and Internet service providers (ISPs), which manage the "pipes" that deliver digital content and thus provide crucial infrastructure for this revolution. Sensing that change is in the air, some ISPs have integrated with content companies, Comcast being the most notable example. Now a sprawling conglomerate, it is the largest Internet service provider, the world's largest pay-TV provider, and the owner of NBCUniversal, among other properties. Comcast owns both content and conduits in the new digital ecosystem, thereby achieving an unprecedented measure of control over most aspects of the media environment. Exactly how much further it will be able to extend this control remains a politicized question, as its conduct falls to the scrutiny of increasingly lax government regulators who set the boundaries for acceptable conduct in a highly consolidated industry.

The digital distribution revolution is therefore a dynamic and multifaceted process, affecting almost every aspect of the film and television industries. It is changing the ways in which content is imagined, formulated, financed, produced, promoted, packaged, marketed, measured, delivered, interpreted, enjoyed, and recirculated. It is changing our ways of using media and our ways of socializing through media. The distribution revolution is therefore the subject of intense deliberation within the industry, among policy makers, and among the population at large. As these conversations unfold, it has become apparent that the seismic changes taking place today are among the most momentous in the history of modern media.

REVOLUTION REDUX

Throughout the interviews in this book, the role of "disruptive" technology is a recurring theme with both executives and creatives suggesting that technological innovation has been the driving force of change in the new millennium. Government policy and popular culture likewise portray technology as a determining force, even though technology is, by definition, an instrument, a *tool* for achieving human goals. Moreover, the public at large embraces the commonsense notion that technology is an autonomous, seemingly natural force, despite the fact that triumphant technologies throughout history have either been fostered by powerful interests or are ultimately put to work on behalf of influential elites. Scholars, on the other hand, tend to be skeptical about the singular influence of technology, preferring instead to see it as part of a broader set of social and economic forces. When they hear "The technology did it!," they usually wonder what other factors shaped that moment of change.

Given the fact that technology looms large in the conversations that follow and that the title of this book implies the centrality of digital technology as the driving force of change, it is important to explain why we see this moment through a substantially different lens. Although we do indeed believe that today the forces of change have coalesced around a cluster of new technologies, we see these innovations as part of a longer history of social, cultural, and economic transformation. That is, the digital distribution revolution emerged in part as a consequence of corporate maneuvers that stretch back almost two hundred years. Moreover, this commercial competition took place in the context of common perceptions about the role of media in society and political struggles about free expression and the public good. Technological innovation is furthermore intertwined with long-standing popular aspirations to expand and improve audience access to media entertainment. Indeed, throughout the history of electronic communication there has existed a recurring tension between institutional ambitions and popular aspirations. On the one hand, audiences and inventors dream of technological utopias, while on the other executives and regulators work to harness and exploit the latest innovations.

Consequently, our collective imagination of technological potential has always outrun technical and institutional capacities. The very idea of delivering audiovisual imagery to the home dates back to the nineteenth century; so too does the fantasy of personal portable devices. When the telegraph was first introduced in the 1840s, many Americans imagined that the cacophony of dots and dashes would someday give way to wireless handheld devices that would be available to all, putting one in touch with distant events, long-lost friends, and spectacular new forms of entertainment.[1] Likewise, at the dawn of cinema, radio, television, computing, and even telecommunications, each technology promised to upend social hierarchies and bring together a worldwide community of humankind, but each was eventually tethered to dominant institutions, becoming a source of vast profits and an instrument of political advantage.[2] It's striking that despite the seemingly relentless pace of "technological disruption" since the early 1900s, many of today's major players have been with us for much of that time: AT&T, AP, Reuters, Paramount, Fox, NBC, CBS, Time Warner, and IBM, not to mention a plethora of military institutions that developed and made extensive use of each new communication device.

As for members of the general public, they enjoyed only limited control over what, when, and where they engaged with information and entertainment. Indeed, the commercial and strategic value of media content was produced through *scarcity*, that is, the selective circulation of content. Gateways to access were in the hands of a few, and the distribution of content was strategically controlled. Even though the film and broadcast industries churned out a seemingly endless stream of novel content, much of it featured recognizable stars and genres that were delivered to particular audiences in particular locations at particular times. These "windows" of exposure were calculated to exact higher tolls from those with greater access, thereby exploiting the full profit potential of each bit of information or entertainment.[3] During the first half of the twentieth century, media institutions privileged first-run and live entertainment. Although information and entertainment were widely available, one had to attend *Gone With the Wind* during its theatrical run or listen to *The Jack Benny Show* on Sunday evenings or catch the news each night at six.

Here lay the seeds of the distribution revolution that we are experiencing today, for what we are now witnessing is the latest iteration of an ongoing tension between the diverse desires of audiences for cheap and easy access and the twentieth-century business models that sought to manage media flows and audience consumption. Today, however, media companies are competing to develop new business strategies and technologies that at once offer audiences greater access while nevertheless monetizing content as fully as possible. In this new environment, older conventions of network broadcasting compete with innovative approaches to subscription video on demand, and both compete with the relentless specter of piracy—a relatively novel audience alternative, regardless of its ethical implications. Consequently, media distribution models are moving from mass to niche and from synchronous to asynchronous, a transition driven at once by competitive forces, government regulations, and popular aspirations, as well as by technological innovation.

Some of the earliest inklings of change began during the 1950s, when the syndication of old movies and off-network reruns gave audiences a chance to break from the scarcity principles of first-run media.[4] *I Love Lucy* reruns became a pervasive and perennial fixture of television schedules worldwide. Viewers also gained access to movie studio vaults, mining the glittering appeal of Hollywood's golden age and offering new generations an expanded range of entertainment options.[5] Cable television became the next important antecedent of today's distribution revolution. When it was first introduced to the general public during the 1970s, cable's most enthusiastic proponents promised five hundred channels of novel and alternative content, but such aspirations outran capacity, since few could agree as to who would finance and develop such a system.[6] Through much of its early history, cable television offered little more than old movies and network reruns, providing simply another window for the exploitation of existing content. The range of choices nevertheless expanded, and innovative programming eventually emerged.[7] As cable television gained traction, audiences furthermore embraced remote control devices that allowed them to surf among an expanding universe of channels. With remotes in hand, they dodged commercials and restlessly flipped between programs, making television executives nervous about their waning ability to manage mass audiences.[8]

Yet even though these technologies disrupted the media economy, they matured in the midst of policy changes that helped to shore up the power of major companies. During the 1980s and 1990s, for example, the federal government responded to intensive lobbying from studios and networks to lift restrictions on the size and scope of media corporations. Top media executives argued that such changes were necessary as waves of deregulation in countries around the world opened new markets, spurring technological innovations in satellite, broadband, and computer communication. Many executives and investors contended that only the very biggest conglomerates would survive the brave new era of synergy and transnational distribution. By and large, they got their way, touching off a wave of mergers that brought producers and multichannel distributors under the roof of sprawling conglomerates.[9]

While CEOs anguished over the big picture, they also worried about changes in audience behaviors. The home videocassette recorder (VCR), an innovation pioneered by Japanese electronics manufacturers, allowed audiences to record, share, and time shift their viewing of favorite movies and television shows. It also allowed them to zip through shows and zap commercials, challenging the fundamental principles of film and television distribution in the United States. This seemingly technological disruption was actually touched off by competitive conditions in the electronics industry. By the 1970s, Japanese firms were the world's leading producers and exporters of radio and television sets, but these core markets were becoming saturated and profit margins were shrinking. Some companies sensed that personalization was the way forward, sparking the development of the audiocassette recorder, the portable cassette player (Walkman), and the VCR. Sony Corporation, one of the principal innovators, was motivated largely by competitive conditions in Japan and by the increasingly globalized market for consumer electronics. The resulting technologies proved profoundly disruptive to American media companies, but the actual driver of change came from the activities in hardware industries abroad.[10]

Other forces were at work as well. The field of telecommunications was at the same time being deregulated, unleashing a host of hungry new competitors and spurring new frontiers of technological innovation. Audiovisual signals were digitized, compressed, and multiplexed, thereby enhancing the speed and volume of delivery. Error correction software improved the quality and reliability of signals, eliminating static and enhancing fidelity. During the mid-1990s, these technologies suddenly made it possible for satellite transponders to carry eight times as many channels as before. Optical broadband likewise expanded the carrying capacity of terrestrial and transoceanic cables. As capacity grew, ferocious price wars began that would ultimately topple some of the biggest telecommunications competitors. This proved to be a boon to consumers, however, driving down prices and allowing cheaper access to telephone and computer communication. Consequently, many of the disruptive technologies that would prove crucial to the digital distribution revolution were forged in the crucible of competition among huge telecom providers operating in a newly deregulated environment.[11]

These developments proved to be "revolutionary" both because they gave consumers more control and because they helped propel the nascent globalization of media. Japanese companies became important players in American film and television; U.S. media companies expanded their satellite services abroad; and European entrepreneurs jumped at the chance to roll out new satellite and cable services in a direct challenge to the public service monopolies that prevailed in countries throughout their continent. As the distribution business became rife with opportunity and uncertainty, global competitors scrambled for control of content libraries. Sony bought Columbia Pictures in 1989; Matsushita purchased Universal shortly thereafter; and News Corp. Australia preceded them both by picking up 20th Century Fox in 1985.[12] Italian, French, German, and British media giants made similar maneuvers. These mergers, acquisitions, and alliances heralded an unprecedented transformation of media institutions and practices.

Despite such tumultuous changes, the major media companies adapted. They pushed through legislation that allowed them to grow; they loaded up their content libraries; and they locked down top talent in film, television, music, and publishing. They also responded—often reluctantly—to changes in audience behaviors by establishing business models that turned new technologies to their advantage. As VCR ownership proliferated, they developed a robust video rental business. With the evolution of DVDs, they established a lively sell-through market, allowing fans to purchase and collect favorite films and television shows.[13]

Introduced in the late 1990s, DVD players were rolled out in a far more orderly fashion than VCRs, with Hollywood studios (Sony now among them, having bought Columbia Pictures) and electronics manufacturers negotiating a set of standards that tamed the technology before it got to market. As digital discs, DVDs were far cheaper to manufacture and distribute than videotapes. Digital encoding also improved picture quality and made it easier to incorporate copy protection technologies that were energetically supported by the major media companies.[14] Royalties gushed in and DVD revenues became a source of outsized profits for film and television studios. The stock market value of media companies soared and the future seemed even brighter as the penetration of digital broadband to the home began to pick up, promising synergistic connections between various forms of information and entertainment. Such premonitions helped justify the grossly inflated value of America Online (AOL) and Time Warner when they merged in 2000. Those heady expectations were fueled in large part by passionate declarations about the revolutionary and disruptive effects of digital technologies. Left unsaid was the fact that technological innovation was now a strategic form of competition *and* collaboration among the major media companies.

In the midst of these dramatic corporate transformations, audience behaviors were changing in the home, on the street, and, increasingly, online, as media consumers (who more and more were referred to as "active users") were gaining greater access and control. Most controversial was the rapidly growing phenomenon of P2P music sharing over the Internet. In 1999, Napster captured the spirit of music fans who eagerly ripped, stored, and shared their favorite songs without paying a penny to the major music companies. Such technologies were made possible by the complex convergence of forces outlined earlier, but this took on a new dimension in the hands of a younger generation that was explicitly resentful of enduring limitations on access and what it saw as exorbitant prices. Some railed against the huge corporations that stood between performers and their fans, while others simply relished the most attractive price point of all: free. Music companies represented by the Recording Industry Association of America unleashed a torrent of lawsuits, lobbied for stricter regulations, and sought to shut down the biggest providers, but netizens developed ever more imaginative ways to turn technologies to their advantage.[15] Public debates raged over the moral and legal implications of these new behaviors, but some of the darkest dialogues took place privately among film and television executives, knowing full well that it was only a matter of time before *their* content would be shared online as well. They hoped to delay the day of reckoning by reflecting on the failures of their counterparts in the music industry. Many agreed that music executives had been too greedy, had resisted change, and had too readily taken their customers to court. When the digital distribution revolution came to film and television, they hoped it would look different. And of course they had more time to think about it because the relatively slow bit rates of the 1990s Internet made it difficult to deliver acceptable film and television programming online.

Nevertheless, as early as the mid- to late 1990s, a few small companies began to experiment with video-on-demand and online video distribution.[16] These early innovators were operating well ahead of the Internet's ability to deliver a robust range of content in a reliable and attractive manner. The web nevertheless became the basis for the extraordinary success of Netflix, which offered viewers a substantial and growing catalog of DVD movies that they could select online and receive via postal delivery. Unlike the brick-and-mortar movie rental shops that the major studios had come to embrace, Netflix offered a monthly subscription service with no late fees. It also offered the most diverse catalog of titles, largely by exploiting a legal principle that allowed it to rent DVDs without securing a licensing agreement from syndicators. Customers could browse through an immense digital catalog, build a personal list of preferred titles, and rate the quality of each film they watched. Netflix in turn used this data to make recommendations for future selections, creating a profile of each subscriber's tastes and a profile as well of each title it offered. This groundbreaking level of personalization and expanded access was, like other antecedents, a product of forces external to the film and television industries. Founded by Silicon Valley engineers, Netflix pioneered many of the principles and practices that would come to define the digital distribution revolution in the entertainment industry.[17]

The remarkable growth of Netflix and P2P services, as well as the growing penetration of broadband services in the home, sent clear signals that the film and television industries would only prosper through an affirmative response to the potential of digital distribution. Yet as late as 2003, Michael Eisner, then Disney's CEO, told a gathering of broadcasting executives that media companies remained profoundly conflicted. "Hollywood studios," he said, "spend enormous sums of money encouraging people to see their films and TV shows and then spend more money devising ways to control and limit how people can see their films and TV shows."[18] Eisner was among a growing number of executives who believed another disruptive moment was fast approaching for the motion picture business. Two years later, YouTube fulfilled that expectation, launching a streamlined, user-friendly video-sharing service that was quickly populated with unauthorized clips of popular film and television content. The company resisted legal challenges from copyright owners, saying that YouTube could not be held responsible for the various personal uses to which its services and platform were put. The argument was similar to the one that Napster used to defend itself from legal challenges, but the difference was that YouTube, as of 2006, became a division of Google, a company with extensive resources and one of the most aggressive legal teams in America.[19]

Just as frustrating for media executives was the fact that they had spent tens of millions of dollars trying to develop their own online content delivery services only to see them wither by comparison to interlopers from Silicon Valley. The emerging threat posed by YouTube was no doubt fresh in their minds when they were approached by iTunes executives seeking to license content for a video download service that they planned to launch in 2006. Disney was one of the first to sign on, followed by several other major studios and networks. Depending on the title, iTunes offered customers digital copies that they could own or rent at prices that were lower than most video stores. It was soon followed by Amazon and Netflix, with each offering similar services to their growing legions of customers. Nevertheless, iTunes dominated the commercial online video market during the early years of the digital distribution revolution. In 2008, it delivered 87 percent of online movie sales and 53 percent of online movie rentals.[20]

Innovations in online retail and rental services were then followed by an advertising-supported service launched by Hulu in 2008, a joint venture of NBCUniversal, Fox, and Disney. Although most major television networks were already streaming video content on their branded websites, Hulu signed licensing agreements with a host of content providers, becoming the first major aggregator of ad-supported programming and making it a one-stop shop for high-quality video streams of popular TV series. Hulu grew dramatically and within a year became the third most popular video destination on the Internet. But tensions arose between the partners and the executives within their respective companies. Was Fox getting a fair return on its investment? Were NBC's own websites suffering in comparison to Hulu? Would Disney be better off developing its own services that leveraged the company's distinctive brands and customer base? Licensing deals also became more expensive and complicated; some providers angled for the best deals possible, while others withheld content, favoring lucrative cable licenses and proprietary services instead. The joint-venture partners also grew restless about ad revenues, which grew quickly at first and then began to slow, forcing Hulu executives to reluctantly introduce a premium subscription tier of service in 2010 that revived revenue growth but undermined the popularity of the service with many viewers.

VOD via cable providers has also been growing more popular, as companies try to offer more instant, nonlinear programming options in hopes of holding on to customers before they become "cord cutters." The subscriber base and libraries of SVOD platforms such as Netflix and Amazon Instant Video have also seen tremendous growth as the digital distribution landscape expands. These two companies alone have done much to define the market for subscription film and television in just a few short years, with Amazon's service beginning in 2011 and Netflix going from a DVD-by-mail rental company founded in 1997 to the largest online provider of streaming film and television shows and an original content producer by 2013. In fact, while many think of Netflix as a streaming platform, the company's own website now describes itself as "the world's leading Internet television network,"[21] a label that undoubtedly disrupts whatever complacency is left at the major studios and networks and puts the rest of the industry on notice. How long before the "Internet" distinction is no longer necessary? As Bruce Rosenblum, chairman of the Academy of Television Arts and Sciences, recently said, whether people watch on a mobile device, a tablet, or a flat screen, "It's all television."[22]

These historical developments provide some larger perspective for the interviews that follow. Some lessons have indeed been learned, while others have been forgotten. Disruption or innovation, depending on one's perspective, has come with bandwidth explosion, more powerful laptops, personal mobile technologies, and the advent of cloud computing. It is indeed a revolutionary moment, perhaps because there are no inevitable outcomes, but if history offers any instructive pointers, the desires and aspirations of audiences will consistently be more expansive than—and quite often defy—industrial imperatives to control the parameters and potentials of media technologies. To that end, it behooves us all to keep an eye on how networks and creativity are managed; to monitor the effects of consolidation; and to remember that those who control distribution have for centuries had the power to define the size and scope of markets—in this case, the digital space for media entertainment. Finally, it's important to keep an eye on popular aspirations, for there is still a great deal of negotiation taking place between those who dream big about the future of digital media and the institutions that seek to tame them.

Such overarching issues animate each of the conversations in this collection, all of which were conducted as part of the Carsey-Wolf Center's Media Industries Project (MIP) at the University of California, Santa Barbara. As a dedicated scholarly research program into the governing logics and everyday practices of media institutions, MIP is engaged in a diverse array of activities, including these interviews that over the past few years have explored the wide-ranging impact of digital distribution on the entertainment business. Although gaining access to professionals in the entertainment industry can be challenging, we found that the subject of digital distribution evokes such passion among film and television professionals that many proved willing to speak with us about it at length and on the record. Each interviewee agreed to meet with our team for a period of ninety minutes, and some interviews lasted longer or resulted in follow-up conversations. Prior to each interview, we sent our interlocutor a list of prospective topics, but the actual conversation was free ranging and expansive. We preferred to follow emerging lines of discussion rather than stick to a structured survey format. Each session was recorded and transcribed, averaged 12,000 words, and was then edited down to 5,000 words for inclusion in the anthology.

Ideally, the interview sessions provided opportunities for our subjects to step outside of their daily work routines to reflect more expansively on the shifting media landscape and to consider emerging challenges on the horizon. As it becomes apparent in the chapters that follow, some hewed closely to their organization's official positions, while others were quite willing to engage in speculative and critical exchanges. In some cases our invitations to take on controversial issues were declined or deflected (sometimes repeatedly) and those sections were deleted during the editing process. As critical researchers, such twists and turns in the interview process are themselves intriguing, but we have distilled the following chapters into what we believe is the essence of each particular conversation, providing a concise rendering of the most intriguing exchanges in individual sessions. Taken as a whole, this book offers a range of perspectives that document the profound and pervasive changes engendered by the digital distribution revolution in the film and television industries.

This collection also draws prominent attention to an underexplored aspect of the entertainment industries—media distribution. Despite distribution's primary importance to Hollywood's creative strategies and financial success, comparatively little has been written about this particular aspect of the business, in part because the promotion, marketing, and delivery of feature films and television shows were remarkably stable during the latter part of the twentieth century.[23] Certainly the rise of the multiplex theater and the arrival of cable TV were disruptive in their own ways, but the depth and scope of change seem greater today, generating widespread discussion of the profound transformations now under way. Consequently, this book provides a glimpse into a distribution revolution in progress. It examines the film and television industries as they wrestle with economic, cultural, and technological change. Each chapter details the internal tensions and differences within companies, between media sectors, and between corporate and creative communities. In doing so, the book counters common perceptions of media conglomerates as well-oiled machines that are confident of their hold on markets and audiences worldwide. Instead, these interviews underscore the importance of innovation and experimentation in an era of tremendous risk and uncertainty, as well as opportunity.

The book is organized into three parts. The first section features interviews with top executives at leading Hollywood studios, providing a window into big-picture strategic thinking about the major concerns of media conglomerates with respect to changing business models, revenue streams, and audience behaviors. The executives explain how challenging it is to successfully manage and distribute studio content in an environment of almost limitless choice, at a time when digital devices have effectively put "a video store in everybody's pocket." The second section focuses on innovative enterprises that are providing pathbreaking models for new modes of content creation, curation, and distribution. These interviews offer perspectives from individuals operating outside of the global conglomerate. While a few come with established Hollywood credentials, the companies they run are very much the new kids on the block—mapping out a digital future for the entertainment industries that attempts to integrate the disparate strategies and practices of Hollywood and Silicon Valley. The final section offers insights from creative talent, those who have been profoundly affected by the revolution at hand. They reflect on issues of creativity, compensation, and everyday working conditions, enumerating the many ways that life inside Hollywood has changed over the past ten years. Taken together, these interviews demonstrate that virtually every aspect of the film and television businesses is being affected by the digital distribution revolution, a revolution that has likely just begun.

NOTES

1. Catherine Covert, " 'We May Hear Too Much': American Sensibility and the Response to Radio, 1919–1924," in *Mass Media between the Wars: Perceptions of Cultural Tension, 1918–1941*, ed. Catherine Covert and John Stevens (Syracuse, NY: Syracuse University Press, 1984), 199–220; Lynn Spigel, *Make Room for TV* (Chicago: University of Chicago Press, 1992); Susan J. Douglas, *Inventing American Broadcasting 1899–1922* (Baltimore: Johns Hopkins University Press, 1987); Carolyn Marvin, *When Old Technologies Were New* (New York: Oxford University Press, 1988); Jeffery Sconce, *Haunted Media* (Durham, NC: Duke University Press, 2000); Lisa Gitelman, *Always Already New* (Cambridge, MA: MIT Press, 2006); James Carey, *Communication as Culture* (New York: Routledge, 1992).

2. Daniel Czitrom, *Media and the American Mind* (Chapel Hill: University of North Carolina Press, 1982); Brian Winston, *Misunderstanding Media* (Cambridge, MA: Harvard University Press, 1986); Timothy Wu, *The Master Switch* (New York: Vintage Books, 2011); Susan Smulyan, *Selling Radio* (Washington, DC: Smithsonian Institution Press, 1996); Robert McChesney, *Telecommunications, Mass Media, and Democracy* (New York: Oxford University Press, 1993); Thomas Streeter, *Selling the Air* (Chicago: University of Chicago Press, 1996); Richard John, *Network Nation* (Cambridge, MA: Harvard University Press, 2010); Ithiel de Sola Pool, *Technologies of Freedom* (Cambridge, MA: Harvard University Press, 1983).

3. Douglas Gomery, *The Hollywood Studio System* (New York: BFI, 2005).

4. Derek Kompare, *Rerun Nation* (New York: Routledge, 2005).

5. Gomery, *Hollywood Studio System;* Thomas Schatz, *Boom and Bust* (Los Angeles: University of California Press, 1999).

6. Thomas Streeter, "The Cable Fable," *Critical Studies in Mass Communication* 4, no. 2 (1987): 174–200.

7. Megan Mullen, *The Rise of Cable Programming in the United States* (Austin: University of Texas Press, 2003); Patrick Parsons, *Blue Skies: A History of Cable Television* (Philadelphia: Temple University Press, 2008).

8. Sheila Murphy, "ALT-CTRL: The Freedom of Remotes and Controls," in *How Television Invented New Media* (New Brunswick, NJ: Rutgers University Press, 2011), 103–122; Robert V. Bellamy and James Walker, *Television and the Remote Control: Grazing on a Vast Wasteland* (New York: Guilford Press, 1996); Robert V. Bellamy and James Walker, *The Remote Control in the New Age of Television* (Santa Barbara, CA: Praeger, 1992).

9. Ben Bagdikian, *The Media Monopoly* (Boston: Beacon Press, 2004); Herbert Schiller, *Culture Inc.* (New York: Oxford University Press, 1989); Edward Herman and Robert McChesney, *The Global Media* (New York: Continuum, 2001); Robert Britt Horwitz, *The Irony of Regulatory Reform* (New York: Oxford University Press, 1989); Jennifer Holt, *Empires of Entertainment* (New Brunswick, NJ: Rutgers University Press, 2011); Eli Noam, *Media Ownership and Concentration in America* (New York: Oxford University Press, 2009).

10. Paul du Gay, *Doing Cultural Studies* (Thousand Oaks, CA: Sage, 1997/2013); Edward J. Epstein, *The Big Picture* (New York: E.J.E. Publications, 2005); Frederick Wasser, *Vini, Vidi, Video* (Austin: University of Texas Press, 2002).

11. Christopher H. Sterling, Phyllis W. Bernt, and Martin B.H. Weiss, *Shaping American Telecommunications* (Mahwah, NJ: Lawrence Erlbaum Associates, 2006); Susan Crawford, *Captive Audience* (New Haven, CT: Yale University Press, 2013).

12. Stephen Prince, *A New Pot of Gold* (Los Angeles: University of California Press, 2002); Jon Lewis, *American Film* (New York: W.W. Norton & Company, 2007); Thomas Schatz, "The New Hollywood," in *Film Theory Goes to the Movies,* ed. Preacher Collins and Hilary Radner (New York: Routledge, 1992), 8–36.

13. Chuck Tryon, *Reinventing Cinema* (New Brunswick, NJ: Rutgers University Press, 2009); Barbara Klinger, *Beyond the Multiplex: Cinema, New Technologies, and the Home* (Berkeley and Los Angeles: University of California Press, 2006).

14. Lawrence Lessig, *Free Culture* (New York: Penguin Books, 2004), and *Code Version 2.0* (New York: Basic Books, 2006); Peter DeCherney, *Hollywood's Copyright Wars* (New York: Columbia University Press, 2012); Tarlton Gillespie, *Wired Shut* (Cambridge, MA: MIT Press, 2007).

15. Patrick Burkhart, *Music and Cyberliberties* (Middletown, CT: Wesleyan University Press, 2010).

16. Stuart Cunningham and Jon Silver, *Screen Distribution and the New King Kongs of the Online World* (New York: Palgrave Macmillan, 2013), 16.

17. Gina Keating, *Netflixed* (New York: Penguin, 2012).

18. Cited in Cunningham and Silver, *Screen Distribution,* 21.

19. Jean Burgess, Joshua Green, Henry Jenkins, and John Hartley, *YouTube* (Malden, MA: Polity Press, 2009); Pelle Snickars and Patrick Vonderau, eds., *The YouTube Reader* (Stockholm: National Library of Sweden, 2010); Joshua Jackson, *YouTube: Redefining Cultural Production* (dissertation, University of Wisconsin Press, 2013).

20. Cunningham and Silver, *Screen Distribution,* 24.

21. "Company Profile," Netflix, accessed September 3, 2013, http://ir.netflix.com.

22. Gary Levin, "With Emmy Nods, Netflix Is a TV Player," *USA Today*, July 18, 2013, http://www.usatoday.com/story/life/tv/2013/07/18/netflix-emmy-awards-house-of-cards/2552867/.

23. Notable contributions to the literature on film and television distribution include Justin Wyatt, *High Concept: Movies and Marketing in Hollywood* (Austin: University of Texas Press, 1994); Derek Kompare, "Reruns 2.0: Revising Repetition for Multiplatform Television Distribution," *Journal of Popular Film and Television* 38, no. 2 (2010): 79–83; Alisa Perren, "Business as Unusual: Conglomerate-Sized Challenges for Film and Television in the Digital Arena," *Journal of Popular Film and Television* 38, no. 2 (2010): 72–78; Philip Drake, "Distribution and Marketing in Contemporary Hollywood," in *The Contemporary Hollywood Film Industry*, ed. Paul McDonald and Janet Wasko (Oxford: Blackwell, 2008), 63–82; Jeffrey Ulin, *The Business of Media Distribution* (New York: Focal Press, 2010); Dina Iordanova and Stuart Cunningham, eds., *Digital Disruption* (St. Andrews Film Studies, Scotland: Iordanova, 2012).

Studios

. . . . .

EDITORS' INTRODUCTION

In what has been called "a new golden age," particularly for television, the media industries have also been experiencing a period of tremendous change and uncertainty. Developing technologies and new distribution platforms have necessarily required innovation and new creative strategies on the part of content providers in the digital era. The distribution revolution has indeed presented a host of new challenges for the studios, from engaging the ever-elusive online audience to the art of revaluing content for a digital marketplace. These challenges are among some of the topics discussed by six executives from Sony, Warner Bros., Fox Television, and Disney in this section focusing on "The Studio." Their perspectives represent some of the most knowledgeable and forward thinking in the media industries today, as they have been leading the charge for multiple divisions of a conglomerate or even entire studio operations in the transition to the digital ecosystem.

As the major media conglomerates deal with a dynamic range of variables involved in distributing their content digitally, these studio representatives provide a window into big-picture strategic thinking about the most prevalent business models currently in development, their historical evolution, and the often conflicting desires of audiences and content companies in the digital era. These conversations ultimately draw our attention to the increasing number of moving targets that studio executives have to maintain command of in order to distribute their content successfully in the digital era; they must simultaneously adjust to a landscape of new technologies and platforms along with evolving consumer habits; respond to new marketing and branding imperatives while adjusting to rapidly changing business and development strategies; juggle ever-present piracy concerns with pressures from the international market for more content; and face growing competition from a host of aggressive new players in the content distribution business, some of whom they already rely on to distribute their own products.

Uncertainty and innovation are two common dynamics discussed by these executives as opportunities to enact new measures of control over the market. Similarly, they also see the need to retrain consumers regarding new habits of engaging with their content. Mitch Singer, chief digital strategy officer at Sony Pictures Entertainment, views innovation, or "disruption," as it is sometimes called, as an opportunity and not a threat; for Singer, the current moment of uncertainty presents an exciting range of options for consumers and studios that must be balanced in relationship to a complex constellation of third-party services, piracy concerns, and licensing agreements. For Kelly Summers, former vice president of business development and new media strategy at Disney, one of the major challenges brought on by early digital platform innovation was the fact that although many new interfaces were being developed, the user experience was often inferior to that of traditional linear video. Combined with piracy concerns and a massive amount of unlicensed material in circulation, this set of circumstances led to a devaluation of digital content—an issue with which the studios struggle to this day.

Most of the executives interviewed in this section have had to constantly reevaluate release windows, as strategies continue to evolve and shift for both film and television content. The path from theatrical to digital video disc (DVD), electronic sell-through (EST), and video on demand (VOD) and then on to the networks and library markets has been one of the most significant aspects of navigating the digital distribution revolution. Aside from making "the concept of windows more visible," as Summers notes, it has also made them remarkably complicated. All options regarding when, where, and how content is for sale and/or rent have yet to become immediately obvious to consumers. It also becomes clear from these interviews that the various studio strategies or approaches to digital release still remain rather inconsistent in this era of experimentation. Disney's construction of its carefully guarded "vault" of animated content, which is behind the studio's policy of releasing home video titles for a limited time only, after which it is put on moratorium for an unspecified time, has continued to dictate the studio's approach to distribution in the digital age. The studio is also the most brand-protective and maintains a high degree of exclusivity with its online properties and platforms. Gary Newman, chairman of 20th Century Fox Television, on the other hand, sees each property demanding a unique strategy, depending on various considerations that include the genre of the program, its syndication potential, what season the show is in, and ultimately its calculated value to the studio's overall library.

Windowing considerations also led many interviewed in this section to comment on the common problems of large media conglomerates as their many quasi-independent silos adapt to the new demands of digital distribution. Our conversations often returned to such structural concerns, including how executives must mitigate against one revenue stream cannibalizing another when determining how to maximize exposure and income across an array of digital platforms (e.g., timing the release on digital platforms so that it doesn't cut into or take away from potential DVD revenues). Newman addresses this issue when looking at the needs of the Fox networks versus the studio and discussing how certain subscription video-on-demand (SVOD) platforms compromise the show's value for streaming on the network platform. Elements of this complex calculus engendered by the ubiquity of mobile and streaming platforms are further complicated by the human element of windowing, or what Thomas Gewecke, chief digital officer of Warner Bros., sees as fundamental changes in how consumers perceive themselves, their choices, and their control over content. Since digital ownership is usually positioned somewhere along a spectrum depending on how it is viewed (downloaded, streamed, left to reside in the cloud or transferred to a local drive, etc.), the capabilities encoded in digital content and the ramifications for studio strategy are also partially dependent on consumer attitudes toward that spectrum of ownership, and how they position themselves in relation to such content.

These various digital distribution options and their appeal to audiences as well as their importance to studios' bottom lines are another recurring topic of discussion. Gewecke compares the considerable differences in the electronic rental market and EST for both film and television, as well as various SVOD and other streaming platforms, including UltraViolet, regarding their importance to connected viewing. Singer similarly emphasized EST as the future but maintained a steadfast belief in the resilience and staying power of physical media as well. Newman is quite bullish on the SVOD business, and Richard Berger, senior vice president at Sony Pictures, talks about the virtues of mobile devices and apps in the studio's digital strategy, which effectively put "a store in everybody's pocket."

The studios' desire to control the digital environment in which their content is consumed has also become quite pronounced as the ecosystem has evolved. Disney has clearly been the most successful at that, eschewing collective platforms such as UltraViolet for its proprietary Key Chest digital rights management (DRM) system in the cloud. The executives also comment on the role of social media, television networks, and even large-scale retailers such as Walmart (through disc-to-digital programs) as supporting and impacting the future of digital distribution, but those relationships are currently a work in progress.

If there is a common sentiment in this group of executives, it is that they ultimately see digital distribution as a very complex puzzle full of tremendous choice, one with increased responsibility to engage with consumer demand. The result is quite an interesting moment for the studios that has resulted in tremendously popular content being available on more screens than ever before. Whether or not that constitutes another golden age, it does indeed appear to be a new era for those at the top—one that demands significant flexibility, extraordinarily steady nerves, and a willingness to break the "old" rules as well as the ability to design new ones.

Gary Newman, Chairman, 20th Century Fox Television

Gary Newman has been chairman of 20th Century Fox Television since 2007 and has overseen the television studio with Dana Walden since 1999—with great success. Some of the studio's recent hits include *Modern Family, Homeland, Glee,* and *Sons of Anarchy.* Twentieth Century Fox Television also is responsible for *24, Family Guy,* and *The Simpsons,* the latter now the longest-running prime-time show in television history.

Newman began his career as an attorney and worked in the legal and business affairs departments of Columbia Pictures Television and NBC before joining 20th Century Fox Television. After rising to become the studio's executive vice president and top-ranking business officer, he was tapped to run the studio with Walden. Newman's experience and instincts have helped build Fox into a leading supplier of programming to all six broadcast networks. He has also pioneered mobile content strategies, and with Walden he established the practice of releasing series on DVD immediately following the broadcast season—now industry standard practice.

We interviewed Newman in his Century City office where he talked to us about developing new formulas for successful distribution strategies, the different needs of studios and networks in the current environment, and television's "new golden era." Flowing between historical perspective, high-level business strategy, and pointed illustrative details, Newman explored the complexity of the contemporary marketplace with a great deal of nuance and presented a clear—and an optimistic—vision of the digital landscape that content providers are currently navigating in the TV industry.

MEDIA INDUSTRIES PROJECT: *You and Dana Walden are chairmen of 20th Century Fox Television. How does that partnership work?*

25

GARY NEWMAN: I tend to focus more of my time on the business and distribution side of what we do, but our philosophy is that either one of us should be able to sit in any meeting and be fully up to speed and lead it, so I end up getting quite involved on the creative side, as Dana does on the business side. As the heads of a content creation company, our primary focus is creating new series, whether it is selecting the writers, shaping pitches, or overseeing projects from the script stage to the editing room and beyond. We work through all the difficulties of production, from hiring talent to negotiating license fees with networks to getting shows launched and pushing the networks to market, schedule, and support our shows successfully.

Once we get a show launched and secured, I immediately turn my focus to the distribution of it, which a decade ago was a relatively simple thing. There wasn't a lot to do in the first four years of a series' life until the network exclusivity period ended and you were free to sell the show into syndication. Ten years ago we were just beginning home entertainment releases of shows, but even that was always after four or five years of production, and sometimes just the pilot or special episodes—no one thought to release entire seasons back then. Now, things have changed so much. We map out and execute our distribution strategies right from season 1 with streaming, electronic sell-through (EST), and releases on DVD. The international distribution of shows, which has always been the province of the studio, has become a more important part of our financial equation. Then there are ancillary businesses that are only applicable to certain shows, whether it is the music of a show like *Glee* or the licensed merchandise for a show like *The Simpsons* or *Family Guy*. Those are businesses that begin right away, and it is up to the studio to manage them.

What do you focus on when you're building brands: the content, the studio, the Fox networks, News Corporation?

I think about branding on a show-by-show basis. I visualize each show as a wheel, with the center of the wheel being content and then the spokes go out to the different platforms. So I think of the brand as the content itself.

Part of what has changed over the last decade is that it is no longer sufficient to focus solely on the performance of a series on the broadcast networks. Performance on other platforms has become more important, and those platforms tend to be the studio's businesses, not the network's. We have gone from being a company that serviced networks to being a company that services consumers. That being said, we can't service the consumer if we can't initially launch a show on the network, so the network is still a big part of the equation. But it is no longer the only part.

The network business is quite challenged right now. I believe retransmission consent fees are going to ease some problems. As the networks get their dual streams of revenue, which is I think an absolute inevitability, then some of the pressure we have been feeling at the studio from the networks will ease. Network executives think our ancillary distribution is harming their ability to go into the advertising community and say, "The only place your clients can associate with *Glee, Modern Family,* or *Family Guy* is on our air." That model gave them an enormous premium. I think some of the pressure on us will be relieved because the networks will have revenue coming in through retransmission consent fees.

I can't in my mind picture a business model for studios that doesn't include the network. The network is critical. Our business doesn't work without networks. While the show will always be the brand and the center of the wheel, the network is one of the spokes without which the wheel falls apart.

Ten years ago the network was more or less the client?

The network was certainly the dominant piece of our business model by far. If you looked at a pie chart of our revenue fifteen years ago, the network revenue was the single-biggest element, with syndication second and international third. We found in the early part of this last decade that home entertainment revenue became a major part of the pie. International was probably fairly comparable to the network slice, and sometimes syndication remained important. Now it's shifting again. I think DVD revenue is down across the industry. International has remained strong, although it is a very challenging world economy right now. The United Kingdom, which was such a vital part of the international television business, is still really in trouble, and our numbers in the United Kingdom aren't nearly what they were three to four years ago. The makeup of the pie keeps shifting.

Could you explain your philosophy about the relationship between the creative decisions you make and the distribution strategies you pursue?

We are all about the creative integrity of our shows first. If you don't develop things that are unique, distinctive, and engaging, then it doesn't matter how brilliant your distribution strategy is; you're going to have nothing. We don't ask writers to develop ideas in "hot" genres. We believe our best chance of creating great programming is to have a writer come in and tell us what they are passionate about, what they know, and what is personal to them. A great example is Ryan Murphy and *Glee*. Trust me, we didn't ask him to come up with a musical, particularly one set in a high school. It was just a show he was passionate about, he knew the world intimately, and it really came alive when he sat in our office and pitched it.

That being said, when we hear these ideas, one of the things we think about is whether it will be commercially viable or not. It certainly needs to pass that test as well. Still, we do take fliers. Sometimes we just love a show so much we believe that somehow the market is going to open up for it. *24* is a great example of that. No one had produced such a serialized drama. And, in fact, no one ever tried to do a show in real time, which seemed preposterous to us when it was first pitched. Looking back at its first season, even though its ratings were strong enough for a renewal, we had no idea if we would ever make any money on it.

The network figured out very quickly that it wasn't repeatable, that people didn't want to watch it a second time. In fact, at the end of the first season they had us write a script that would be a template for *24* without any of the serialization; each episode would be a stand-alone story. We saw very quickly that the show wasn't nearly as compelling without the real-time format and the serialization. We all said, "Well it was a good experiment, but we love this show as it is; we think there is something special, so let's just keep going."

When the network green-lit a second year, we released the first-season DVD, which was the first time a show had ever done that—released a season box set at the end of its first season on the air. We released it at the beginning of September, one month prior to the premiere of season 2. We believed there were potential viewers who had missed the initial episodes and thought it was too serialized to join during the season. We wanted to capture those viewers by allowing them to watch season 1 and see a trailer for season 2. The show had great buzz, the press liked it, and so we thought it would be a great marketing strategy. We really had no expectations of making any money on the DVD. And when it just blew off of the shelves, we realized that something very special had happened. The DVD was a great marketing platform for season 2, but it was also a remarkable way to monetize a show early in its life span.

But it's important not to allow the business side of things to drive the creative side. At the end of the day we have to have passion for the shows we produce, and produce them even if we are unsure whether they will have ancillary value. Our very best properties almost always were the ones that scared us, that we weren't really sure would be economically viable.

24 was that way; *Glee* was that way; even *X-Files* was that way, as we elected to produce that series when conventional wisdom told us that one-hour dramas were dead.

Family Guy *seems to be a good example of the changing dynamics of distribution. It didn't look like the show was going anywhere and then the DVD market told you something very different. What happened in the case of* Family Guy?

First, it was a network decision to cancel the show. The studio loved it and we would have continued production. After it was cancelled, a few things happened. Steve MacDonald, who works in our syndication division, loved the show and was frustrated he couldn't take the fifty episodes that existed and sell them to a cable network. Typically fifty is too few episodes for a cable network to syndicate because they want to be able to strip it five days a week, and fifty episodes is just ten weeks of programming. But Steve convinced Cartoon Network to "buy" it and he convinced me to let them have it for free for the first two months. After that, Cartoon had an option to continue for another period of time for a very low price, which I believe was $25,000 per episode. So this was a very small deal, but Steve hoped to ignite interest in the show so that when the contract with Cartoon Network was up he would be able to raise the prices.

The deal with Cartoon Network happened at about the same time we began releasing the show on DVD and our sales were through the roof. A part of the reason we were willing to sell the show so cheaply to Cartoon Network was that we had a DVD release coming up and we wanted to create awareness on Cartoon Network. We figured our consumers were watching that network, or at least the children of our consumers were, and they would convince their parents to buy it. So we thought of the sale to Cartoon Network as a synergistic marketing campaign for our DVD.

At about the same time I took my older son, Jordan, back to Yale on a college trip. I spoke at Pierson College and took questions from students after my presentation. Twenty hands shot up and almost every question was about *Family Guy:* "Would it come back?" "Why was it not on the air?" "Do I know Seth?" It was just that confluence of events, coupled with our great relationship with Seth MacFarlane, who was still in business with the studio. Seth never let go of the dream of bringing back *Family Guy.* He used to call me or come in and see me every few weeks to convince me to bring *Family Guy* back to television.

Eventually we just decided that we should do something. So I went back to talk to the network but they just flat out passed. They had no interest in bringing it back. So I went to my boss, who oversaw both the network and the studio, and I would bug him every couple of weeks about it. Eventually, I said, "What if we can figure out how to do this without a network and still pay for it?" He said, fine, never imagining we could do that. We got our DVD division to give us estimates on the value of new episodes, we got Steve MacDonald to go to Cartoon Network to see how much they would pay for new episodes, and we made deals to bring the show back. Because we knew our network could easily change its mind, and because it would be helpful to us to have the network relaunch the series to create awareness, we negotiated a Cartoon Network deal with a potential window for the Fox Network, in the event they changed their minds. Of course, once we got into production, they did change their minds. We had gone into production on forty-eight episodes, which is what Cartoon Network was prepared to buy. The Fox Network only agreed to buy the first thirteen. Later, they agreed to take all of the episodes. And it turned into one of the studio's most enduring and valuable series.

Over the last seven to eight years we have recognized that we are in an even more hit-driven business. It isn't about market share, it isn't about volume, it's about very brand-specific properties. Shows that are serialized, or are genre or animation, and that appeal to a young and male-skewing audience still perform great on DVD. We are not going to be able to sell serialized programming in syndication to broadcast stations or cable networks so you must rely on home entertainment

There is a level of complexity to our business that simply didn't exist when I started. I know it sounds simplistic, but twenty years ago all we cared about was the network and its needs. Almost everything went from network to syndication and that was pretty much it. As that changed, we began to look at each show separately to determine whether there might be other paths to financial success. At the same time we need to be careful to protect the core parts of our business.

So every decision we make about digital options we put through the prism of: Is it going to cannibalize another business? And if the answer is yes, we might ask: Are we getting compensated for it in a way that makes that risk appropriate? It is important that we don't trade customers who are providing great margins for customers who aren't, because we simply won't be able to afford to make the kind of programs we want to make. That being said, this movement to consumer convenience, ubiquity of content, and portability is vital. It is here to stay, and no one is interested in trying to block that. In fact, we want to support it. We just want to make sure we get compensated for financing and producing the content.

As a studio head, what does the revenue pie look like today? Where do you make your money?

You will probably get a different answer from every studio because it really depends upon what shows you have. I can only speak to what we have, but our home entertainment revenue, which includes physical sales (DVD) and digital revenue (such as that from Netflix and Hulu), has remained relatively flat with where we were during the height of the DVD market a few years ago. Whereas DVD revenue was 90 percent of the piece and digital was 10 percent, it's now approximately the same. Consumers are still paying for our product, but the revenue is just coming in differently, and, for us, that's very encouraging.

Right now, digital sales are more of a domestic phenomenon. International revenues haven't really grown yet the way domestic revenues have, although we expect that to change over the next several years as Netflix expands into foreign territories. Anyway, where people thought you were going to trade analog dollars for digital dimes, that hasn't really been the case. We are finding that digital growth has exceeded what we would have expected, and so we feel pretty bullish about the home entertainment sector.

Do these revenue shifts affect your release strategies? Is syndication still the most important?

No. That's no longer the case. *Sons of Anarchy* is a perfect example. It will never syndicate, for many reasons: the content is a little rough; it's very serialized; it's only thirteen shows a year. So, after four seasons, we only have fifty-two episodes. But we have such a fantastic deal with Netflix for the show—it is very much comparable to what you would hope to get from syndicating an episodic procedural drama. We also have *Sons* on Amazon and have a great deal there too. These new distribution opportunities enable us to do shows that, as a studio, we are very passionate about. We love serialized storytelling: *24, Lost, Prison Break, Homeland.* These shows create so much passion; it's satisfying to our creators and it's satisfying to our executives. And these shows tend to receive awards, and they travel great internationally.

What constitutes a "fantastic deal" with streaming outlets?

In this particular case I am referring to deals that were not part of our output deals. We made separate deals for significant amounts of money and they were nonexclusive deals. So it didn't prevent us from making a deal with Amazon, didn't prevent us from making deals with cable networks and stations for shows. So it was purely additive to what we were doing. SVOD (subscription video-on-demand) platforms have become important partners to us and we want their businesses to flourish, and I think they are wrestling with the issue of are they an out-of-season library platform, or are they akin to a premium cable channel with original programming? I imagine if you asked those platforms what they want to be, they want to be like HBO or Showtime. They want to be akin to a premium service.

They made these great library deals with most of us and I think they probably don't really value it very much. I think what they feel drives their business is probably 10 or 15 percent of their programming, which is why we chose to hold out some programs that we thought had greater value than the library deal. Netflix agreed to make those deals. As we look to the future with them, we would hope that we can find some sort of win-win scenario where we are really well compensated for the shows that are driving business—those shows that people want to consume six in a row on a Saturday night. That kind of show seems to be what really works for them, and we want to be paid well for those shows, but we also need that library outlet. I think there needs to be some adjustment in these deals to recognize that there is greater value in some shows and probably lesser value in others and the one-size-fits-all payment doesn't really make a lot of sense.

So Netflix has actually helped your studio. It's not just digital dimes.

You're right. But the deals we negotiate with them are still evolving, and it's complicated because Netflix is essentially charging the same to a viewer whether she's watching the most popular show or the most niche show. To me that's a little bit of an imperfect marketplace. But we are starting to break through it. They negotiate output deals for most of our shows, but we held certain shows out of that, *Glee* and *Sons of Anarchy* and *Burn Notice* and *White Collar*. With these shows, we made different types of deals that are more lucrative to us. We refer to them as syndication deals rather than the output deals. I know the same is true with shows at other studios, such as *Mad Men* over at AMC and Lionsgate.

But not all studios executives are enthusiastic about the prospects of SVOD. They feel it devalues the content quite a bit.

Well, they are probably talking about half hours and procedural dramas where you hope to still get that syndication play. We kept *Modern Family* off Netflix. We don't really have too many procedural dramas, but with our half hours, as early as the first season we are having that discussion about maintaining the scarcity value and preserving it for syndication versus putting it through an output deal and generating some money early in the life cycle. We also have to balance this against the need to get as much sampling and exposure as possible during the first couple seasons. So I can imagine with a half hour that you would hope to eventually syndicate, putting the first season out on Netflix just to create as much awareness as possible, but if you succeed in season 2 and you feel like you have a show that's really catching on, then you want to pull back on SVOD platforms so that your syndication buyers will sense the audience demand for the show.

It's an interesting calculus to keep on refining.

What makes it complicated is that the networks have their own issues and sometimes those issues butt up against our strategies. If you were talking to a network president, they would say to you, "Among the biggest issues we have is we are not capturing all the people who are watching our shows. All we get credit for are people who are watching it during its first three days and who are watching commercials." It's a little disingenuous because they are also being paid retransmission money from the cable operators. As for the cable operators and satellite operators, they don't care whether people are watching commercials. They're looking at the gross audience, live plus seven. That's why people still report live plus seven, because it is relevant for that calculus.

So if you are running a network, you are trying to put your program on as many platforms as you can and attach your advertising, but that flies in the face a little bit of the scarcity issues that we have as a studio. Some networks even try to go further; they put shows on platforms where there are no commercials. So you have the Fox Network putting programming on Hulu Plus, which is an SVOD platform. And we feel as a studio, that's cannibalizing the desirability of our shows for SVOD at the end of the season.

We're currently trying to negotiate this issue so that we have an understanding that the networks can stream during the season and we can do SVOD out of season.

If you are sitting at a studio I guess you sort of think we've got a few different types of shows. We have half hours and procedural dramas that will syndicate, and getting them out a year earlier can be valuable. Then we have shows that are highly serialized and you are going to want to make an SVOD deal early. So that was probably their calculus.

So *Modern Family* was a huge syndication property, *Big Bang* a huge syndication property, but with shows like *Sons of Anarchy*, it's not likely to draw much in syndication, so the ability to put it on SVOD is a fairly significant financial opportunity for us. If your show stays on the air for six seasons, every year you are getting an additional payment, maybe several hundred thousand dollars per episode. When we talk to the networks, we ask them to let us look at each program individually. On all programs at the end of season 1, let us put it into SVOD if we choose to. At the end of season 2, we have a decision to make. Either we stick with SVOD, in which case we don't get early syndication rights, or we take it off SVOD to help snag early syndication rights. We feel we are the most informed party to make the choice. Let us do it, and we'll live with the notion that we can't do both. I think the reason that the networks don't want you to do both is they think their rerun opportunities are limited when the shows are overly exposed. So that's kind of what's going on right now in the industry.

What do you use for metrics when negotiating these kinds of deals? When you're doing a deal for Glee, *for example, what are the numbers that are on the table when you're negotiating with Netflix?*

Well, we're still in the early stages. There is no SVOD history to look at and say, "During the last two years, *Glee* did this for you." We purely look at their subscriber base. That's public knowledge. You know how many subscribers they have and you have a sense of what they are paying, and you sort of think about what you should get on a per-subscriber basis as opposed to a per-view basis. You look at what cable networks are paying for programming and you know what their carriage is, and you are trying to draw some parallels to that.

Amazon was hard because they didn't have nearly the number of subscribers, and a per-subscriber deal wouldn't have worked. They are buying shows like *Glee* and *Sons of Anarchy* to grow their business. We set the bar pretty high for Amazon, and it's going to be a loss leader for them to build their business.

Does Netflix share any of its viewer data with you?

We do seem to have some knowledge of what is being watched. I don't know if we get that from them or if there are some independent research things done.

You have previously told us your most lucrative customer was the one that paid to download the show as opposed to the one that watched it on any other platform or even broadcast. Does that still hold up?

That's an interesting question. Honestly I'm not sure. It's hard for me to imagine that an iTunes customer is not still our most lucrative buyer because the cost of making content available there is pretty low, and even though iTunes takes a cut, I think that's probably our single-biggest profit margin. But that's a business that really isn't growing very much.

Recently, the SVOD business has grown much more in terms of overall revenue. The revenue coming in from SVOD dwarfs any other form of digital revenue. It dwarfs what we get from streaming, which is ad-supported, and it dwarfs what we get from EST, which is a per-customer transaction.

Despite this growth, DVD margins still remain pretty good. They have compressed a little bit just because the market for DVDs is a little tougher. With shows like *Sons of Anarchy*, we still provide lots of great extras on those DVDs and people want to collect them and own them. So we have not seen a falloff on some of our top titles. They continue to hold their levels or even grow.

Does your studio monitor social media, and does it tell you anything that is helpful in the creative or distribution decisions that you make?

Our head of research will send us "blog reports" on our shows periodically, which is just her judgment of what the audience is saying out there on the Internet. It's such a wide space that it's hard to measure in anything that feels like reliable numbers. You are just trying to get a sense of the general mood and feeling about shows. I think it is useful, though. You are hearing your most passionate fans, or if they are not all fans, at least the most passionate people with regard to your programming. I think it's interesting to see how they feel about the twists and turns that your characters take, particularly in serialized shows. We don't look at it as instruction as to what our shows should be. You just try to get a general sense. Are they responding, are they interested in a story line, are they interested in a character? Is the character engendering emotion, positive or negative? These sorts of things.

It does enable feedback from the audience in a more timely fashion. You are not relying just on your own instincts anymore and I think that's a good thing. If you start seeing that fans are not liking a story or they are not believing a story or they are bored by a relationship or whatever it may be, we want to know that and at least consider whether we ought to make an adjustment in the shows sooner rather than waiting to see our ratings impacted.

Some critics have suggested that television may be at a tipping point due to the disruptions caused by digital media. In some of our interviews, they draw comparisons to the newspaper business. Do you think the television business could be headed for a serious and unexpected decline?

I guess first I would say, I'm not sure I agree with that sort of speculation. You have an issue with advertising revenue but now you have this retransmission consent revenue, which is very substantial. You have other platforms where consumers are paying one way or another, either through subscriptions or per viewing. So I don't think we are in a world where we are likely to find ourselves with one-tenth of the revenue.

On top of that, the most creative talent in the business of entertainment is coming to television. You have movie directors, movie writers, movie stars—all wanting to come to TV because fewer movies are being made and there is greater freedom in TV. If your issue is you don't want to be limited by network standards, there is this incredible cable market. If your issue is you only want to work for four months a year so you can do your independent movies, there are many opportunities to work on a series with only thirteen episodes a year.

That being said, if the economy tanks, if some of our hopes and assumptions about the businesses turn out not to be so and we do find ourselves in a tough television economy, it will be very hard. We've been through economic downturns before. We've been through years when ad sales have dropped and you tighten your belt. You force yourself and your show runners to produce more economically. You develop shows to be produced in states where you can get tax credits. You produce in countries where you have a favorable exchange rate and the dollar is strong. You cut your development overhead. But I'm not sure it makes sense to draw an analogy between the newspaper business and the television business. I actually disagree with the assertion, because I feel like TV's in a golden age that is going to even get brighter.

Richard Berger, Senior Vice President, Global Digital Strategy and Operations, Sony Pictures Home Entertainment

Richard Berger sat down with Media Industries Project (MIP) for an interview in Sony's Culver City offices to talk about how digital technologies have been used to distribute Sony's content. As senior vice president of Global Digital Strategy and Operations for Sony Pictures Home Entertainment, Berger is in charge of developing digital strategy and overseeing digital distribution operations. He also evaluates emerging platforms and "disruptive" technologies that create new digital business opportunities. Our conversation focused on the emerging digital locker service, UltraViolet, and some of the complex choices consumers are facing as the viewing context grows increasingly mobile and fragmented.

Berger's perspective on these issues has been shaped by his multiple responsibilities and varied career at Sony. Before joining Sony Pictures Home Entertainment, Berger was senior vice president of New Media & Technology at Sony Pictures Entertainment, where he was responsible for establishing digital policy across all Sony Pictures digital distribution businesses. He previously worked in the Sony Digital Entertainment Department and the office of the chief technology officer at Sony Corporation of America on digital media strategy and anti-piracy efforts. He also worked in Sony's Interactive Services Group and Sony Music Entertainment's New Media Department and developed Sony Music's first Enhanced CDs. He is well seasoned by struggles over digital technology across multiple media industries and, as a result, is uniquely qualified to characterize the importance of the current moment in distribution.

With such extensive experience at the company, Berger was able to provide us with insightful commentary on Sony's view of the current marketplace, as well as offer compelling historical insights into early industrial approaches to compatibility, interoperability, shifting business models, and the evolution of digital rights management (DRM) technologies. His challenges at Sony are representative of what many studios are facing as distribution goes digital.

MEDIA INDUSTRIES PROJECT: *There is a lot of industry and popular discussion about the launch of UltraViolet right now. Can you talk a bit about its origins?*

RICH BERGER: Internally at Sony, we started the "interoperability" discussions back in the early 2000s. At that time, I was working at Sony Corporation of America. This was when the discussion was focused on how to get our content to play on all of the consumer's Sony devices. In 2006 I moved over to Sony Pictures Entertainment. I worked for Mitch Singer (now Sony's chief technology officer) in a corporate group called Digital Strategy & Technology. Among other things, we were responsible for establishing digital policy across all of Sony Pictures' digital distribution businesses. As the conversations evolved, and Mitch and I started working more closely on this together, we realized that when people buy digital content, they are going to want it to play on all of their devices (Sony and others), just like when they buy a CD or DVD. It was here where the initial ideas for UltraViolet first originated. At the time, we called it "Open Market" because we were trying to create an open ecosystem for content.

In reality, the need (and the idea) for UltraViolet really snuck up on us. Remember, the predominant digital business model at this point was rental, aka, video on demand (VOD). When you rent a movie on demand, it is usually accessible for twenty-four hours. You rent it, watch it, and then it goes away. In this environment, no one really thought about interoperability across systems and devices. It just wasn't needed. As digital began to grow, service providers would come to Sony Pictures and say, "We are building this platform, and we want to license your content for it. Here is how we are going to offer it." Then, we would talk to them about the usage model, sometimes for months. This really became much more complex when we began to offer electronic sell-through (EST). Then the usage model discussions were about "How many copies can you make?" and "What devices can it be played on?" "How do you access it?" and "How long does it last?" We were trying to enable a new business but needed to guard against unauthorized sharing of content, so managing the digital rights was an important part of the conversation with our licensees. Remember, this was not too long after Napster completely disrupted the music industry.

We didn't realize it at the time, but the more digital services that we licensed our content to, each with different formats and usage models, the more we contributed to a fragmented marketplace for EST. If you bought a movie from one service and another movie from another service, each one had a different usage model and played back on different devices.

During the early and mid-2000s there were some industry initiatives working to enable interoperability, like the Digital Living Network Alliance, but these groups never really figured out how to address commercial content. Those that tried had focused on the technology needed to get content securely out of the DRM on device platform A into the DRM on device platform B. There was never consideration for how studios licensed content and defined the usage models for each service platform that sells the content. So even though the technology to enable interoperability was there, the rights granted to each service never permitted the content to flow from platform to platform.

As EST started to emerge as a viable business model, we realized that the entire industry was thinking about licensing EST content in the wrong way. The studios were licensing content, but the "digital product" was actually being defined separately by each service provider. We thought that buying movies digitally should be more like buying DVDs. The industry created the DVD Forum to define the DVD as a standard format. Consumers don't think about it because it is obvious. The stores that sell DVDs all sell the same movie product. *Spiderman* on DVD is the same product when I get home regardless of whether I bought it from Walmart or Best Buy. And, because DVD is a standard product, any device manufacturer can build a player that will play that DVD. The creation of this product "standard" was essential in establishing DVD as arguably the most successful media format ever defined.

Yet for digital (EST) movies, we as an industry didn't initially follow the DVD/standards model. I think it was because EST licensing followed the VOD licensing model. VOD was always offered as part of a single-service provider's offering. But in a sell-through model, why should each digital retailer create and sell their own, distinct version of *Spiderman?* If you think about it, the *Spiderman* digital EST offering is a different product on Amazon's digital service than it is on CinemaNow, or Vudu, or iTunes, PSN [PlayStation Network], or Xbox, and so on. This is like a format war on steroids. Digital movies, specifically those that are being sold in an EST model, should have a common format and a common usage model. We should make it a standard product like we did with DVD and Blu-ray. This standard digital product would be available at multiple stores with a single, recognizable brand.

This was the breakthrough idea behind UltraViolet. Because UltraViolet is a standard product with a uniform usage model, the interoperability is built into the digital rights at the time the studio licenses it to service providers. This is great for consumers who want to collect movies and great for the industry because now there can be an "open market" for EST that has the potential to really scale.

For it to really work, we knew Sony Pictures couldn't do it alone. We needed an industry consortium with multiple representatives across the entire content delivery ecosystem, each with a stake in the game. So, with a group of other studios, electronics firms, and technology companies, we formed the Digital Entertainment Content Ecosystem (DECE) in 2008. Its primary goal was to develop a set of standards for the digital distribution of movies and TV shows in an EST model. We set out to "productize" digital EST.

Flash forward to 2011. Seeing the official launch of UltraViolet has been great for me personally because I have been there since day one, developing the concept, pitching the idea to the other founding companies, forming the consortium, working through the product's evolution together with the other DECE members, and finally, launching the first Sony Pictures UltraViolet titles.

Tell us about your current role with Sony. What are some of the challenges for your division?

In March 2010 I joined the newly formed Global Digital and Commercial Innovation group within Sony Pictures Home Entertainment. We are the commercial group responsible for licensing deals for the transactional digital business (EST and VOD). I focus on our digital strategy and product development. If we think of our product as the digital rights that we license, how can we innovate that product? What are the best usage models? What are the interactive features attached to the digital rights we license? These are the questions we are trying to answer. For UltraViolet, we are the group that will bring Sony Pictures' UltraViolet titles to the market.

One of the biggest challenges we have as an industry, in general, is to figure out how to encourage people that migrate from physical to digital to continue buying and collecting our movies and TV shows. You will consistently hear this from every studio. I believe UltraViolet is a big part of the solution. We just need to make sure to get the economics right for consumers and our customers (the retailers). We need to make sure consumers have a great experience at a fair price. With the launch of UltraViolet, we have dramatically transformed the way consumers can collect movies digitally. And, as more companies launch content, services, and players as part of the UltraViolet ecosystem, the value to the consumer gets better and better.

What are some of the challenges you face with retailers?

Traditionally, agreeing on a usage model and content protection has been a sticking point during negotiations with retailers. What's the product? What's the content protection? How do you enforce it? Well, guess what? With UltraViolet, that's all set. Everything is standardized. In our bilateral licensing discussions with our retail partners, we simply point to the product specs for the UltraViolet usage model and content protection. Then we can spend our time focusing on the business terms, which makes the overall conversations a whole lot easier.

Initially, it was challenging to explain the benefits of UltraViolet to our retail partners, but it is really rewarding when the conversations change from why UltraViolet to when UltraViolet.

How does the global market factor into the equation? Can you discuss some of the challenges you confront?

The global market adds a significant amount of complexity. As services expand into different territories, you can't always just replicate what you did in one territory for another. Whenever there is variation in the digital supply chain, you have to create new work flows to support it. Obviously, as you expand and there are more variations, your complexity increases. Standards can really help.

Aside from the language differences, there are many different rules and regulations for content ratings, privacy policies, and content protection standards that are challenging. Piracy is more problematic in some regions, which makes certain business models and offerings more difficult to establish.

UltraViolet certainly simplifies how you distribute content to multiple platforms. But are there still individual differences across those platforms that are important to you?

Certainly we want to license everything to everybody. But some platforms attract different customers than others, and that results in different content preferences across those platforms. We have a whole team here that figures out how to best promote titles, especially if we think they are great fits for certain platforms. In some cases, it's not one-size-fits-all. Take the PlayStation and Xbox services, for example. Both are gaming platforms. People who use them to watch movies are different than people who use iTunes or Amazon. This is apparent when we notice certain titles performing better on certain platforms.

Other platforms, like Facebook, have proven to be great for discovery. Discovery doesn't necessarily happen through fan pages or official pages that we create but rather through your friends. Once something goes viral, you are likely to get a recommendation from a friend to check it out. And that recommendation is more effective than if some company says, "Oh, please, check this out!" I think all the studios are dabbling in social networking environments to see how to best utilize them.

Is there a difference in how you approach digital strategies for film versus television?

Probably the biggest difference in digital strategies has to do with the different release windows each follows. Film for the most part starts in theaters and then moves into the home in a transactional model, followed by a series of pay-TV windows and eventually a free/ad-supported window. TV starts with the network broadcast and fans out from there.

My group is focused on the transactional business—VOD and EST. Unlike movies, we currently only offer TV content in an EST model, not in a VOD model. That said, another division of Sony Pictures focuses on TV content in pay/subscription and free/ad-supported models.

How do you identify the ways in which consumers are experiencing digital content? Do you engage with fans or online communities?

We of course conduct many consumer attitudes and usage studies. These studies help identify key user trends over time. We also conduct a variety of focus groups to gather direct consumer insights with more specific objectives.

Additionally, we work very closely with our retail partners to find new ways to reach the consumer through various promotions and offers. We are also deploying various direct-to-consumer touch points that will enable us to establish a direct relationship with the consumer. What we learn will hopefully enable us to make more intimate offers over time.

Part of the allure of owning a movie is sharing it with your friends. But as soon as you share it in digital space with one friend, you share it with your entire social network. How are you responding to this challenge?

UltraViolet has some built-in sharing with it. It's a family model where members of a single UltraViolet account can share content. We will need to look at new kinds of models going forward, but traditionally sharing has given studios a lot of discomfort. Think about how we have evolved. The usage model for DVD is "copy never," right? For the most part, people have been okay with that model, but increasingly they are thinking, "I would like to have a backup of this DVD because it could get scratched." Now we've resolved the problem by giving consumers multiple copies for multiple devices.

What has helped enable more flexibility?

DRM actually enables these kinds of models. It is the DRM software that enables you to make multiple copies of a movie based on a single purchase. These copies can only be played on devices you own.

That sounds like less flexibility.

DRM gets a bad rap because the policies that have been traditionally applied to it have been very restrictive. Initially, studios used DRM to prevent people from making copies. In fact, we used to call it copy protection. Now the digital rights or usage models we grant are much more flexible. Unlike DVD, the rights that a user gets when they buy a movie digitally permit unlimited copies on the devices they own. Now think about the terminology: digital rights *management*. We think of it as an enabling technology. It enables a usage model like UltraViolet. If you bought a movie with the model UltraViolet offers, what more would you want that you are not already getting? Your digital rights are stored in the cloud. You can download, stream, make copies, remotely access your content from the service of your choice. Essentially, anything you would legitimately want to do with your content, we enable.

Policies applied to DRM are much more evolved now. Now we don't care if you copy it as long as it's within the confines of the usage model we've laid out for consumers. For example, if we offer a rental for $3.99, should you be able to keep that forever? No. The rental is for twenty-four hours and after the twenty-four hours is up, the rental expires. DRM enforces that model. Now, if you want to rent a movie for twenty-four hours but keep it permanently, then DRM will not be your friend. If we didn't have DRM, we couldn't offer digital rentals as a lower-cost option for consumers.

Is there a concern that DRM enables too many competitive options? For example, what if consumers won't buy a digital copy because DRM has enabled companies like Netflix to offer unlimited streaming?

I don't think so. We want to give consumers choices. If you really want to watch a movie when it first comes out, you can go to the theater and pay to see it on the big screen. If you want to watch it when it first becomes available in your home, you can rent it or buy it. If you want to wait a little longer and not pay separately for it, you can receive it as part of a subscription package. Eventually, if you wait long enough, you can watch it for free with ads. We couldn't offer different models—a rental model, a sell-through model, different release windows—without DRM.

I don't know what the magic number of choices is, but if you don't offer enough choices you are going to have a problem too. I think the industry is trying to figure out where the market is going. New technologies constantly disrupt traditional distribution models. Rather than fight it, I think we are embracing it. We are actively trying to figure out ways to innovate with new distribution models and monetize them. We've learned a lot over the past ten years. If there are too many options, consumers will tell us by not opting in.

How do you introduce your digital strategy to consumers who are still buying physical discs?

We are introducing UltraViolet to consumers as an offer on the Blu-ray they purchase. This strategy helps bridge the gap by introducing our digital product to consumers who buy the physical disc—redeeming the offer will enable them to add the movie to their UltraViolet digital library. It's the best of both worlds. Ultimately, our goal is to provide something for everybody. We won't stop making DVDs or Blu-rays any time soon. They are great products, and for consumers in the United States, the most efficient way to bring HD (high definition) into your house is to buy a disc because bandwidth constraints remain an issue.

Another executive told us the most valuable consumer was the consumer who purchased his or her product on iTunes because it had the highest profit margin. Is that the same for you?

Yes. Regardless of the retailer, EST is the highest margin transaction for us. That is why we need to make the EST value proposition as good as we can so if the consumer wants to buy it digitally, they will have a great value and experience. Of course, not everyone is going to buy every movie. It's about getting the right mix of transactions, both rentals and sell-through.

Apple has moved aggressively into cloud computing, and it opted not to plug into UltraViolet. Is that a serious challenge, or do you think Apple has done itself a disservice?

Apple is not currently a member of the DECE consortium, but membership is open, and Apple can always join any time they want to. UltraViolet has just launched. It is in its early days. The media is always quick to ask how Apple fits into the UltraViolet ecosystem. That is probably a question best answered by Apple. That said, without any Apple participation, we have already seen that UltraViolet movies can be streamed and downloaded onto Apple devices, including the Mac, and iOS devices (iPad, iPhone, and iPod touch).

Consumers have a choice when buying movies digitally. They can buy their movies on iTunes and have a great experience within the Apple ecosystem, or they can buy their movies from an UltraViolet retailer and have a great experience as well. The key difference is that UltraViolet was designed from the beginning to be playable on a wide variety of devices made by multiple manufacturers and accessible via multiple services. That is the difference between an open standard and a proprietary service. The consumer's UltraViolet collection is separate and distinct from any one single-service provider or device platform. The consumer can choose which services and devices from which to access their UltraViolet collection.

We've spent some time talking about sell-through, but what models are emerging for rentals and subscriptions?

Have you ever rented a movie on a Friday night but fell asleep before finishing it? Then, by the time you sat down on Saturday night to finish watching the movie, time expired on your rental and it was gone. We are looking at extending the viewing period of VOD rentals from twenty-four to forty-eight hours. A simple change in digital rights, but a great improvement in the consumer experience. Additionally, we are looking at early home premieres of certain movies as a premium VOD offering.

Do mobile devices have a place in your digital strategy?

Mobile is an important part of the digital distribution strategy. It's important to us, and it's important to our partners. We don't license sell-through content to a single platform. It's multiscreen—simultaneous access across multiple screens. Mobile has increasingly become a part of that. It's a great value for consumers.

We also look at mobile from an applications perspective. We think about ways we can engage with our consumers through these devices that they carry with them all the time. For example, we have an app called My Daily Clip—every day, users get a free clip of the day. It is a great way to feature our new releases and surface great titles from our huge catalog. If they like the clip, they can share it with friends and click the buy button to purchase it. When people share the clips, they can go viral, and that is a really great way to make people aware of our content and create impulse purchase opportunities.

There's also consumption to consider as mobile screens are getting larger and larger. What can we do on tablet screens? What can we do for commuters? I think mobile devices are great. It's like a store in everybody's pocket.

Kelly Summers, Former Vice President, Global Business Development and New Media Strategy, The Walt Disney Company

Kelly Summers is a former vice president of Global Business Development and New Media Strategy at Disney, where she led content commercialization for new media distribution platforms, created new product concepts, incubated new ventures, and oversaw technology commercialization efforts for the studio. She currently manages her own consulting firm, Bella Rafe Media, advising start-ups on digital distribution strategies and digital product development.

Summers began her career working with entrepreneurs in start-up environments and first explored digital media distribution in 1997 when seeking to commercialize price discovery technology and develop online transaction markets. After business school, Summers joined the Walt Disney Company and by 2006 had closed Hollywood's first iTunes movie deal, bringing the Disney family of brands to the popular digital platform. She sat down with us for an interview during a visit to (UCSB's) Carsey-Wolf Center and drew on her experience at Disney to discuss the challenges of windowing strategies in the digital era and her thoughts about digital delivery's potential to devalue content. Summers was also able to talk to MIP about the unique concerns of Disney and its approach to navigating the many options in online distribution while simultaneously contending with issues of brand identity protection. She brings the perspective of a film studio to the conversation—one that has been notoriously savvy about controlling its "vault" of content—and addresses questions about how to best leverage those assets in the digital space.

MEDIA INDUSTRIES PROJECT: *Moving from Disney to a consulting role, how has your perspective changed with respect to distribution issues and what's going on inside the industry?*

KELLY SUMMERS: There is higher energy around digital on the outside. When you're sitting on the inside, you're always going to be looking at the financials. The joke has often been made: Are you going to trade your cable dollars for digital pennies? There just wasn't the same kind of energy around digital on the inside, because the traditional revenue streams are significant. On the outside, you spend a lot more time with people who are really trying to change things by creating better consumer experiences, monetize content in new ways, and try to evolve the industry.

Do you think the cable industry in particular is one of the really big factors that makes studios like Disney cautious about innovation?

I think so, simply because of the size of the checks that they write. They are significant. As cable services renegotiate their deals, obviously those writing the big checks want to secure as many rights as possible, which if granted can tie the hands of a content owner. They may not be free to innovate.

We need to think about what happens if we unbundle content . . . and that's always the criticism of cable: "I'm paying for all of this stuff when really I just want one channel." But from the industry perspective, you see unbundling being really good for the consumer but not necessarily great for the industry. In digital or any content development product, bundling still has an important role to play to keep price erosion from continuing and keep the margins healthy and businesses growing. It's an interesting balance you have to play between being really consumer-friendly and keeping the media business healthy. It's an ongoing challenge for everybody.

Tell us about your last role at Disney.

My last role with Disney was trying to figure out what the go-forward strategy for the studio ought to be. We executed digital distribution deals where it made sense, but the question at the time was, will this new deal really move the needle for the company? Digital distribution was not growing as much as everybody thought it would. So I was looking at what can Disney do that is unique? It has a unique brand, it has some unique technology, and it has content that fits a certain demographic. It also has existing programs that are direct-to-consumer. So I began to look at how we could start to stitch these elements together: What assets does the Disney Company have to create something a little bit more compelling in the digital environment? And that's what led to a project called "Disney Studios All Access."

The idea was to take existing platforms where Disney has a connection to the consumer and stitch them together to create a more compelling experience.

One of the connections is the movie studio's reward program, Disney Movie Rewards, which has millions of members who enter codes online to gain and redeem points.

There is also a product called "Digital Copy." That's where people buy a Blu-ray or DVD, and if they buy a certain SKU [stock-keeping unit], usually the premium SKU, they can receive the digital version of that movie as well. Usually it's a third disc in a package that has an iTunes or [a] Windows media-formatted movie—and, more recently, the UltraViolet version—and the movie file transfers directly into the consumer's digital library or is stored online for on-demand access.

Even today, most consumers sort of cling to the notion of holding on to a physical object. Whether they realize it or not, or admit it or not, they really like to have it on a disc. As recently as 2010, the majority of consumers were still getting their digital content through packaged media, despite all the hoopla on iTunes and all the energy around Netflix and everything else, so Digital Copy is a fairly powerful lever.

At Disney, we looked at those two programs and said, "Okay, there is a code that's unlocking reward points and another one unlocking digital access." Let's pull those two things together.

There was also a proprietary technology called "Key Chest," which is essentially a way to record your digital rights, so there's another sort of platform to play with.

And then of course there is Disney.com, with 30 million unique visitors a day—a huge audience.

None of these elements—Rewards, Digital Copy, Key Chest, and Disney .com—were necessarily operating in an integrated way, so the idea was to bring all of these things together in a really powerful way, where consumers could have one code that is going to unlock your points, unlock your digital access, and also unlock that version of the movie at Disney.com. And Key Chest would manage and record those rights across platforms.

So that's the concept with the project known as Disney Studio All Access, branded "Disney Movies Online" at the moment. It was a very internally focused initiative requiring a great deal of collaboration across departments and business units—not an easy process. And it gets even more challenging to think about how to deploy it—or any direct-to-consumer service for that matter—in external environments due to the channel conflict issues that arise between technologies or platforms such as iTunes, Android, or Vudu.

Was Walmart concerned that there was a competing Disney version of products in its Vudu store? Because if I can get this streaming version on Disney.com, I don't need to go to Vudu anymore.

There is always that concern from any retailer about being disintermediated by direct-to-consumer activity. Disney has been in direct distribution for a long time so those conversations have had their day. Disney has been selling DVD and Blu-ray directly through their Movie Club, DisneyShopping.com, and their own retail stores for years. There are consumers who want to deal with brands directly and those who want to have all of their business with Amazon or Best Buy. It is really more about choice.

Did Disney tend to have a lot of leverage when dealing with retailers about situations like this—more so than other studios? It's a fairly distinctive product line in many ways.

In physical retail, big brands look at things like whether their product brings additional foot traffic into the store, and does it increase the market basket for the retailer? Brands do a lot of research to try and answer these questions, and assuming the brand is a powerful one, they will have leverage in talks with distributors.

In the digital space, the big challenge for branded content is aggregation—where the brand identity gets muddled from being listed alongside the competition with little or no differentiation. Or the platform itself wants to push its brand over the content owners. Content owners have tried to combat this—some have pulled or refused to place their premium-branded properties with aggregators. For example, Viacom pulled programming from Hulu, and Disney-branded video isn't found there either. Others try to extend their brand into digital storefronts by requiring a "store within a store"—this is why you see most of the digital services enabling users to search by studio or network.

Can you talk to us about windowing? How has Disney experimented with windowing?

Disney accelerated the release date of the *Alice in Wonderland* DVD. You may have read about the drama that ensued and threatened boycott as a result of this experiment. It was a stressful period but an important test. I think the key takeaway for anyone wishing to test windowing is to back the proposal with research and do it in collaboration with distribution partners. In other words, no surprises.

Going forward, you may see more tests like this, particularly in television but also for some hard-to-market films, experiments like placing advance screenings online before the show or movie premieres in traditional channels.

One of the things that Disney tried to do was organize so that all distribution works together in one place. Most studios basically have one division running theatrical, another division running home video, and another running TV and Internet distribution, with everyone working in silos, operating and making decisions that are best for their own unit. Disney was the first to formally structure its studio to look at distribution holistically and manage product from theatrical on through the entire windowing scheme.

Who were the people that needed to be brought into line in order for that to actually work? What are the various tensions that may arise in doing something like that?

With any massive restructuring it's important that there is total alignment and buy-in at the senior management level and, in my view, that the tactical elements of change—things like collaboration and new process—be part of everyone's performance measures. The reward structure needs to be aligned with new expectations. Tension can arise when a group that is rewarded on its own P&L (profit and loss) performance is now expected to share process with another team that is measured differently or is not well versed in the vertical and therefore can't contribute meaningfully, and slows process. The gears start to grind.

But it starts at the top, and if the leaders of these organizations are not fully on board, then politics take center stage and you don't get the results you're looking for. At the time of the Disney studio restructuring, the then-current leadership aimed to have the sales teams essentially merge.

Those distinctions went away?

Well, yes, in theory.

How can they go away? They seem endemic to the system.

Exactly. Each distribution organization managed not just three different channels but three very different industries—exhibition, retail, and television. These are very different industries with their own sets of norms. So, it's not simple or easy, and a lot of work went into figuring out how this gets done. But prior to the change, these folks weren't sitting around a table together having a conversation about how to maximize returns across all windows, and the change was meant to address that. It appears the thinking at Disney has evolved since then, as the home entertainment sales organization has moved out of the studio and into the consumer products division. The newer idea is to gain more efficiency by having all of Disney's retail business managed in one place.

Have you seen this at any other studios?

It seems every studio is trying to get the organization right, and so we continue to see various combinations of restructuring every few months or so.

One of the biggest areas of tension is the one around release windows. What are the time frames for each release window?

Domestically, theatrical runs anywhere from three to six months, and then DVD follows anywhere between three to six months depending on the strength of the title. DVD release dates would be the same as the electronic sell-through date. Then there is the video-on-demand (VOD) date, which is increasingly day and date with DVD and EST (electronic sell-through). Pay One follows about eighteen months after that and runs its course, which can be anywhere from eighteen to twenty-four months. Then you go into a network window, which is about seven years, where you sell the film across all the various networks. Then you go to the Pay Two window, which also runs from eighteen to twenty-four months, and then you are into the library VOD business, which is when a film goes into a library about seven to ten years after its initial theatrical release. International markets have their own windowing schemes that reflect how the business has evolved in their markets.

It's helpful for people to have a grip on these time frames because they are always shifting and changing.

It hasn't always been very transparent, but digital and new media certainly make the concept of windows more visible. Traditionally, consumers didn't know about these windows or talk about them because when you were buying or accessing a movie, generally you were separated from it by place and time. Buy it at Walmart. Watch VOD on your Comcast box. Rent it at Blockbuster.

With digital, not only is the time converging but the places are converging too. To buy a movie you had to go to a physical retailer; now, to rent something digitally, you have your cable box, but you can also buy it from iTunes and Vudu, all of them sitting right next to each other on the same day. So when a studio follows the traditional windowing scheme, it might be saying to consumers, "It's only for rent and not for sale," but people wonder why, and that sparks a conversation about windows and what these studios are doing. It doesn't make any sense to most consumers, but the economics make a lot of sense for the motion picture studios.

Along those lines, how do these changes affect the moratorium strategy that worked so well in the past for Disney?

That's a great question. At Disney we often discussed what the role of the moratorium strategy should be in a digital world. If we weren't making it available, then the pirates would do it for us. I can't say with any specificity what is happening with the moratorium strategy other than there is an awareness of exactly what you are talking about and whether it's still relevant. How do you take the concept of the Disney vault and sort of age it up and modernize it?

When you were leading global digital distribution, how did you see Disney operating differently in the digital space compared to your competitors? Disney has always had its own unique brand in ways that other studios have not. How did you see that translating into different strategies?

Early on and very much by design, we did not have a presence on every digital platform that was out there. When the category emerged around 2006–7, it seemed every week there was another press release from a studio about another big deal that was being closed.

But in my view, some of these platforms were simply not ready for prime time, and they definitely were not delivering a great consumer experience. So my concern was, if these are the places people go, or what they begin to associate with new media consumption, it wouldn't be good for the digital category because it would just perpetuate the devaluing of content online. So I stayed away from a lot of those platforms and didn't license our content to them because I wasn't interested in having bad consumer experiences proliferate the digital channel. We did fewer deals. We set criteria around the consumer experience probably more so than our competitors.

The second part of the strategy was really refocusing on what we as Disney can do for the consumer within the digital channel, since the consumer experience is different depending on which platform you buy from. For example, if you go to iTunes you are going to have a certain level of utility and access to unique content. You go to PlayStation and it's different. You go to Amazon and it's different. Who is determining the consumer experience in those cases? It's the digital platform service provider. Given

Disney's emphasis on the creative product, we weren't accustomed to turning control over consumer experience to retailers. This was also a factor in our development of direct-to-consumer digital strategy—it was another way we could say, "Okay, you guys can distribute the film, great. We'd love to have you as retailers, but we, Disney, want to build an experience behind that purchase that can be consistent across platforms." Conceptually, the idea was, we are going to build into this and all retailers had to do is let the consumer opt in and record their rights so they can have access to all of these features, reward points, and games within Disney.com.

During the Net Worth conference at UCSB, you expressed concern about digital devaluing content. What do you mean by that?

It touches on the product development issues that arise when the product evolves but doesn't necessarily get better. When DVD was in its heyday, people would run out to shop for the latest DVD, read the back to find out about the bonus features, buy it, bring it home, and watch it—it was an event and all so exciting. That didn't exist in the VHS days. From a product experience standpoint, there was a big leap between VHS and DVD.

Online digital arrived around the same time as Blu-ray, and so the next step in the evolution of home entertainment product was split among more options. Some consumers liked HD [high-definition] and went for Blu-ray. Others thought that immediacy was more valuable, and so watching SD [standard-definition] online was preferred. As consumer preferences shifted, we saw the industry struggle to establish Blu-ray as the DVD replacement. There wasn't, and still isn't, the same "gotta have it" factor that we saw when DVD replaced VHS, even though Blu-ray has the best audio and visual quality elements of any option.

With each successive technology, the experience got better. But with digital, it didn't. Digital was worse than DVD. The quality on the Internet was awful at the time, thanks to a combination of things—what hardware a consumer might have, which digital rights libraries were installed, what the encoding bit rates were, and other variables like the speed of a consumer's connection. These were all things that as product owners we weren't controlling, so the experience actually got worse. On top of that, the platforms delivering content didn't want to spend a lot of money to push high-quality files. We've come a long way now, but that wasn't the case at the time.

So the consumer is looking at this digital thing going, "Why is this costing so much? It's not even as good as what I have, I can't take it anywhere, it's not working on my device," etc. So, that played a large part in devaluing digital. Add to that piracy: If you can get it free, why pay anything? Certainly DVD piracy exists. But I think for the average family, people were not out buying pirated DVDs. They just aren't as accessible as websites hosting illegal content. And the pirate websites looked so legitimate that kids were using them and not even realizing the sites were illegal, and the parents were looking at them and saying, "Oh, it looks legit." Families weren't going to a shady street corner to a guy selling stuff out of a trunk. They're online, and it appears reputable. So now you have a zero price point for piracy compared to a $15 or $20 price point for legitimate digital, but consumers can't tell the difference between them. That plays a part in digital devaluing content too.

The convergence of VOD and the sell-through business so that they actually collide in time and place was also new. "Over here at the local Walmart, the movie is $15, and over on my cable box it's $3.99." You do the math and find you can watch it four times before you have to buy it. Let's just say all of those things play a role in bringing down the overall value. With each successive technology, we want a better consumer experience and to grow the overall business, but things going digital hasn't always enabled that.

Then there are aggregators. Aggregators devalued it too.

Well, some are better than others. I mean if you look back at the traditional video-on-demand business and the traditional TV distribution services like the Comcasts of the world, not a lot of work goes into the interface and the consumer experience. Those platforms actually tend to be—and research has shown this—one of the least favored. People hate their cable companies, and they especially hate their cable bill, and they will parse the cable bill and call in to complain in a way they won't with any other bill. Keeping that cable bill down is something that everybody is focused on. Yet cable's business model is basically to garner as many subscribers as they can and market all the different packages and grow that bill at the end of the month. It's not a transactional business; it's a subscription business. When you are a subscriber and you are in a subscription business, your focus isn't on the kinds of things that transactional businesses would be focused on, which is consumer experience, marketing around the event, driving sales volume, etc. It's not about selling a video on demand; that's a much smaller part of their overall business. But then you bring in the digital guys, iTunes, and Vudu with these glorious user interfaces, the big cover art, and branded platforms that are much easier to navigate, and there is no comparison. Platforms like Netflix and iTunes have so much positive brand recognition with consumers, which is very different from the traditional multichannel video programming distributor. From a distribution standpoint, the majority of the business still lies with traditional players, not with the new digital, but that's where the consumer's experience is superior.

Where do you see the growth for the industry? VOD seems to be the direction that . . .

A lot of consumers are going? Definitely. If you're managing distribution across channels, you have to be looking at the concept of bundling . . . finding ways to increase the overall value proposition for consumers by creating a product with so much utility that you can garner a premium price and actually shift consumers from your low-margin products to the premium-bundled product.

Digital Copy is an example of a bundled product. If you're smart, you don't give away the digital file for "free" but instead look for ways to augment the package and raise the price. Good marketers know how to do this. Other examples that have been talked about include packaging a product that includes a movie ticket, a DVD, and gives you online access as well. Of course a product like this would require a great deal of collaboration across distribution units, and so it is difficult to execute. I think the smart companies will figure this out—there is a lot to be gained by raising the value proposition for content, not to mention creating ways to have a deeper relationship with your audience.

Regarding synergy, there was that period when so many of the major media conglomerates were bulking up and there was so much enthusiasm around the idea of synergy, but recently some companies, like Time Warner, have been doing an about-face by downsizing the organization and refocusing it. But, with Disney, do you think it has been different? Do you think it has been more successful with synergy? Or is Disney also asking those questions about the right mix of businesses and about the right size for organization itself?

Yes and yes. There was constantly the question of "Are we in the right businesses?" I wasn't in all of those conversations, obviously, but from my experience at the most senior levels there is this idea that whatever activity is being done, it is being done to lift all boats. I think it's a different culture than the previous regime where you had business unit heads literally fighting one another instead of working together, and I think when Bob Iger came in, that was one of the biggest issues he wanted to address. He wanted to get collaboration and synergy going. I think he's been very effective in doing so and in sending that message. So I think the culture has changed quite a bit.

As for right sizing, there have been a lot of acquisitions lately, so it's not only about what still fits but what needs to be added. What's going to help the company grow? You have seen a stream of acquisitions on the new media side and of course there are a lot of new relationships with companies such as Hulu, and Sheryl Sandberg, COO of Facebook, and for a time, Steve Jobs on the Board. So I suspect they continue to stay connected to where a lot of the newer things are happening, and that can help influence things at the corporate development level.

Is piracy still a significant concern? It seems like the narrative has been that piracy is a concern when viable options aren't available to the consumer, but now there are many viable options. Does that mean we should expect to see piracy decline?

Piracy is still a concern, and every studio has a different perspective on how to combat it. When I was leading digital distribution, we were more focused on how we could make the experience better for people who were buying legitimate copies. Rather than constrain usability, we sought to enable as much flexibility as we could. My group wasn't concerned so much with what the professional pirates were doing because they weren't our customers. Other departments were very concerned. So you look for balance.

One of the questions I know many studios are looking at is how they can take advantage of the fact that all this pirated content might be sitting on YouTube or some of these other platforms. What can be done to perhaps monetize that or make people aware of other legitimate options? Those are ongoing efforts. There is always going to be the work being done to find out when this movie got released, how long did it take to get to Russia, Thailand, and so on? They have these big maps where they track these things. They will continue to be researching and studying that to try to clamp down on stuff getting out, but I think it depends on the market.

In the United States piracy represents a much smaller portion of overall consumption than other markets where it's a very big concern. South Korea is a huge concern. Italy and Spain are becoming really big concerns. Those latter two are markets that perhaps only two or three years ago were largely legitimate markets, but with the advent of online digital and with maybe weak regulation, consumers in those two markets have come to believe there is not really anything wrong with what they are doing. If these markets go to piracy, it's really hard to get them back. We know this from

South Korea, where only 1 percent of the overall consumption is legitimate. It's 99 percent illegal! How do you bring them back? Are they lost forever? And how many more markets will go the way of South Korea?

At Disney we ran a lot of tests in South Korea. We tried accelerating windows significantly because there weren't as many sensitivities. A lot of people might believe that to counter piracy, you just have to make the title available sooner and cheaper and you will turn things around. That is not true. You don't automatically get this lift. There is more to be done than simply adjusting those two levers, price and windows. And it's a massive undertaking in terms of overall product experience. I have yet to see proof that lowering the price or accelerating the windows are the solutions. I believe the real solution is in creating a superior product experience and marketing it effectively.

What are the most important challenges that studios are trying to address today, and over the next five years?

Most everyone is taking a look at production budgets and what can be earned back against those budgets. How many films get made a year? How can they be monetized? Can it still be done in the way it used to be done, or has all this change materially affected it? How does digital change the overall business model for film entertainment? You have your windows and you will be able to earn your return, or at least an acceptable return, on that, but those windows continue to collapse and pricing continues to vary or decline, so what does that mean in terms of the number of big pictures we can produce and distribute? How do other components fit into this bundling aspect? Maybe it's not just the movie anymore—maybe it's the movie plus this other experience. Maybe it's just the movie plus the virtual world. Maybe it's the movie and . . . ?

The smartest teams are thinking about the product in a whole new way as well. How can you create this value that doesn't exist today and really morph the definition of product and of distribution? But, in general, everyone is taking a look at what is being spent on production and marketing and trying to figure out how to influence all the emerging business models in a way that contributes to a healthy movie business.

Thomas Gewecke, Chief Digital Officer and Executive Vice President, Strategy and Business Development, Warner Bros. Entertainment

As the first chief digital officer for Warner Bros. Entertainment and executive vice president of Strategy and Business Development, Thomas Gewecke is the point man for one of the most challenging aspects of the studio's business strategy: how to position the company for success as digital distribution threatens to cannibalize Hollywood's traditional business models. Gewecke now coordinates all of the studio's various digital and global business strategies. If that weren't enough, he also oversees WB Home Entertainment's Direct-to-Consumer, Business Development, and Flixster groups. He is not a man with a lot of spare time.

This is a brand-new position established in the wake of Kevin Tsujihara's ascension to CEO in 2013. Prior to this promotion, Gewecke had been president of Warner Bros. Digital Distribution (WBDD) for five-plus years and was in charge of guiding the worldwide development and execution of activities in the wireless, online, transactional video-on-demand/pay-per-view and electronic sell-through sectors. Under Gewecke's leadership, WBDD launched such innovative offerings as On Demand movies day-and-date with their DVD release (2007), "App Editions" of films (2010), and film rentals directly through Facebook (2011).

Gewecke previously worked for Sony BMG Music Entertainment as executive vice president, Global Digital Business. Prior to Sony BMG, Gewecke was senior vice president of Business Development in the Digital Services Group for Sony Music Entertainment. Gewecke has clearly taken the lessons from the music industry's earlier mistakes and used them to his benefit at Warner Bros. We interviewed Gewecke soon after Tsujihara took over as CEO and right before he was promoted to his new post as chief digital officer. He helped explain the perks of cloud-based digital ownership, how digital distribution plays out differently for film and television content, and, among other things, why we can't rent TV shows on iTunes anymore.

MEDIA INDUSTRIES PROJECT: *Can you tell us what your job is now as head of Digital Distribution, what the key elements of your role are now, and how it has changed over the last five years?*

THOMAS GEWECKE: The role has evolved over time. I oversee Digital Distribution in the Home Entertainment Group at Warner Bros. The Home Entertainment Group is charged with making our content available—movies, television, and often games content as well—through a wide variety of home consumption channels (DVD, Blu-ray, and others). I oversee the digital distribution aspect of that, which includes making that content available through digital rental, video on demand (VOD), streaming services (such as Netflix), and through what we call electronic sell-through (EST), which is the digital downloading or digital ownership of a product.

Part of my job is to help maximize the availability of our content on a worldwide basis through digital channels; one of our most important business strategies from a commercial standpoint (but also from an anti-piracy standpoint) is to maximize the availability of our catalog, which is one of the largest in the world, through legitimate commercial digital channels. We seek to make our content available through a wide variety of business models and in a number of different sequential windows for the purpose of having availability to many, many different consumers at different price points and at different times. We have employed a lot of strategies over time to try to rapidly increase the amount of content that is available in digital form, and managing that commercial aspect of the business is one portion of the job.

A second portion is trying to understand the very rapidly evolving technology landscape and how particular technology changes are affecting our consumers, the business models that we rely upon, and the types of products that we create. This technology strategy or digital strategy element is increasingly important and part of not just my job but really of the job of everyone else in the Home Entertainment Group as well. It's something that we're trying to make part of the basic way of thinking about business, because we're in a marketplace where technology is really fundamentally transforming how consumers experience and find and discover and choose to purchase or consume our content. It's changing that experience at a very rapid and accelerating pace. We have to be continuously asking the question "What do consumers want to do with our content?" even if it is not what we have traditionally sold to them and continuously adapting our business to be aligned with the disruption and innovation that is happening in the marketplace.

Stepping back, we look at the function of digital distribution and think it really has those two pieces: helping to drive the commercial models through which consumers rent or buy our content in digital channels, and then trying to assess and understand and anticipate what the impact of technology is or is not going to be on consumers' experience of our product—and bring that into our process for developing, marketing, and distributing our product as rapidly as we can.

So along those lines, can you talk to us about practically setting up how important VOD versus EST is to your division and company? We're also interested in how that plays out differently for film and television properties.

Sure. It's definitely different for film and television product. For movie product, there is both a rental and what we call a sell-through business, sell-through being the ownership part of the business. We have multiple strategies around driving the business to be as large as it can be in those categories.

In the rental space, we've seen this very rapid evolution from physical to digital. Over the last three or four years, the percentage of total consumer spending in the rental category that goes to digital has grown very rapidly. It's now easily over 40 percent of the dollars spent by consumers in the United States. If you look at the total contribution to the company, it can be higher than 40 percent for some titles.

There have been a number of trends in the marketplace. If you look at companies like Blockbuster and other traditional brick-and-mortar rental or retail outlets, they have obviously become a smaller part of the marketplace over the last two or three years, and if you look at companies like Netflix, they have really shifted their focus to subscription streaming from disc-by-mail subscription. So the physical rental marketplace has really become much smaller than it was. Redbox, the company with the red kiosks, has been the fastest-growing part of that marketplace. But we've also seen really dramatic growth in video on demand. If you were to add the subscription business—Netflix, Amazon Prime and Comcast Streampix, Hulu, Verizon, Redbox Instant—into the mix, the digital percentage would be much higher. Well, over 50 percent of the total business of renting, if you include subscription, would be in digital format. The rental business, if you look at the most expansive definition, is fully on its way to a digital transition. Obviously it takes many, many, many years to finish those transitions, so there is certainly still a large, multibillion-dollar physical rental business. But the direction, I think, is pretty clear.

If you look at the purchasing of movies, something like 90-plus percent of all consumer spend on purchasing is still physical in the marketplace, and that varies by title, but roughly speaking, about 8 or 9 or 10 percent of the total consumer spend has now gone to digital. That's a lot higher than it was before, but it's still much, much smaller than the rental category. Part of the reason for that is that it's only been possible recently. The digital movie rental business is a much more established business and has been in existence for twelve, thirteen, or fourteen years, including the cable and satellite distributors of video on demand. On the other hand, digital ownership of movies is a relatively new thing, just the last four or five years, and it's only in the past two years really that some of the core infrastructure that was necessary to make it a really large business has come into place. So it's grown very rapidly. The marketplace is growing at a nice double-digit percentage every year, but it's still a relatively small part of the business, and making this a bigger part of the business is one of our biggest priorities.

If you look at television, there is not a rental business, so we only have a digital sell-through business.

Why is that? Why has the rental of television been eliminated in some ways?

In the digital world, there just hasn't been a demand for it. There have been some efforts to explore digital rental from time to time over the years, some experiments, but they haven't really gotten much traction among consumers. The price point for television is already very attractive. A single episode costs two dollars. If you imagine a rental version of the same product, maybe it would be a dollar or something like that. It's not that dramatic of a change in pricing. Consumers have a real desire to own content like that. The marketplace for television rental really has not ever emerged.

There are other reasons as well. If you look at the broader ecosystem of television content, the sell-through model makes a lot more sense as a complement to the other ways in which television content is distributed. If you look at traditional broadcast or cable distribution or some of the SVOD (subscription video-on-demand) distribution channels that are in place, it's not clear that à la carte, the episode-by-episode rental model, really adds much value to those options. There are plenty of linear television and linear television-related on-demand and subscription-on-demand options for television, so the transactional option that makes the most sense is really the sell-through one. As a result of that market configuration, the stats are that about 35 percent of all transactional consumer spend for television is now digital as well. If you look at the television DVD business and then the television EST business and then add those together, the EST business is now about 35 percent of the total. That's also been growing rapidly over the years.

In addition, there are new merchandising technologies. For example, iTunes launched a service about a year ago called "Complete My Season," which is very similar to their "Complete My Album" feature in the music library, where if you purchased a few episodes of the season and you want to get all the rest, there is a special discounted price that honors the fact that you've already purchased the previous episodes. It makes it easier for consumers to upgrade from a few episodes to the whole season, and that's been a part of the driver as well.

So the landscape, just to finish this, for those three categories of transaction—movie rental, movie sell-through, and TV sell-through—are very different. They are clearly in very different stages in terms of how far along the path we are from the physical to digital transition, and our view is that movie rental and TV sell-through are moving rapidly along the digital path, whereas with movie sell-through, we've still been in the situation where we need to get the product and value proposition to a better place. The difference and contrast between those three areas is one of the reasons we have such a strategic focus on things like UltraViolet and cloud-based ownership and are really redefining what ownership should mean in a digital and cloud-based world to try to make sure it is a sufficiently compelling and appealing product for consumers, because clearly the transition isn't as far along in that category.

To the extent that you're successful at developing the kinds of delivery mechanisms and business models that are going to improve the rental experience, one has to ask the question, why would anyone own? What's the value of the ownership proposition in this kind of environment?

Well, it's really interesting. This is one of the most commonly asked questions, and we think it's really based on a misperception of where consumers are from a media ownership-desire standpoint. If you look at the business of digital media in general, look, for example, at music, where for a very long time the overwhelmingly successful commercial experience was a digital download and ownership one, and while new services like Spotify have increased the significant share of subscription, in most marketplaces ownership is still overwhelmingly the largest consumption choice, both from a unit and a revenue standpoint. If you look at digital books, where there certainly are book rental models—Amazon has one, for example—the fact is that ownership of e-books has been the primary mode of commercial transaction for consumers, and people want to own music and they want to own books. If you think about things like photos, there really isn't a rental construct in photos, but if you imagine how consumers think emotionally about photos, they very much feel that ownership over that kind of personal product is really important.

There has been a rental option in the home entertainment space in movies for decades, starting with VHS. Renting is one of the business models in the film environment, but we think consumers really, really do want to own their favorite movie and TV content. There are all sorts of benefits from a distribution standpoint. For example, in many cases we make ownership content available earlier than we make rental content, although different studios have different strategies. From a consumer standpoint, we think that the reason there has been more growth in digital rental than digital ownership in the last three or four years is not because consumers don't want to own, it's because the product of digital rental has been innovating much more rapidly than the product of digital ownership (although I think that has been changing in the past year and a half because of the new strategies and models that are in place). Video on demand has been in the marketplace for a longer time. There have been more new retailers launching with new and different approaches to the interface and transactional model for video on demand. There has been a growth in the physical rental category over the last three or four years driven by a dramatic reduction in price in the form of the new model that Redbox introduced when it introduced its kiosk-based network.

What we've seen when we've gone out and done lots and lots of research on consumer attitudes toward digital ownership is that it's not any inherent issue around ownership; it's that consumers want to feel like they're (a) getting the right product for the right price, so they have a good value and a good deal, and (b) when it comes to movies in particular, where movies are more expensive today than television shows and the consumer experience of the movie is that they're making a meaningful time commitment to have what is intended to be an in-depth, important, central entertainment experience, it's very important that the quality of the product and experience be exactly what the consumer wants.

So over the past year and a half, as we have added things like HD and enhanced HD quality, as we have begun to create earlier windows for EST, the industry has been experimenting with price in various places—you've seen a variety of price points. There are more and more retailers that have much, much larger libraries available than was the case a few years ago, there has been tremendous growth in the number of ways in which you can get a digital-owned movie to the television screen, and that's been very, very important, because the longer the piece of content is, the more important it is for the consumer to be able to get it to the television screen. The more they're putting it on a large screen, the more important the HD and enhanced HD quality of the content is, and so forth. So as we have made the product better and more available and much more accessible on the television through connected TVs, connected game consoles, and a variety of other things—airplay on iTunes, things like that—the marketplace has grown steadily.

The other thing that has been really important is to get much more clear about what it means to own something digitally, particularly given the file size of movies and television shows. If you download an entire season of a TV show in HD, you may be putting 50 gigabytes of content on a hard drive. And a movie can easily be 3 or 4 gigabytes or more. And even for consumers with very large hard drives, that can still be a very meaningful amount of storage space when you start to buy a lot of content. So cloud storage and the ability to access content from the cloud across devices was really a core prerequisite for making digital ownership of movie and television content work for consumers.

The challenge for cloud ownership is that consumers have lots of questions about what it means to own something in the cloud and lots of questions about the distinction between the physical, tangible possession of something and virtual cloud-based possession of something, and that's partly because of the new technology and the new commercial phenomenon, but partly also because those are clearly distinct things and we have spent a lot of time over the last year and a half working with consumers and doing research to try to make sure that we can define what cloud ownership means in a way that will really help make consumers feel as though what they are buying when they buy from the cloud is a permanent guarantee, an always there, always available product that they own in the same way that they own something when they hold it physically in their hands.

Do you foresee a future in which one of the features might include share-ability for those digitally owned files?

Yes. Think of your own experience. What's the difference between holding a DVD in your hand and holding a digital copy of a movie in the cloud? One of the answers is that with a physical DVD, I can take it over to a friend's house, I can give it to somebody, I can sell it to somebody. Those are all things that we have historically not let consumers do with digital files in order to deal with the fact that a digital copy can be made millions of times, and it's not the same as a physical copy, where if you give it to somebody, it's not in your possession anymore.

So we are looking into some very interesting ways at partnering with companies, like Facebook, but also building into the standard industry definitions of what digital ownership is, concepts like sharing and possibly even in the future exploring how you might create secondary marketplaces for digital content. It's important that you create the right type of environment for those kinds of transactions. It's important that you have, for example, strong identity of the type you have through a Google Plus or a Facebook, so that the consumer is able to authenticate who they are and their ownership of the content that they are working with. It's certainly possible in today's digital, social networks to imagine a model where you log into, for example, Facebook, you authenticate that you own a collection of movies by logging into the UltraViolet cloud, and then you have the right to share your movies with your friends but with some reasonable rules. Maybe when you lend a movie to a friend you don't have it anymore until they give it back to you. Or maybe it's a broader, more generalized sharing right than that where you can share with a certain number of people at any given time. But we think those are very important and interesting consumer benefits that you can bring to the marketplace, and they would be a great tangible way of catching the idea of digital ownership in a way that would make it a compelling and appealing product.

Can you tell us a little bit more about your experience with the Facebook venture? What has been the most successful aspect of it? And have you achieved your objectives, what you set out to do? What were the unexpected developments in rolling out that service?

A better answer now would be that we have a wide array of offerings on Facebook. We have hundreds or even thousands of fan pages, destinations on Facebook for fans of shows or movies or characters—for example, Superman or Batman—to go and receive information about those properties and franchises and get updates and in some cases post their own thoughts or comments. We have a very large number of consumers who have joined and expressed an affinity for one or more of those pages—well, over a half-billion consumers around the world have self-identified as a fan of one or more of our properties. So first and foremost, we're working very closely across this wide spectrum of properties with Facebook as a marketing partner.

We've also done a large number of different kinds of distribution experiments. We've made movies available for rental on Facebook. We have a number of places where we link to movie ticket purchasing opportunities for new movies. We make physical merchandise available through Facebook. We are exploring opportunities to participate in Facebook's gifting program to let consumers give movie gifts to one another through Facebook, and other things like that. It is a very important platform for connecting directly with our consumers.

Along those lines, how have your efforts with UltraViolet and Flixster and even Warner Archive Instant changed or responded to what you've all learned about connected viewing from the past few years of developing these platforms? We're also wondering how you're thinking about connected viewing moving forward. Are you more interested in developing internally owned platforms, or working with external partners, or a combination?

Right. That's a great question. Figuring out the balance between those things is one of the core strategy discussions that we have all the time. Connected viewing continues to be extremely important, and the stakes are very meaningful. The percentage of homes that have a connected television is just growing all the time. We're expecting in many cases a majority of the viewing of our content is occurring on a connected or connectable screen. The consumer may not be using it as connected, but increasingly it's connected or connectable. If it's not on the television but instead on the tablet or a smartphone or any number of other portable mobile devices, then it is also most likely on a connected screen, and increasingly people are just carrying around connected screens with them. The phenomenon of connected viewing is increasingly ubiquitous.

On the other hand, from a product and service standpoint, we've still only scratched the surface. In the vast majority of cases, the fact that the viewing is occurring in a connected environment does not change what the consumer's experience of it is very much and is not changing what we're providing to them and is not necessarily changing what we're measuring or how we're serving that customer. But clearly it could.

The connection is there. The technology platforms increasingly are there. The data collection is increasingly there. Increasingly the consumer is logged into an authenticated, strong identity while they're doing the viewing, and so they have the technical ability to authorize a service to provide enhanced content or enhanced viewing or second screen content activity of some kind. We think that the technology infrastructure is in place, but a lot of the product innovation is still to come.

If you think a little further afield, today it's connected screens in the form of Internet televisions and iPads, but in the very near future, it's going to be things like Google Glass, where the consumer will be potentially wearing a lens or have access to one that is continuously connected, meaning that while you could have a second screen experience that's on your tablet while you're watching your television show, it can also be that the second screen experience is simply overlaid on top of your vision, if you want it to be, while you're watching whatever you're watching, and dynamically updating and changing based on recognition of whatever it is you're watching. The nature of what second screen is could go from being a super customized application that was designed in advance as a sort of companion, and it could really evolve rapidly into something that is more of a generalized, automated, programmatic service that tends to constantly enhance your viewing experience with all sorts of metadata and related content and search-driven content and information services that are connected to your identity and to things like your viewing history, your DVD collection, whatever else you have stored in the network, and have authorized services to access and leverage in order to provide an experience for you. That almost sounds like science fiction, but in fact, we're scant years from that being a mass-market reality based on the technologies that are being developed or are already in the marketplace.

What is up next for UltraViolet, and how are things developing with your strategy for continuing to roll that out?

We actually feel very good about that. There's nothing easy about Ultra-Violet because UltraViolet is an industry standard developed by a consortium of more than eighty companies, and it has all of the characteristics of such as standard. It is something that was collectively designed, and it has taken some time to roll out and time to perfect. However, over the last year and a half, it has really gotten very meaningful consumer traction. There are more than 11 million consumers that have created accounts, and we're seeing really rapid growth over the past six or seven months, particularly in the number of movies that are stored in UltraViolet. There are six or seven retailers who have now launched in the United States and Canada and the United Kingdom and a lot more who are coming.

We're particularly excited by the emergence of these in-home disc-to-digital services. There are about 10 billion DVDs on consumer shelves in the

United States, another 10 billion outside the United States, and, by and large, they haven't been ripped into digital files by consumers. Some people do that, but it's not legal, and there aren't any retail-based outlets that are authorized by studios. It's a big opportunity. Most consumers digitize their photos and digitize their music and want to digitize their movie and DVD collections but haven't really had an opportunity to do so legitimately. These new in-home, disc-to-digital services, there are three right now, one operated by Best Buy, one by Walmart through Vudu, and one by Flixster. They allow the consumer to sit at home with their computer and insert a DVD into their computer's DVD drive and the movie is instantly recognized and matched to a copy in the cloud and associated with the consumer's account, and he or she pays a small fee for that. It's a way to very quickly convert your collection into a digital collection in the cloud through the UltraViolet system. The other related thing that is going to happen is that multiple retailers who have a decade or more of order history—online retailers who have sold DVDs and therefore have a record of every DVD you've purchased, or traditional physical retailers who have rewards or club cards or other systems that associate transactions with identity—are going to launch services that will allow you to, for a very cost-effective price point, convert your historical purchases into the UltraViolet cloud automatically.

In the same way you can take a shoebox of photos into a camera store or a Walmart and participate in a service that converts those photos to digital form, very shortly you're going to be able to do the same thing with your historical DVD collection, but in a much easier way. We've got an automated, push-one-button-and-get-your-entire-order-history-converted-to-the-UltraViolet-cloud effect. We think that will be very appealing to consumers but also take us to a new place where consumers have large collections of movies in their lockers online and are therefore able to look at them, curate them, share information about them, share them as we launch sharing-capability services, and have them be a starting point for discovering new content.

What do you know about the demographics of the 11 million registered UltraViolet users?

Less than we'd like because they come in from lots of different sources. The nature of UltraViolet is that there are many different retailers and they all acquire customers and register them with UltraViolet, but UltraViolet itself is not necessarily a collection of demographic information, just a central registry of ownership. Each retailer holds its own deeper customer database. So we don't have perfect information.

But, generally speaking, it certainly has been a cross section of DVD and movie enthusiasts. The movie-buying and renting marketplace is a broad one. There are well over 100 million DVD-buying households in the United States. A very large percentage of American households purchase at least some DVDs or some movies every year. Obviously the number of people going to movie theaters or consuming in either the digital or physical form is very high, so we expect a broad, national cross section of consumers ultimately to be the UltraViolet constituency. There is a skew toward younger demographics in general, although we see really meaningful growth and adoption of some of these technologies in the fifty and over category as well, particularly when you think about things like curating collections and beginning to digitize content that you have collected over a period of time, and investing time in that activity.

As you're expanding the options for people to access content legitimately and expanding the platforms that your content travels on, how is that altering windowing strategies in a larger sense, and also how is that altering your relationship with cable companies? Because in some ways you're making it easier to cut the cord, right? If they have platforms that allow them to access your content, they don't need to necessarily subscribe to cable anymore . . . so can you talk about how your different strategies are changing your relationships with various sectors of the industry?

In our case, the case of movie and television content in the home entertainment window, we don't face much of an issue with that because our content typically is available through cable and satellite networks and MVPD [multichannel video programming distributor] in an on-demand format anyway. We aren't providing something that creates an incentive to cut the cord or anything like that. We're not changing the economics of the linear bundle at all. It's a bigger problem if you're a cable network and you look at whether you want to distribute your entire linear broadcast across an over-the-top platform. Then you really are potentially creating a situation where the entire linear stream is available outside of that pay-TV environment. And that's a bigger thing.

Along these lines, how are SVOD middlemen figuring into your strategies at this point? Are conglomerates moving more into in-house streaming platforms like Warner Archive Instant, or are they moving more in the direction of the external partnerships that you have been talking about?

Long term, it's a hybrid. In the near term, it's overwhelmingly a marketplace of third parties. Companies like Netflix, Amazon Prime, and Comcast

Streampix are large and important commercial partners who are really similar to our traditional syndication and network partners. They are buyers of content in later windows and make it available in a streaming format, both movies and television products. We view them as very important parts of the ecosystem. We are in increasingly larger relationships with them.

Warner Archive Instant is really an example of a different thing. It's not, in our case, an effort to create a competitive alternative to something like Netflix. Netflix is a very broad service that reaches tens of millions of people. Warner Archive Instant is intended to be a small service really directed at a very niche audience of very passionate fans of classic movie and television content. There's a place for us to showcase and make available older content that's very, very high quality, in many cases iconic content that nonetheless is old and doesn't have a really meaningful commercial distribution path in our traditional channels. These are products that aren't carried as DVDs in the Walmarts and Best Buys of the world, which is why we make them available only on a manufacture-on-demand (MOD) DVD basis. They really aren't carried by SVOD services either, for the most part. The audiences they reach are too customized to make them suitable for mass-market distribution channels. In the era of the Internet, of course, we can really begin to micro-target, and it's economical to make this content available to smaller audiences, and that's what we're trying to do with Warner Archive Instant.

The thing we did with Kickstarter and *Veronica Mars* is an example of the same thing. That's a project where we've partnered with Rob Thomas, the creator of the *Veronica Mars* show, and we've been running this campaign on Kickstarter to help fans support the movie by pre-buying T-shirts and DVDs and digital downloads and other products and other experiences. It's been very, very successful. It's broken a bunch of records.

That's a show that had 2 to 3 million viewers per episode. It has a core fan base of . . . we're not sure of the size but certainly many hundreds of thousands of people. So far, 70,000 people have pre-ordered one or more of the items as a way of demonstrating that they are commercially supportive of the idea of the movie. It's a very innovative way of trying to efficiently match a decision about investing in production of a new property with the fan base itself. It just was never possible to do that in the past in an efficient way. Platforms like Kickstarter make it very efficient to do that now and to connect with those fan bases and work with them to decide what makes sense to produce and what's commercially viable.

Warner Archive Instant is one example of that. We have a big database of people who have purchased MOD classic discs from us over the years, and we know from our research with those movie enthusiasts that they want a service like this but we expect a very small audience in a very targeted way. The Kickstarter example with *Veronica Mars* is another example where we're super-serving a fan base of 70,000 to 100,000 people in a way that very efficiently allows us to match a green-lighting decision with an advanced proof of commercial viability.

Would you do the Kickstarter model again?

Yes. It's been incredibly successful so far. It has also engendered a whole national debate about what crowdfunding is, and does it work or not work for projects of this kind. It's been very interesting.

From our standpoint, this is really a talent-driven initiative. This is not a Warner Bros. business strategy first and foremost point of entry. It's an idea that Rob Thomas, the show's creator, and Kristin Bell, the star of the show, crafted. We are a commercial partner and stand behind the effort. We're distributing the movie. We're the studio partner. As a way of connecting with fans, it is crucially built around the idea of the show's creator and star.

This is the first time anyone has done anything like this. We're in absolutely uncharted territories. It's the third-highest fund-raising project on Kickstarter of all time. The number-one and number-two things are the Pebble Watch and the OUYA game console. We're trying to get to the record of most backers ever, and we think it's a great experiment.

You have made millions from this campaign. What costs will that money cover?

It's all going to the production of the movie. Warner Bros. is ultimately funding the whole thing, so it goes into the production budget that is controlled by Warner Bros. Rob is the director and writer. He is the one shooting the film, casting the film, the one signing off on the budget. It's his project. The money goes first to pay for the stuff people have purchased. We're up to something like 65,000 T-shirts. We have to pay for the cost of the pre-ordered merchandise and DVDs and so forth. And the rest of the money goes literally into paying actors and key grips and cameras, locations, and all that stuff.

We would like to close with a question about the bigger picture. A couple of things that we noticed about Time Warner over the past year is the continuing move toward focusing its businesses, offloading more of the publishing component, taking the conglomerate and putting a laser focus on screen media, and then, on the other hand, at the studio, the elevation of Kevin Tsujihara to head of the studio. Can you talk about the overall strategic vision that's at work here?

Well, it's hard for me to speak on behalf of Time Warner, but from a Warner Bros. standpoint, we are first and foremost in the business of making fantastic content, and we then distribute that content. We feel like we have the best creative studios, the best company for creating content—movies, television, and games—in the world. And we're in a marketplace where the distribution frameworks are just changing very, very rapidly. So our strategy overall is to keep being phenomenal at the creation of content, and we have been and want to continue to be very thoughtful leaders in innovation and distribution.

We think being at the very top of our game in terms of anticipating and reacting to that change is really important, and it's how you maintain growth in an entertainment business like this by really being focused on what technology and business model changes really mean.

Do you think that distinguishes Warner Bros. from its competitors in the market, or do you think that's the general drift of the industry at this point?

I think everyone faces the same environment. I think that Warner Bros. has been particularly good at and has invested substantially in trying to both be very agile and very fast in perceiving and reacting to these changes. I think you have to. We're a very large company in some ways, and the natural condition of larger companies can be to move more slowly, and it's very hard to grow the way that you need to grow if you move too slowly in a market that's changing very rapidly. That core tension between large-size, established models, a certain amount of understandable inertia sometimes, and a very rapidly changing marketplace is a core business dynamic that we manage. I think Warner Bros. does that very well.

Mitch Singer, Chief Digital Strategy Officer, Sony Pictures Entertainment

Mitch Singer is the chief technology officer for Sony Pictures Entertainment and executive vice president of New Media and Technology for the studio. He is responsible for coordinating digital policy across all of Sony Pictures' businesses and staying ahead of the technological curve. In addition to developing strategies for engaging consumers with content across platforms and devices, Singer also coordinates Sony Pictures' anti-piracy activities worldwide.

Singer has been involved in digital rights management since the initial launch of DVD technology and has been the lead negotiator for Sony Pictures in content protection technology licensing. In June 2008 Singer became president of the Digital Entertainment Content Ecosystem, an international and cross-industry consortium of more than twenty leading studios, consumer electronics, and technology companies that are working to define and build a new digital media framework of industry standards. They plan to enable consumers to acquire and play content across platforms, services, and devices.

Singer joined Sony in 1990 as counsel and subsequently went on to become vice president in the Television Legal Group, head of Columbia TriStar Home Entertainment Legal Affairs, and senior vice president in the Sony Pictures Intellectual Property Department, where he was responsible for issues such as copyright, trademark, new technology licensing, and content protection.

In our interview, it is clear that Singer is primarily invested in digital ownership, yet he recognizes that consumers are more committed to video-on-demand (VOD) and streaming media options. He is very aware of the conflicting desires of audiences and content companies in the digital era. Singer's understanding about the need to balance those tensions with various licensing agreements, the needs of third-party services, and a host of other technological concerns combines for a thoughtful "big-picture" perspective on the future of digital distribution.

MEDIA INDUSTRIES PROJECT: *Can you tell us a little bit about your job and how it has changed over the past ten years?*

MITCH SINGER: I am the chief digital strategy officer of Sony Pictures Entertainment. I have a couple very high-level aspects of my job. First, I coordinate our worldwide anti-piracy activity; we now refer to that as digital theft policy. It takes quite a bit of my time to ensure our content is not prematurely distributed around the Internet.

Second, I review every single license agreement that we do on a worldwide basis in connection with digital distribution to ensure that third-party services have our content. They must deliver our content to the consumer in a secure manner, fully encrypted, and then when the consumer has the content locally, we must have some control against widespread unauthorized distribution of our motion pictures.

Lastly, when I see new technologies being developed, and interestingly, especially in the piracy world, I ask, "How can we use those technologies to enhance the products that we're delivering to consumers?" This aspect of my job gave rise to UltraViolet (UV).

When you're reviewing license agreements with third-party services, what are you looking for? Are there trends that are emerging? Are there red flags that you keep an eye out for?

Everybody wants to develop the best service that they can for their consumer and differentiate what they offer from their competition. I totally understand that. So one of the things I look for, first and foremost, is whether the content is being delivered to the consumer in a secure way. Does the content have appropriate protection across devices within the domain of the service's control so consumers have easy access to content but, at the same time, widespread copying and redistribution is difficult? The second thing I look for is a usage model. Obviously we want to limit the number of devices to which content is delivered. Services, on the other hand, want to expand the number of devices for content delivery. We're always looking to strike the right balance that gives the consumer a great opportunity to collect content within the service ecosystem and at the same time do it in such a way that the threat of unauthorized distribution is minimized. And of course I also want a commercial guise to get these various retailers to migrate to UV so that we can offer an even better usage model for consumers than a service can offer as a typical proprietary satellite.

What about the consumer experience? Or is that something that stays within the realm of those distributers or partners whose licenses you're reviewing?

First and foremost, it's important for the studio to license content in a way that consumers actually want to consume it. So the user experience is very, very important. User experience is always about the extent to which they can copy and play content within the home. So from a service provider's standpoint, they want the broadest rights possible. From a studio standpoint, we want to make sure that the consumer has a great experience from the service silo, but we don't want to grant broad rights that increase the threat of unauthorized sharing.

How do you develop a sense of what the consumers want?

I'm an avid consumer myself. So I start with my best judgment on what consumers want to do with content. Then, there's lots and lots of research that gives insights into consumer behavior. You also get that information from talking with service providers because they know what their customers are doing.

Let's talk digital theft policy. How have things changed in the past ten years?

I think the biggest change is how we view new technology. Disruption is no longer a threat. It's an opportunity. Ten years ago I was an intellectual property lawyer for the music industry; we firmly believed we could stop people from stealing content through peer-to-peer decoys and litigation. We understood those technology changes that were rocking our business models as huge threats. Now, we're slowly starting to ask, what opportunities do these changes offer? The industry is educating itself around disruptive technology more than ever before, and you can see attitudes slowly shifting. So, for example, we still protect our content from digital theft, but now we're looking at those tools as a way to empower the consumers as well. In a way, it's another form of security—make sure the product is secure first and foremost but start to use that same technology to expand what's possible with our content and limit the trend toward unauthorized services.

Do you think this new attitude extends to the way that the industry perceives media users who are operating in a digital environment?

If you look only at the last couple of years, consumer spending on home entertainment products has remained fairly constant. But what we're finding from an industry perspective is the percentage of those revenues that come back to the studio is less than what it was before. That's because there's a trend toward more subscription and video on demand and a movement away from ownership.

Music is a great example. Early music models—Pressplay or Rhapsody—were subscription models. But consumers still wanted to own music, and that drove the popularity of iTunes, which is not a subscription model at all: it's an ownership model. Over the last couple of years, however, we're seeing the trend shift again with the advent of subscription services like Spotify and Pandora. Netflix and Hulu are facilitating change for movies and television shows as well.

But I don't think this trend is irreversible. Collecting is in our DNA. Cavemen collected antelope antlers in their caves and drawings on their walls. It defines who we are. I collect like crazy at home. My girlfriend hates me for it. I have a bookshelf full of movies. If you look at my collection, it tells you something about me, perhaps more than I can tell you myself. Look at my Facebook page. It'll tell you what music I enjoy and what television shows I watch. You'll learn more about me. Collecting books, music, and movies really just defines us as human beings, and I firmly believe we have an innate desire to own things as long as that process is frictionless.

Here's what I mean: the motion picture industry launched the DVD in 1997. It gave the consumer the ability to collect our movies in a much more efficient manner than any technology before it. It was very easy. It was very convenient. They fit perfectly on a bookshelf. I could share it. Rental, however, had a lot of friction associated with it. I had to get into my car and find the local Blockbuster. I wasn't even sure the title was going to be available when I got there. I had to browse the shelves to find it. I had to wait in a line. I had to bring it back on their terms. If not, I was charged a penalty. All those things? They cause friction. At the time, then, buying was frictionless and renting had friction.

As the digital model emerged, friction switched. Video on demand, which replaced the physical rental model, was frictionless. I press the rent button. I pay my feed. I watch the movie on my television screen. There are no late fees. I don't even have to leave my sofa. Buying content, however, was more complicated. If I bought it from one platform provider, I swore allegiance to that platform. I wasn't able to view it across my devices. I couldn't share with friends without also sharing the device. I couldn't play it on a big-screen television. It was harder to keep track of what content existed where—there was no more bookshelf where I kept all my titles, or now there were multiple bookshelves on Amazon, iTunes, PlayStation, Xbox. There was no way to aggregate my collection.

In this environment, it makes total sense that you'd start to see video on demand and subscription increase, and you'd start to see the ownership model decrease.

You've just articulated the rationale for UV. It's an impressive consortium. How did you manage to put it all together?

There was a lot of support from multiple players early on. They all put in so much time and effort that if they weren't there, it may not have actually happened. I was just one of many.

Why was it so easy? Well, crucially, we have monopolists in the marketplace, and there's nothing that prompts companies to join forces more than a monopoly. When you have iTunes representing 70-plus percent market share, and other companies are struggling to gain a foothold, an opportunity for a pan-industry ecosystem sounds like a pretty good idea.

Really, though, I think it's a result of the attitude change I spoke about earlier: disruption as an opportunity, not a threat. Companies needed to understand that proprietary ownership or a proprietary service doesn't work for collecting content, and I'm happy to say it was fairly easy to get partners on board who shared that vision. Everyone agreed we needed to improve the consumer's experience with content if we wanted ownership to remain a valuable investment. Frictionless sharing is a key example. In UV, you can sign up to five additional members in your account, and every member has unique credentials, but everybody can share content. So, my sister, my son and daughter, my girlfriend, and my brother are the five people in my account. I live in Los Angeles. My son goes to UC Berkeley. My daughter lives with her mother in Houston. My sister lives in France. My brother lives out in Northridge. My girlfriend lives with me. She doesn't even use it. But the bottom line is I now have a choice. I can rent content and just watch it myself, or I can hold the content and collect it and know that the moment it's in my locker, my sister can enjoy it with her family in France.

So we now have a technology that enables what consumers want in a way that protects the content on terms that make the studios comfortable.

How did you arrive at an agreement among content providers that five was the right number for "household" sharing, and how did you figure out what the implications would be on pricing?

Obviously there's no discussion around pricing within the UV consortium because we would raise anti-trust concerns. Pricing is never discussed. The number six, including the original signee, for the most part was arbitrary. Some content providers wanted three. Some device manufacturers wanted ten. So we came up with a compromise. The key thing to remember here is that even though you can share your account with other members of your household, each of those individuals has his or her own log-in credentials. We know households share credentials today. Families don't have multiple Netflix accounts. But if you're sharing your account with your mother, I guarantee that the service's recommendation engine is completely broken. With unique credentials, UV can make much better recommendations based on individual viewing habits.

But that doesn't fully address the question whether the industry did enough thinking around whether sharing with households negatively impacts revenue. It's no surprise to admit DVD sales have been declining and Blu-rays aren't making up the difference. In order to invigorate sell-through—we knew we had to migrate from physical to digital—we had to offer the ability to share as a feature of ownership. We think sharing will drive ownership and reverse the trend toward subscription services and video on demand. Now I'm sure there are people at the studios who are not going to be happy that I'm sharing content with my sister in France. But I guarantee you that my sister, who's a professor on a professor's salary in France, isn't going to go out and spend twenty dollars on Blu-rays or DVDs.

What have been the biggest challenges for UV since its rollout?

We don't sell content. We don't stream content or download content. We're just a backend platform that authenticates what content the consumer has a right to access. No one has done something like this before. If it were easy to do, it would have been done. So the major challenge we find is figuring out how to ensure the system operates at its best when third-party services that plug into UV are trying to differentiate the experience for their particular users. We can only do so much to dictate that experience—how you create your account, how you sign in, how your library is presented. So the fact that we've had some issues with respect to account creation shouldn't surprise anybody. It certainly didn't surprise us. In fact, our most recent release in July 2012 fixed about 90 percent of the account creation issues. We will continue working on the problems we are faced with, and I do believe it will get to a point where it is much more seamless: where it's easy to create an account and link to retailers, to sign up members in your family. But, again, some problems were expected. We have a lot of opportunities to improve.

How do you see different power dynamics evolving in the digital distribution landscape? Some say content providers are king; others say it is those who own the digital pipelines into our homes or those who build the best device.

In the end, the consumer is king. It's the consumer who is going to control where they want their content and how they want to view it. The rest of us need to do our best to empower that.

But the consumer isn't involved with these negotiations.

We're all consumers. I'm a consumer. And there are things about UV that attract me and that I want to make better. Steve Jobs was a consumer and he said it numerous times. His intent was to make the best product for the consumer because he used his own product. I love the story about Steve Jobs scratching the glass on his first prototype iPhone when he pulled it out of his pocket. Within weeks, Apple had the first smart glass. So we're all consumers and we're building the best ecosystem because we consume content too. Here's the bottom line: I can't really isolate one particular industry over the other as being more powerful, more controlling.

You're focusing a lot on ensuring that the environment is frictionless, and ensuring that folks can share. Are there other aspects of ownership that are also important to consider?

The other parts of ownership really come down to choice, freedom, and flexibility. Consumers in all of our research have told us that they like the idea that UV gives them the freedom to determine which service to watch the content from, and which device to watch it on. In some recent research, consumers have basically told us they'd switch retailers to find UV content because they don't like being locked to a platform. I thought that was very telling. They want content across devices anytime, anywhere. That's what it means to collect content today. But that's not what it meant four years ago when I had to buy it from one service and manage my own aggregation. I had to remember where I bought the content. For any of us with kids, they would come in the room and say, "I want to watch *Spider-Man*," and I had to think, well, is that an iTunes copy, or is it sitting on the PS3? Maybe it's on the Xbox in your bedroom. Now those questions are gone. With UV, once I acquire the content, regardless of how I acquire it, physical or digital, regardless of where I acquire it, from which retailer, it's all aggregated in the same place. As more devices and services come out, consumers will have even more choice. They're no longer locked to a platform, and I think that's key to making ownership meaningful to them.

What keeps Apple's iTunes service from joining the UV environment? What do you think are the reservations?

Apple has done a phenomenal job of creating the most seamless experience for consumers. Whether it's Apple TV, or your iPhone, or your iPad, if you buy content you can watch it on all of your Apple devices. I don't expect that iTunes and Apple are just going to give up what they've built overnight. In the end, consumers are going to choose how they want to collect content. It may very well be that consumers that have Apple devices and love Apple can continue buying content from Apple. Those consumers may not care that they can't watch content on an Android device. But there are other consumers who are entering the digital market and they might have the same investment in the Apple ecosystem. What we're doing is giving them an alternative. At some point in time I would hope Apple will see that an open market for digital content is good for consumers and they will migrate iTunes into UV where consumers can buy it from iTunes, play it on their Apple devices seamlessly through the iTunes interface, and iTunes puts a token in the consumer's UV account, allowing them to share with other family members who might actually have an Android device and want to share the library on their tablet. When we get to a point where we're a little more mature with UV and we've worked out all the bugs and we get up to 10 million consumers, or 20 million consumers, then it makes the choice for iTunes a lot easier. We're less than one year old now and we're still working out the bugs. It's still a little early to look at iTunes and ask why aren't they joining.

Do you think UV will open up household media budgets a bit more, or is there some sort of innovation coming along that might transform the way people think about their household media budget?

To be honest, I don't think about it in terms of a household budget. I think about how I can help make sure consumers always have a choice between subscribing to watch our movie, renting the movie, or buying the movie. I think annual DVD sales peaked at 1.1 billion discs in North America. We're now down to 700,000 discs. Is it from the recession? Is it because consumers are substituting a video-on-demand product for a sell-through product? Is it because there are apps today and so much other entertainment online that consumers can view in lieu of our motion pictures? There may be all kinds of reasons that the number of discs being sold in North America has declined over the last few years.

What I do know is that there's a large number of consumers who love collecting our movies, and we've made it really easy in the physical world and really challenging, at best, in the digital world. My focus is: I don't want to lose a consumer from collecting our movies because we haven't given the consumer the kind of experience they want and the kind of experience we can, in fact, deliver. That's really what I'm looking at. What if a consumer had a choice between renting and buying a movie? I'm going to take subscription out of the equation for the moment because it is long-tail content and generally that content is outside of the transactional window. But when a consumer has a choice to either rent a movie and watch it or buy a movie and collect it, the question for me is: How do I get the consumer to click on the "buy" button versus the "rent" button and put it in their locker? That's been my focus, and that's the trend that I'm really looking at.

In 2010–11 the revenue from physical sell-through versus physical rental—we're talking buying or renting discs—was about a 2:1 ratio in favor of ownership. In the digital realm, that revenue ratio is reversed. It's closer to 1:3 when comparing digital sell-through to digital rental or video on demand. I'm most concerned that the majority of the revenue now comes from video on demand. So I don't think, "Oh, my God, the consumer has a limited amount of disposable income. Let me get every possible dollar!" I know consumers have a lot of choice about content, and when they choose between renting versus owning, I want them to choose ownership because it's the highest per-view transaction for our industry—that's my concern. What we don't yet address, and what consumer research suggests we may need to start addressing, is pricing. But that's not something UV can do. We can't deal with pricing. That's up to each individual studio. Jeffrey Katzenberg recently came out and said he thought the ratio between ownership and rental should be 2:1. If it's five dollars to rent, it ought to be ten dollars to buy. That's a very interesting way to think about the equation. Not only do you have to make sell-through more attractive, but in order for a consumer to pick the ownership model, they have to ask themselves, "How many times am I going to watch the movie? If I'm going to watch it more than three times, I'm going to buy it. If I'm going to watch it less than three times, I'm going to rent it." So that ratio between sell-through and rental is an important number. I don't think anyone knows what the number is yet. Katzenberg thinks it's 2:1. I think it's 2.75:1. And if it's a movie like *Spider-Man*, it might be 5:1. Who knows?

How do you think digital ownership will affect windowing strategies?

We've had a few titles now that we've actually put out for digital sell-through ahead of Blu-ray, DVD, and rental. When the sell-through model is a couple of weeks ahead of the rental, or the Blu-ray or DVD model, it ends up increasing sales. So I think windowing is very important. It's difficult to convince the consumer to buy something when he or she sees the digital sell-through price is seventeen dollars but the rental price is four dollars. I believe that what we're going to see as an industry trend is the electronic sell-through window starting to develop ahead of the existing physical window. And, again, we've seen a few studios—Sony Pictures included—that have started to experiment with that.

One last question: What is the future of DVD and Blu-ray?

I get asked that question all the time. It might have been two years ago when Steve Jobs said he wasn't going to put a Blu-ray drive in any Apple device because physical media is dead. I think he was a bit premature in that declaration. We're about thirteen years after the development of MP3 compression in the music industry, yet CDs still make up about 40 percent of global revenue. So I think physical media in film and television will remain for some time, especially Blu-ray. You're not going to get the same quality from bandwidth any time soon. Right now, there are only a small number of consumers who can stream high-def media into their homes. But for the majority of consumers? It's not going to happen for a while, so Blu-ray will be the preferred mode for quality viewing. That's why it's so important to bundle a digital copy with the physical disc. I can bring home my Blu-ray for a beautiful high-fidelity view on my big-screen television, but at the same time, I get a token in my locker that allows me to share that content across devices and with my family members. It gives me the same content but I can take it with me because it's also in the cloud.

Many disagree with me on the resilience of physical media, but based on what I've seen in music and the fact that even vinyl is still around, I think the disc won't go extinct anytime soon.

This discussion reminds me of an important point: We're not in the DVD distribution business. We tell stories. That's what we do as a studio: We tell stories. And how those stories get into the home—as a disc or as data—we don't really care. If it's brought into the home on a physical media, or if it's delivered over the Internet, we just want our stories in as many homes as possible. So we want as many delivery options to exist for a long time.

Upstarts

EDITORS' INTRODUCTION

Some media executives understand innovation as an end to established business practices and professional relationships: What was once familiar melts into the ether as digital platforms and services "threaten" more traditional ways of making, selling, distributing, and consuming content. In this sense, innovation, which is often labeled "disruption," replaces widely accepted truths with emergent realities and overwhelms veteran industry players with an impending sense of complete and total change. Both Gail Berman and Jordan Levin, who are television industry veterans, frame this particular perspective as generational. "I think that if you are an older executive," Berman says, "You are just trying to wait it out, hoping to retire before this whole thing collapses." Levin calls it "riding the dinosaur down," an expression that captures what he sees as the tendency among seasoned executives to stick with what they know and defer dealing with change to younger media professionals. Whether such assessments are true, Berman, Levin, and the other industry leaders interviewed in this section certainly see themselves as part of the latter group, a growing community of upstarts who are actively mapping out uncharted territory. Innovation, for them, has created a space to rebuild the twenty-first-century entertainment company from the ground up and reimagine what it means to produce and distribute content for a different breed of consumers. As each of the following conversations makes clear, though, innovation is not the clean break with the past that some executives fear. Rather, it expands the possibilities for entertainment content in a context that blends established practices, such as programming flow, with more novel possibilities, such as taste-based algorithms and peer-to-peer content delivery solutions.

Of course, everyone in this anthology contributes to an evolving digital media culture and economy. Yet this section represents perspectives from those whose efforts are less fettered by the machinations of the major Hollywood studios. They enjoy some distance from the layers of bureaucracy that oftentimes filter the rhetoric of executives at larger media firms. They also worry less about conflicting interests—there are fewer competing divisions and risk-averse shareholders to appease. At times, they don't even speak the same language as their studio counterparts, a symptom of the increasingly interconnected cultural geography these firms trace between Hollywood and Silicon Valley. As individuals who are working to more fully align these supposedly contrarian institutions, they pose a bit of a conundrum to established producers and distributors. They are rivals who compete for the same viewers and contribute to the ongoing fragmentation of audiences into smaller and smaller niches. Yet they also are an increasingly popular market for content companies to push their wares, even though their success threatens more traditional, and more lucrative, licensing agreements. All the while there's evidence from our conversations that these firms are important incubators, laboratories from which lessons learned can be adapted by more "mainstream" businesses. Nevertheless, without the financial cushion of a major media conglomerate, it means the stakes are much higher. They have more to lose if their business models don't deliver, adding additional pressures to the risks and experiments they make in the digital space.

From an entrepreneur in the adult entertainment industry to a high-tech engineer, and even some former studio heads, each of the executives in this section brings her or his respective expertise to bear on a common set of questions about producing and distributing content across digital platforms, mobile devices, and multiple screens. Accordingly, the following conversations pose fundamental questions about the continued relevance of broadcasters and cable channels in an environment where content is increasingly available anytime, anywhere, and on any device. Time-shifting technologies and the emergence of streaming alternatives further disconnect content from the temporal structures of network schedules, shifting the power of "appointment viewing" into the hands of audiences and raising the profile of "binge viewing" and other nontraditional consumption patterns. Likewise, as content becomes more and more available on digital delivery platforms, the future of the network as a key distribution mechanism remains uncertain. A number of interviewees invoked *Mad Men* as an illustrative case study. Lionsgate, which licenses original episodes to cable network AMC, elected to sell syndication rights not to another broadcaster or cable channel but to Netflix, where it consistently ranks among the streaming service's most watched series. This deal rewards both Lionsgate and Netflix, but what value (if any) extends to AMC is a thorny issue. Netflix's Ted Sarandos argues that the success of the series on his streaming service both opens up a new market for material notoriously difficult to syndicate (i.e., highly serialized drama) and drives new viewers to the network after they "catch up" with the series online. Yet as the deal also betrays other distribution possibilities, it challenges the network's position as an exclusive outlet for content.

In fact, Sarandos offers one of the more disruptive visions of this future, positing that networks will lose their grip on content in favor of app-based interfaces or web channels. Others in this section agree: Network brands hold little purchase in television's ongoing evolution. Instead, they detect the rising primacy of content brands—fans will seek out *Breaking Bad*, for instance, but know little and care less about the show's network home. Various opinions are offered here about how best to program in digital space, from a know-it-when-you-see-it intuition to the reliance on increasingly elaborate algorithms that reduce creative risk. Some clearly borrow from their experiences in film and television when they argue for the continued supremacy of narrative flow, regardless of device or platform. Yet others have established their entire companies around the notion that different screens require different content, making success contingent on matching the right content to the right context and, most importantly, to the right audience. Engagement, immersion, and connection are common buzzwords, capturing a certain zeitgeist among these entrepreneurs when describing the ideal relationship between their content and consumers. Digital strategy consultant Betsy Scolnik argues that online community engagement and digital brand management are the two most fundamental concerns for content creators, tasks currently misunderstood as marketing and promotion by the networks but entitlements that showrunners must learn to fight for in television's streaming future. Scolnik's entire business is built on this premise, a vision of the future in which audiences make meaningful connections with content, not *despite* the multiplatform world we live in but *because* of it.

Whether it's a more open dialogue between producers and consumers or highly personalized interfaces, the upside of fragmentation, it seems, is the ability to create screen media that connects with audiences on a more fundamental level. Even for digital distributors, identifying the easiest, most meaningful means to engage viewers is a primary concern. On the one hand, this is the stuff of dot-com entrepreneurialism found in the origins of a company like Sweden's Voddler—just three guys in a basement interested in making video streaming more efficient for users. On the other hand, digital delivery also is a much more urgent matter in which innovation is the only option to prevent extinction. Christian Mann's experience in the adult entertainment industry is a paradigmatic case. Once a new generation of entrepreneurs came of age on the Internet, the proliferation of free "tube sites" upended the sector's revenue streams, requiring leaders like Mann to adapt their business models to better compete with online rivals. Whether driven by experimentation or necessity, these executives reaffirm the central import of personalization—matching specific content with increasingly particular tastes—and open a window into the opportunities and challenges this operational logic poses for today's upstart media company.

Gail Berman, Founding Partner, BermanBraun

In 2007 Gail Berman cofounded (with former television executive Lloyd Braun) the independent production company BermanBraun, which develops content for broadcast and cable television, feature films, and the web. BermanBraun enjoys a first-look deal with NBC Universal Television, but its partnership with Microsoft has produced its biggest success: the celebrity-focused website Wonderwall, which generates more than 15 million unique visitors a month. Other web properties have followed and include partnerships with such tech companies as AOL and YouTube.

Berman admits that her new venture often requires her to translate the basics of entertainment for the engineering culture with which her company so often partners, as much as she needs a crash course in their own terminology. Nevertheless, her company is one of the few creative startups successfully mediating the relationship between Hollywood and Silicon Valley. Berman, an entertainment industry veteran, says she brings a certain narrative sensibility to the digital space, a knack for programming great content that has clearly served her well in previous roles. She is the first and only female executive to hold the top posts at both a major film studio and a television network. She became president of Paramount Pictures in 2005 after five years as president of entertainment at Fox Broadcasting Company. At Fox, Berman launched such television hits as *American Idol, 24, House, Arrested Development, Bones,* and *Family Guy.* Berman's career started in the theater; she produced her first Broadway play when she was only twenty-three years old.

We spoke to Berman about her stage to screen to multiplatform career when we met her at the offices of BermanBraun.

MEDIA INDUSTRIES PROJECT: *How has the emergence of online content platforms affected your understanding of "the audience"?*

GAIL BERMAN: As younger people enter consumer culture, viewing habits are changing. There is no question younger consumers are multitaskers. They enjoy participation and interaction. We have to think about these things as we pursue digital products. What is the audience looking for online, and how do they want to interact and participate?

In creating Wonderwall, for example, we sat for a very long time in front of a whiteboard and talked a lot about these issues. No one was crying out for a new celebrity site, but we were proposing that if we could give the audience what they really liked about celebrity and do it better than everyone else online, we could succeed. The audience liked big photos, they liked to participate, they liked photo galleries, they liked ease of use, they liked editorial bite, but it didn't have to be tawdry and it didn't have to represent the lowest common denominator. There was, it seemed to us, a space that we could fill based on what we knew about audiences and what we knew about how they liked to interact with this kind of material.

We asked ourselves, how do we create the best audience experience? How do we make the site easy to use? How do we give them a photo that appears immediately after being clicked, without buffering or anything else that annoys the audience to death? How do we make a site the best way we know how, using the technology available and making it scalable? How do we make it so that it can be used by millions of people and it can be updated five times a day? How do you do all of that?

We didn't come at it from a technological perspective; we came at it from an audience perspective. What does somebody want to see in a site like this? What is the consumer interested in when they are entering the celebrity space? I know it sounds a little didactic, but that exercise was ultimately about making sure the design was not what drove us but that audience concepts drove the design.

Did you think of the people you were trying to address as "audiences" or "users"?

For me, I thought of them as an audience, but I promise you that the technology people we deal with don't think of them that way. I'm not saying that in an insulting way. I was up in Seattle two weeks ago when I was asked to speak to a group at Microsoft. I told them that sometimes I don't know all the technological terminology that they use, sometimes I get the words wrong, but I told them that I think they understand what I'm talking about and they laughed.

I know another way of speaking or another way of looking—that's what I bring to the relationship with Microsoft. I bring a sense of narrative, for sure. I also bring a sense of immediacy. Knowing that the pictures should come up quickly is a programming sensibility. It is about understanding flow. The basic principles of programming are rarely applied in this new space. The challenge is figuring out a way of working with technologists and engineers that communicates clearly so that together you can deliver what you conceive.

I don't think those miscommunications will happen five years from now. Things will be standardized, and we will all know the terminology.

The Internet is dominated by an engineering culture that doesn't really understand content, but sometimes companies built on engineers arrive at a certain point when they start to say, "We do understand content," such as RCA and television.

Or they hire a couple of people who do—letting people with a good ideas like Lloyd and me work on the content and letting the engineers figure out how to get that content into their systems. That's really important if we want to move forward in the online space. Right now, there is still a bit of a gulf between Hollywood and Silicon Valley. I have found it to be challenging from time to time, but it's continually improving, especially as more companies take an interest in how to make online content better. It's not quite smooth sailing yet, but it's getting better.

Few people have the same level of experience across media as you do. Do you see one medium dictating your approach more than others?

I spent the first ten years of my career in the theater, a lot of my career in television, and a short amount of my career in the film business. I have now worked longer in digital than I ever did in the film business. I am just a content girl. I live my life with a gut feeling about content—spotting it, understanding how to get it out of a writer. I am a dramaturge in a lot of ways. I am an editor. I just understand content. That is the thing I do well.

My son can watch something on an IMAX screen and enjoy that, or he can watch it on the head of a pin and enjoy that. He is part of the generation that can watch content anywhere. He is seventeen. He is trained to do that. But he has to want to watch whatever it is. He doesn't care in what form it comes to him, but it has to be something that interests him. That is heartwarming to me—at the end of the day, it is always "about the show, stupid," as we like to say.

The key is to work out how to create something they feel is easy to use, entertaining, and so involving that they want to hang around. It needs to be something that makes them feel they don't need to go elsewhere.

The folks that work for Microsoft and Google are often talking in the trades about stickiness—how long people spend with content. How is that measured and defined?

"Engagement" is what we like to call it. Our sites are number one in engagement. That is very important. And it is certainly measured, believe it or not. There are two different ways people monetize the Internet—there is search and then there is display. These are two kinds of advertising. Search comes from click, click, click; every time you click an ad some place, someone gets paid.

We always like to ask people, "How does Google make money?" Google makes money from search, but not the way most people think. Let's say you want to read about Eric Clapton. You put "Eric Clapton" into the search engine and there are a million different choices returned. You click on one of those choices and you read about Eric Clapton. How much money did Google make? Google didn't make anything. They didn't make a dime from you. All Google cares about is that when you are searching for Eric Clapton you are clicking on an ad that is designed by complicated algorithms to be relevant to you. You click on that and Google makes a nickel. They are in the nickel-and-dime business. That business is all about click, click, click. Google wants to keep you clicking.

Then there is another kind of advertising called "display advertising." Display advertising is about engagement. It is about how long I can keep someone engaged in my content. When we started this business, we realized we are good at engagement. We may not be good at click, click, click, but we are really good at keeping eyeballs fixed on a certain channel. We are good at flow. We can keep audiences from changing the channel. We can keep them from clicking to go someplace else. Or when they go someplace else, we can get them to come back.

We maintained to MSN that we could engage an audience better than anybody else. It was a bold statement, but based on our experiences in the entertainment business over many, many years, and understanding programming in a really profound way, we believed we could do it better than anyone else. You will see that in our numbers. Wonderwall is the number-one celebrity site in terms of engagement. We aren't the biggest celebrity site, because Yahoo! will always have more reach. (MSN has lots of reach too, though, so we are going to be the number-two site.) But we can be number one in engagement. This means that once you get to our site, you are going to stay there longer than on anyone else's site. That is true even in the first month of Glo, which is our lifestyle site. The very first month, we were number one in engagement.

Last time we saw you, you had just returned from the upfronts. It's that time of year again. What do you think about the future of network television?

That is a big question. I went to my first upfront in 1993 or 1994, and in 2000 I gave my first upfront presentation. I did that from 2000–2005, and then I attended again in 2010 and almost nothing had changed. That was staggering to me. People are describing shows during upfront presentations, and when the salespeople get up, they say that the advertisers are not only going to buy the shows but also buy the web as well. So they do talk to advertisers about multiplatform packages, but aside from that, the presentations are the same as the first ones I ever saw. It's very disheartening. How is it possible that everyone is not on board for where everything is headed? I think that if you are an older executive you are just trying to wait it out, hoping to retire before this whole thing collapses.

I think that most established industries are resistant to change. I think that that's just a given. I think TV is still an incredibly popular medium, but the numbers that constitute successful shows now are significantly different than the numbers that constituted success in 2005 when I was running a broadcaster. It doesn't mean that there aren't people interested in TV. It means they are watching it in many different ways, and that the industry itself has to catch up with the audience, and it has been slow to do so. It's done so begrudgingly because as much as the digital space provides so much opportunity—other places to sell content, other places to engage audiences—it also provides headaches for people who are accustomed to working in a different environment. People are trying to cling to successful models that may or may not remain successful. The business is undergoing a significant evolution.

Are there any trajectories of change emerging, or are we still mired in the chaos of transition?

I think we are headed for an app-oriented world, and in that world content will become ever more important. The question that remains, then, is how important are the broadcast networks in this future? How do you launch a program, how do you get advertisers interested in that program, how do you get marketing to make the audience aware of it? These are the challenges we face, and these are the questions that we will need to answer.

Do you see a specific content provider, platform, or service as being particularly innovative?

I think the next five years for Netflix and Hulu will be very important to watch. Will those services continue to evolve in creating original programming? Will original programming ultimately break the back of those services because it's expensive to do? They have to figure out the right models to make it work. I want to believe that content creation companies will figure out how to distribute their product online and become much more comfortable in that space.

I also think the ongoing evolution of technology is fascinating. How are we going to view content in five years? Where and on what? We don't know where it's headed except that viewers are not necessarily watching television in the traditional manner anymore. Tomorrow's televisions will function like a laptop or tablet and immerse viewers in an app culture. I'm not a futurist so it's very difficult to predict how it all turns out, but ultimately I believe that distribution is ubiquitous and content is anything but. That becomes more and more true every day.

Could you elaborate on the phrase "distribution is ubiquitous and content is anything but." What's your thinking behind that?

It's really the catch-up or marathon-viewing phenomenon. Consider shows like *Breaking Bad* or *Mad Men*. So many viewers are getting hooked on those shows on Netflix, and the shows are catching on with audiences much later in their life cycles. These shows have fans, but most of them don't even know what AMC is! Consumption of the show is happening in different ways as different technologies and platforms are emerging, but the content itself is still what triggers the interest, and that content remains the same no matter where viewers find it.

Traditionally, viewers needed AMC to watch those programs. Figure out where to find it on cable, and set up their TiVo to record it if they couldn't watch it when the network had programmed it. Now we're beyond that, which is, "Hey I heard *Breaking Bad* is good so I'm going to get it and watch it at my leisure when I choose to watch it—on a plane or while I'm sunbathing or whatever." So there are multiple ways to get that content, but it's still all about the content.

What do you think about the role of networks in this environment?

It's challenging. When you start to acknowledge that people can get content now in lots of different ways, and that some of the networks don't even own that content, it raises a lot of questions about the relationships among studios, networks, and distribution platforms. So in the case of *Mad Men*, for example, Lionsgate owns it and AMC pays the studio a license fee for the show. But will Lionsgate always need AMC to distribute their material? Will that always be the model for a studio? Right now, it certainly holds true, but what does that mean for the future, and how does a company like AMC—who needs that content—come up with a model that is sustainable with so many other distribution outlets? So Lionsgate can make money from selling the show to Netflix, but how much money does AMC earn from that deal for creating an audience for the show on television? These are complicated issues. And they're bound to become more complicated in the future.

Given that digital production makes up two-thirds of your business, how much control over digital extensions do you give to the network?

I can't let them be in charge, even though they are officially in charge. I can't let them because they don't know as much about this stuff as I do now, and certainly they don't know as much as the people working here. And there doesn't seem to be a tremendous amount of interest from the network in controlling digital parts of the content as it relates to any particular given show.

So what do I mean by that? They still look at digital extensions simply as marketing. So they'll say, "Yes, we are going to have a website for your new show, and, yes of course, we are going to do some sort of background and behind-the-scenes stuff for the new show, and we'll put that online for the audience, which should be interesting." But in terms of moving forward with original content or looking at their digital content in a different way, I have not seen a tremendous amount of change there yet.

What is unique about producing for television, online, or alternative platforms such as Xbox? Does it require a different sense of the audience?

It definitely does. You always have to think about who is watching your stuff, about who is using your stuff, especially if it is interactive, like gaming.

We don't think content is ubiquitous and neither is the audience. If I maintain that content is unique and has unique properties then the audience it is there to entertain is unique as well. The audience comes to a variety of different technologies for different needs they want fulfilled. If I am not fulfilling those needs, no one is going to want to do business with me anymore. You really have to get an understanding of who is using the product.

At the same time, it does not mean that you cannot deliver a television product via Xbox, but if I looked at Xbox as a cable channel, and people are talking about them that way, then who would that audience be? We think of them as serious gamers and people who really like to engage with what Xbox already does. I would venture to say they are male and between the ages of twelve and thirty-four, though that doesn't mean they are completely male. I don't have to look at their demography. I know it. I have lived in this universe long enough to know who these people are. But there are subtleties to this too. I might sit with Xbox and they may tell me that there are X percentage of women between this age and that age they see an opportunity for. I might then think about whether there is something I can begin to put together and create that would be intriguing to that audience. What are the properties of that audience? What do they like to do? What kind of programming are they engaged with now? Then you have to take hints from your audience. What are they like? Where do they live? How much money do they like to spend? You begin to understand that this is a unique audience that represents an opportunity. I don't ever bemoan the fact there is another group of people I have to service. Instead, I am wowed that if we spend a little time thinking about them, we may be able to come with something.

You mentioned Netflix and you mentioned Hulu. What about YouTube? You have three channels on YouTube. Can you talk a little bit about the site?

YouTube is really experimenting in a way that probably few companies have the opportunity to experiment. They've invested money on a trial basis to see how all these channels pan out. How will people find these channels? How long do they have to be promoted? What constitutes a hit? People don't really know. It's constantly evolving, and I mean that literally. It's evolving on a daily basis. YouTube is doing amazing stuff as they try to figure it out as they go—but that's tough.

How is it different to deal with someone at YouTube versus dealing with someone at one of the networks or one of the cable providers?

This is very different. It's a whole different language. It's a whole different set of success metrics. Sometimes we are not even sure what they are looking for. They have an agenda internally that is not as clear as it might be to their content providers because it too is evolving for them. So I'm not sure every day that they know what the success story is.

What do you see a few years down the road for the digital space?

There is a lot developing in the digital space, a lot. It is a weird time to be in a place where no one knows anything. You are just sort of blindly trying things or thinking through things. That is what is fascinating.

We are often amazed that certain people are given large amounts of money to work in the digital space, despite the fact that they don't have proven successes. They understand some buzzwords and they are charismatic. Where it will all come out in the end, I don't know, but it is a really interesting time to be in the industry. It is frustrating because we work blind most of the time. For older generations, in five years if they haven't made the transition they're not going to. It is painful to see colleagues who haven't figured out how to do it.

The funniest part for me is that there is rarely anyone who thinks we are making money at this because they don't want to think that. No one else has, so they figure if the bigger, smarter people couldn't or haven't figured it out, then we have no chance. On literally a weekly basis we do presentations in here for people looking for guidance in the digital space. Just like a classroom. We had the Ziffren organization in here a couple of weeks ago, some of the biggest lawyers in the business representing one big-name group after another, all of them sitting around this table with a projector looking at a screen. The reason they were here was because something was going on and they didn't know the digital business models. They were interested in having us talk them through all of the different variables.

In some ways we are little explorers out there trying to figure things out. It is not particularly fun, and I don't really relish that by the way. I like it so much better when I can turn to someone and just tell them not to do the deal rather than having to talk it through and find out what they are missing and why. Everything is an effort.

What do you mean when you use the term "scalable projects"?

I will be specific and talk about Wonderwall. We need to do something that we can afford to do, something that can move quickly, at the same pace as our audience, and something we can monetize. Wonderwall changes at least five times a day. We have figured out how to do that with a small staff, every day. We monetize it everyday. This approach is different from the traditional approach where if I am going to do a project in thirty-minute serial programs they will cost me X amount of money and take this Y amount of manpower and a certain amount of time. That model is not scalable; I can't do that every day. We have to figure out how to be nimble and do something that a massive audience is interested in with a small staff so we can get massive scale. So we can get massive dollars for it.

I was in the beauty salon and I picked up a lifestyle magazine. Flipping through it I noticed the gossip is a lot of the stuff we do on Glo. It featured an ad for Tom Ford lipstick, which I realized we did on Monday. On Tuesday we were showing something else. On Wednesday, we were showing something else, on Thursday, something else. That magazine comes out once a week; it was equivalent to one day of our programming. How boring! That was my first realization. Every day on Glo we are picking a product for you. Every day we have a new front page that looks beautiful. Every day we are providing the consumer with stories and interesting partnerships and sending them over there and bringing them back here. It is so fantastic, rather than this stale thing that is sitting on a table from a week ago that is showing them lipstick. Is there still room in the marketplace for magazines? I think so, but they better figure out something to do.

Jordan Levin, President, Alloy Digital, and Chief Executive Officer, Generate

Jordan Levin has been instrumental in launching many high-impact entertainment franchises for more than two decades as a network and studio executive, producer, director, and new media entrepreneur. Levin joined The WB (Warner Bros.) as part of the founding executive team launching, building, and branding America's most successful broadcast network that targeted younger audiences. As the youngest CEO in broadcast television history, he helped launch hit shows such as *Dawson's Creek, Buffy the Vampire Slayer, Felicity, 7th Heaven, Gilmore Girls, Smallville,* and *One Tree Hill.*

In 2006 Levin partnered with other leading media executives to launch Generate, a modern entertainment studio with full-service development, production, talent, and research divisions. Alloy Digital acquired Generate in January 2012, and the result is a vertically integrated enterprise that can execute ideas entirely in-house.

Our interview with Levin took place in the Santa Monica offices of Generate. Levin described Generate's business model as a direct response to the needs of a new generation of consumers, a younger audience that consumes in what he calls a "horizontal fashion," across screens and platforms, at different times, in different places, and with a stronger desire to interact with both texts and producers. Soon after we submitted our manuscript to the publisher, Levin was appointed as executive vice president at Xbox Entertainment Studios where he will oversee scripted and unscripted original content development for the gaming console and other devices.

MEDIA INDUSTRIES PROJECT: *We'd like to start by asking you to describe what Generate does.*

JORDAN LEVIN: Very simply, what we do is we make content. At our core we are a production company. If you look at the value chain, we are the factory piece, but how we go about it isn't anywhere near as simple because the media business has become so complex; it has expanded to incorporate a lot of industries that in the past may not have been considered a part of the media ecosystem. We set up the company with a forward-facing, horizontal view of the business instead of a vertical view, which has been historically the way the industry has looked at itself.

So what do I mean by "horizontal view"? It simply means that we started the company over six years ago with the belief that consumers consume "across screen" and they have very little loyalty toward any one screen. So if content lives across screen, you need to set yourself up first and foremost as a content company that meets the cross-screen needs and desires of consumers, advertisers, and content creators.

We also recognized that each screen offers its own varying degrees of interactivity, and that the storytelling experience ideally should adapt to some unique components of each of those screens. At the same time, we looked back at a lot of different structures within the media business and felt like there were still certain benefits to vertical integration. So we set up our company with some of those benefits—not only a strong studio production arm but also a strong sales piece, which is the branded content division, as well as a talent piece, which had been extracted from the value chain around the time the government came in and regulated MCA [Music Corporation of America] under Lew Wasserman.

We have roughly thirty full-time employees and a large rotating group of freelancers. We are a one-stop shop. Usually these big ideas live across multiple platforms—TV, digital, live events, in-store retail, publishing—and we can project manage across all of those various distribution platforms.

So at the core it's about the studio division, the talent management group, and these branded content initiatives. The brand relationships get leveraged across those other divisions. Each of the divisions ends up working symbiotically with one another, so it's a very integrated platform that these divisions sit atop. But, really, it is all centered on production and execution.

How do you contract your clients? If we think about your time with The WB, there was a fairly clear set of relationships governing who the producers were and what the distribution channels were. In today's world of client relationships, this is much more complicated, isn't it?

It's much more expansive now. When Pete Aronson and I started Generate we brought in the management piece, which was an existing company that we merged with at inception. The way we were raised was obviously in a world of relatively few buyers—your choices were limited to three, maybe four, networks and a handful of studios. We were on the TV side, so outside the big three, and maybe Fox, there was really nowhere to go. What we started to recognize was our desire to be a Carsey-Werner-type independent TV production company, but by the time that we had the opportunity to do that, which was back in 2004, we realized for a lot of reasons—deregulation probably being the most important of them—that a lot had changed and you couldn't really be that kind of production company anymore.

On the scripted side what you could expect was a pod deal, which meant that you got paid an up-front guarantee to either have your services be first-look or exclusive under a traditional studio, but your ownership position was passive and you didn't have controlling interest. In that world, you lived or died by whether you got your scripts picked up to pilot and your pilots picked up to series. We never wanted to be in that position. So we kept asking ourselves how we could create an independent production company going forward that wasn't dependent upon hits. Hit-driven economics would be [the] upside to the model, but we felt we could create a sustainable business model without it. The more we thought about it, the more we felt it would be ridiculous to hang out a shingle saying we are a TV company given all we knew about younger audiences from my being at The WB. We figured out that we really had to be a content company first and foremost and needed to develop a suite of relationships with buyers, not just within one medium but across mediums. And we felt that, moving forward, the valuable underlying program assets would be assets that ideally engaged narrower audiences, but engaged them in a much deeper way.

So we started going down the path of believing it would be better to work backwards. How do you create content that's going to speak very strongly to a smaller audience and leverage that across multiple screens? You're going to have to figure out how to use potentially lower-reach platforms to incubate and introduce an idea and establish underlying rights in a world where underlying rights will not only allow you leverage to greater ownership but will allow you to protect the creator to a greater degree, especially on the film side, but TV too. Buyers are more open or eager to buy projects that have underlying rights.

That was the thinking going into the company. But, then, the more we started thinking about creating a company that could think about the world extending across these multiple platforms and having relationships with all these people, the more we recognized it was going to need to require a relatively large infrastructure. This model didn't exist in the past.

The choices we make generally speak to three distinct levers. One: How much money do you want to make? Two: Do you want that money up front, or do you want to bet on yourself and see more money down the road? And three: How much creative control do you want, and how much speed to market do you want? Those three buckets define a strategy for each client. If you want more money up front and want to get to market more quickly, then you are going to pursue the more traditional path. If creative control is more important to you and you are not as worried about getting out to market in a big way quickly, you can try to incubate your content on some of the smaller platforms. It's really the same methodology that talent and talent managers are going to increasingly have to go through. If you are a comic, it's no longer about how to get called over to Johnny Carson's couch; you can get there in so many other ways now. It's just a question of what comes first, what path you want to take.

What impact do young audiences and their consumption habits have for your company, and how do you see yourself in relation to other content providers?

I would preface it all by saying we generally think it's directional. We don't believe one model starts to necessarily subsume another model in the sense that we don't believe that traditional networks or traditional ad agencies are going to disappear. They are just going to have to evolve. I probably have a tendency to get out too far ahead of things and expect that change is going to happen more quickly than it does, but I also don't believe that change is proportionate. I believe that change has a tendency to accelerate unexpectedly once you hit a certain tipping point. I would probably argue that newspapers have started to hit that point with the arrival of the tablet.

As a company we generally say it's as if we are trying to cross a river with a pretty strong current, and we are wading across it with one foot firmly planted in the traditional way of doing things, while with our leading foot we are trying to feel our way around the river bottom. Sometimes we slip and fall and don't know exactly where we are, but we know it's important to get across because once you are committed to going across there is no point in turning back. We are never exactly sure when certain behaviors are going to tip more to the mainstream, but young audiences have always served as very strong canaries in the coal mine.

At The WB, I saw both a younger generation of consumers as well as a younger generation of creators embrace the idea of wanting to have tighter and more immediate dialogue loop between themselves and their audiences; they used chat functions early on to do that. People like J. J. Abrams, Joss Whedon, Greg Berlanti, and Ryan Murphy would get online and embrace the idea of what the audience was thinking and saying. They would talk to them directly, and if they did something the audience didn't like, they would explain why, and vice versa. That's much more immediate and specific feedback than trying to read the tea leaves of ratings. Ratings were just guideposts to whether you were doing something right or wrong without knowing exactly why.

I always found it fascinating that in the late '90s, even at mostly slow dial-up speeds, there was a community that embraced these shows and discussed them online. And there was this group of creators that wanted to communicate with that audience. Creators who very much came out of this background of fuller, more immersive content experiences have served as their sort of guides—you know, *Star Wars*, Marvel comic heroes, video game properties, things of that nature. And consumers would rabidly consume any content pieces you would give them, even in early experiments.

We kept a runner of a story line on *Smallville* alive through text messaging one summer; you could sign up for messages and we sent them until the season premiere. But if you didn't know what was going on, you weren't confused. It just added another layer. At the same time we were programming Kids WB, which had a destination site and a suite of very simple, casual games associated with it. We saw how kids embraced that and even on the WB.com side, there was this constant demand for information around the mythology of certain stories. We also saw how tough it was to reach young people through traditional TV because they were using DVRs to time-shift.

There was this Hollywood Radio & Television Society luncheon I went to over ten years ago where Jeff Greenfield asked the various network heads if they were concerned about DVR penetration, and none of them responded that they were. They felt like DVRs were no different than VCRs and [that] it was an overinflated threat. Jeff Greenfield asked me what I thought, and I was just sort of stunned by that reaction. I said we were absolutely concerned. What we were concerned about was embedding the DVR functionality in boxes being sent out by cable and satellite companies as well as by the providers themselves. Even if you presumed over the next five years you were only going to get to a 20 percent penetration rate, most data shows that 75 percent of that gets ad-skipped. Seventy-five percent of 20 percent of the market when we are at a tenuous place then is just . . . well, we were seeing things early on.

It's my feeling that every generation has a different media imprinting—your media sensibility, or the rules of media that govern your behavior, get imprinted differently. I am in this weird bridge generation in that I grew up in a world of the big-three networks and later the emergence of cable television. I was taught at the University of Texas by professors Horace Newcomb and Tom Schatz. They drilled an idea into my head that the TV experience brings its own narrative rules to the table, and that the TV experience and network experience were predominantly one in the same, in that the rules for TV were defined by the big-three networks. For example, Saturday morning meant cartoons; sports were on the weekends—stuff that we take for granted as making sense, but it only makes sense because that's the way we were raised.

I spent a lot of time in college concentrating on this whole idea that the TV experience was starting to detach itself from the network experience, and that cable was creating this other experience, and that it was imprinting a younger generation differently—to expect sports twenty-four hours a day, for example; especially in the kids' space, kids would be expecting programming twenty-four hours a day. That audience would grow up expecting that a type of programming they like will always be available to them.

In fact, I had children who were growing up through that transition. I would say the big lightbulb moment for me regarding the DVR was with my daughter when I realized she had no perception of live television. If something wasn't available to her and it wasn't on TiVo, she just couldn't understand that. Why is it not there? And then for my son it was about the next generation of video games like Nintendo 64 and the early Xbox. He's a big sports kid, and if a game wasn't on, he would play with his favorite players on Madden or MLB 2K or whatever it was. I realized that for him it was as much about being able to interact with the players with video games as it was to watch them on TV. And then with my youngest daughter, it was at a point in time when we switched to higher speeds online, so we were no longer dealing with dial-up. If her older siblings were watching TV and she wanted to watch *Dora the Explorer*, she was just as satisfied going to Nick.com and playing with Dora as she was watching Dora on TV. She considered it all Dora time.

I think there is a generation gap. For example, I think there is a huge disconnect between the powers that be at the studios, networks, media-buying companies, and CMO [chief marketing officer] levels and their kids. I went to the Adult Swim upfront. Jay-Z was performing. He did a full set. It was at the Roseland Ballroom. Adult Swim did a ten-minute clip of their shows. No one got up to speak or try to sell Adult Swim, because no one is buying a specific show in Adult Swim. They are buying the brand Adult Swim, so who needs to get up there and say, "Buy this show"? All they had to do was have this quirky subversive voice and express it the form of graphic title captions as their upfront presentation and throw a giant party. Instead of doing their upfront in the morning, they did it at night and threw a big frat party, basically. There wasn't a buyer there, with [the] exception of a few senior people, who was over the age of thirty. I remember when we were at The WB I used to ask, "Why don't we do our upfront presentation at night? That's when our buyers are awake." We used to think about things like that. The WB was a unique place because Bob Daly, Jamie Kellner, Bruce Rosenblum, and Barry Meyer empowered a lot of kids like me to do stuff. We didn't really know any better.

I think you are going to have a generation that is going to retire, and I think the recession extended their life span in this business, and I think it especially extended the life span on Madison Avenue. I think that in Hollywood to some degree there is greater independence because of personal wealth, and people stay in these jobs for reasons that have to do with something more than just money. But on Madison Avenue, most of those people in the senior media-buying positions, I believe, were looking to retire because you would hear them say a lot, "You know what? It's all too confusing. It's for the next generation, it's for you guys to figure out. You can't teach an old dog new tricks." I have heard that in our business, and I always find it somewhat shocking. Because everything is so predicated on younger audiences now, you are starting to see this justification for not being able to age-down networks, and instead they are just going to go after the baby boomers. There is an expression that they are going to "ride the dinosaur down." A lot of people are riding the dinosaur down.

What does it mean for advertisers, brands, and a company like yours if Microsoft replaces the broadcast networks, let's say, as the key conduit to consumers?

I believe for advertisers that's a tremendous advantage because, for example, the work we've done with Microsoft has allowed advertisers to create customized content initiatives with targets that MSN platforms can facilitate. Again, it goes back to a more interactive and sophisticated version of the old TV model, where creators work with producers to create a content experience that reaches the audience they want to reach with the specific messaging that they want. I think for the creators the benefit remains to be determined. I think, on the one hand, there is more bandwidth, so there is a greater ease for creators to get content of theirs to market, but again, how is it identified? How do people find it? Coupled with, how do I get paid for it? I think it would be wise for these services to view themselves more as multiple system operators than broadcast networks. The reason I say this is because they have unlimited capacity from a carriage standpoint. But how many things can they promote at any given time? They have the ability to start to evolve into a channeled universe, but they are going to have to fill those channels with something, and user-generated, low-budget content is not going to totally do it. They are going to have to seed that space with original content like John Malone seeded that space by creating Liberty Media.

I think they are going to have to offer a value proposition to the creative community that is at that higher tier, with some version of balancing risk and reward with up-front cash and revenue share down the road, but right now it's too unbalanced. There is not enough of an up-front guarantee. They are still a business that prices its content per minute. Whenever I get that question, my smart-ass answer is, is it a Michael Bay minute or a UGC [user generated content] minute? To price content by the minute is just not a logical thing to do. So I don't know where it goes, because you still have the fundamental "lost in translation" issue between Silicon Valley, Hollywood, and Madison Avenue. The reason we tried to position ourselves the way we did is that we felt consumers were going to pull these three constituencies together into a more codependent relationship. We felt that if we were at the center of being able to understand what each of their needs were in trying to manage each piece, there would be a business in that.

How would you characterize this moment in distribution?

It's obviously a transformative time. I think it's more transformative than the shift from radio to TV, because while that was a different medium, the models pretty much stayed the same. I think social media upends that model, and the fact that consumers have much greater control, the fact that there is relatively unlimited shelf space, the cost basis gets lowered. But I still think scale is going to matter. As long as scale matters, I think you are going to find there is going to be a fixed number of distribution companies, if you will, that have an undue amount of influence and drive the whole ecosystem.

I always approach my thinking first and foremost from the consumer's point of view. And, in that regard, I think it's an incredibly exciting time. The access to content and access to curation around that content is really thrilling to me as a consumer. As a creator I think this transition is probably creating more of a middle class, if you will; the era in which talent gets past the barriers of entry to an agency, studio, or network and they can pretty much coast, I think those days are over. There will be big-A players who make a disproportionate amount, and then for everyone else it will become a little bit more workmanlike. And I think for studios and networks it starts to become a complicated time as the TV business starts to shift into more of a global marketplace. I don't think that global marketplace is going to be controlled as universally by the United States as it has in the past, and I think to some degree all the deregulation that occurred over the last fifteen or twenty years has really undermined America's strength in the overall television business, even though that wasn't the intent.

Do you try to play that shift to a more global marketplace?

Absolutely. We look at the international marketplace as a place to potentially incubate and seed an idea. Theoretically, launching a show overseas with a foreign partner allows us a guarantee of more ownership and leverage back in the United States, which is ideally a stronger position. Our industry just gets more and more complicated. I think we have a lot of really good ideas on how to leverage great ownership, but like anything it becomes more complicated, more time-consuming, and a lot of times we have to ask ourselves if that is what the creative talent we work with wants, whether it's our clients or other creatives outside of our client base, and do we have the time line to really see that strategy through. But, at the same time, I think the reality business is shaping the TV business, where the scripted business used to shape the TV business.

I think the reality business is more international. So we are pursuing reality TV more aggressively, and we have a couple more reality pilots, but because our background is not as reality producers, we have to work through other reality production companies for the most part, and getting to the point where we can drive reality production through our company is going to be a longer-term initiative of proving ourselves. The other way to accelerate that is through acquisition, so that is something we are actively pursuing as well, because scripted shows are rarely going to run through the company. Now that networks don't pay full-cost license fees, which is why all the independent scripted companies are gone, we would have to offset the deficit by piecing it together through foreign sales and brands, which is what a studio like Lionsgate successfully does, but that requires a bigger infrastructure than we have. So reality TV is what's given rise to independents, but it's also given rise to the big international production companies that now dominate the scene.

Betsy Scolnik, Founder, Scolnik Enterprises

Betsy Scolnik is a consultant who specializes in global content, distribution, and communications strategy for the media and entertainment industries. Her company works with the world's leading organizations, from commercial to philanthropic, and has a proven track record of increasing distribution and awareness through building online and offline communities. Her clients have included TED, the Paley Center for Media, National Geographic, the Bill & Melinda Gates Foundation, and AOL Time Warner.

Scolnik also works closely with Wolf Films. She created the firm's first online presence, focusing on extending the *Law & Order* brand across YouTube, Facebook, and Twitter. She nearly doubled the series' online audience and made it the most consistent online promotion week after week with a permanent presence on AOL TV, MSN TV, and TVGuide.com.

Our conversation with Scolnik underscores the increasingly important opportunity that brand management in the digital space represents for content creators to cultivate and engage online fan communities. By giving us a behind-the-scenes glimpse into the digital communications strategy for the *Law & Order* series, Scolnik also reveals the intensive labor and coordination that online brand management takes and the ongoing struggles to get broadcast networks to reimagine social media as a more dynamic promotional tool. We met with Scolnik at the Paley Center for Media in Los Angeles.

MEDIA INDUSTRIES PROJECT: *Given your experience, what are some general lessons we need to know about content in a digital era?*

BETSY SCOLNIK: I would say one great lesson to learn is that when you—and I think most studios have figured this out—purchase the rights to create something, you have to have a plan from the very beginning of how you are going to exploit them. Develop your content for those rights. We got really good at doing that at National Geographic. When we launched a major editorial, the explorers would go in from a print perspective, but we made sure to send camera crews with them and photographers with them who were thinking about television content and online content. In short, plan from the start how you are going to create content and where you will leverage that content. There was this mantra in the middle of the 2000s: "Create once, publish many." Everyone thought that if you can create something once and publish it many times, you were brilliant. I don't think that mantra makes sense anymore. Now I always advise clients to create many things at the same time with specific platforms in mind—I encourage them to think strategically about what they are creating, where they want to distribute it, and how to create specific content for specific platforms. National Geographic was really out in front with this strategy.

Similarly, the other thing we learned was to recognize the digital space as a unique environment with its own content and business models. If you only think of the digital space as a promotional tool—which is what's wrong with the networks' use of it now—you will miss an opportunity to fully leverage the value it brings to the rest of your business. Hence lots of television networks are still struggling to figure out how to be real players online because they can't separate what they are doing on television from what they are doing online. You actually need production expertise for both spaces.

A digital person at a network will tell you that it's like pulling teeth to be included as an equal player within the organization. I'm saying we all have to sit at the table together. We do that at Wolf Films. When we put together a pitch for a new show, we pitch the whole package, including digital. Why? Because we've learned that if you let the network decide what happens online to support a show, they won't do much, or they'll just take a cookie-cutter approach. Then the show you invested so much of your time and creative energy into doesn't get the joy of a real online community, especially across social media. Since 2007 I think that's been the biggest change in the digital space. Today it's not just about creating digital content, which is still important, but also about building an online community around your content brand.

How do you cultivate an online community for content?

An executive producer [EP] needs to own the brand and be able to leverage it to promote the show and build community. The EPs also have to start integrating and defining online experiences as part of the show when they sell it rather than let the network determine the creative expression of that brand online for them. It benefits both the network and the EP.

Unfortunately, content brands are still pretty much owned by the network, and the network is most interested in making ratings. They may say they want to build a digital component, but really they don't. They might use digital for promotional purposes, but they don't even do that very well. So there is no nurturing of the brand's fanatics. The brand's fanatics are actually abused. All shows have the same cookie-cutter sites within the network site. There is no brand personality for the show, and only perfunctory social media interactions, and that's really just for successful shows. They say, "We have a hit, let's do Twitter and Facebook." They have millions of fans for this particular show, and what do they do? They abuse them! They start marketing other shows to them that the network thinks they also should watch. They do that instead of treating those fans as part of an important social community, which is how the show creator would treat them. But the network doesn't see it that way.

I worry *Mad Men* is about to go down this path now that Netflix has purchased syndication rights. AMC is probably thinking, "Shoot, it's not worth my while to invest in this show's community because it will benefit Netflix, and I don't want to benefit Netflix because that's not good for me." They're saying that instead of seeing the value in a community of brand loyalists who have become so engrossed in the show that they know who [Matthew] Weiner is and probably know who every director of every episode is by now too. It just wasn't the same when we grew up watching television. Fans know everything, right? They know showrunner names, episode names, guest stars by episode! They are loyalists! It's really amazing.

Who coordinates social media strategies? Networks? Creators?

I'm coordinating for Dick [Wolf] and *Law & Order*, but this is very rare. This coordination helped grow the *[Law & Order] SVU* Facebook following from about 390,000 to 3.9 million in one year. Dick just had the foresight to see the role social media could play.

Here is what I have learned from doing that. First of all, it's not easy coordinating disparate elements. I have found actors interested but frightened about jumping into the social media realm. So you teach them and they do it and they actually are great about it. It actually has a huge impact on ratings and thrills the fan community. But there are SAG [Screen Actors Guild] issues if an actor does too much work behind the scenes.

It raises questions about additional compensation. In fact, actors are often instructed by their management not to participate. So now there's a vicious cycle—you won't help promote your show, then your show isn't successful, then you don't have a job, right? Sometimes it all comes down to this weird haggling over money.

We had an interesting experience with *Law & Order: SVU*. It's been on the air for a long time, and the showrunner knew the online component was important. He tried like hell to leverage the digital space for *SVU*, and I think he did a pretty good job before we were there to help him. Showrunners simply don't have the time to really think it through or devote the energy the digital space needs. You have to think about supplying the digital space with consistent content, and you have to put that process into your budget. Plus, showrunners are not necessarily marketers, so they don't necessarily know how to make an impact or they might make a mistake— revealing big spoilers or casting problems, for example. And they're not controlled, right? Networks aren't sure if they should step in, or let it go, but often smack down on the showrunners and say, "You better stop that because we don't like it and we are paying your bills and even though we have no right to tell you what to do, we are telling you anyway."

It seems like those who care most about the brand are the creators, but they don't have control of the brand when content is sold to network television or cable. What's the best way forward?

I believe the creator should maintain control of the brand. We are in a new world where creators can start leveraging more power and ownership around how their brands are treated because deals like the one with Netflix are starting to change that landscape. It's just so different now. Who thought Netflix would do that? But here's the hard part. There are now two digital experiences, but only one is dealt with clearly and contractually—the digital streaming rights. But how to handle the digital brand experience is not clear at all. Contractually, legally . . . it just hasn't caught up with reality yet.

I was just talking about this with Dick's lawyer. I asked, "Is there a way contractually to separate digital? There are digital rights to the episodic content and then there is how you handle the brand online. Those are two different digital things to me." Even he was struggling to understand what I was saying. "What do you mean?" he asked. I said, "Well, I understand contractually that the way to retain digital rights is to be paid less for your content. I also understand that's not likely to happen because the networks will just walk away from a deal if you don't give them the digital rights. No creator is going to walk away from an entire deal over digital rights. But how can we deal with these other digital rights to the online experience of the content brand?"

Right now, the problem is that the networks are still trying to figure out how to make the digital space a significant revenue stream. It's still so small compared to the rest of what they do with their content. But they are afraid to give anything up. They are afraid to lose out on whatever the digital space becomes. A creator would lose the deal if he came to the table and said, "I want to be in charge of executing how all of the digital stuff goes. You still have to pay for it, Mr. Network. But I, as the creator, want to manage it." Now you could go in and say, "I will manage it, I will pay for it, and therefore this." But even then I think the networks would walk away from the deal because they are afraid of losing out on whatever value is to be derived from the digital space. You could also go in and say, "I will execute the digital component on your behalf. You can monetize it however you want. I will meet targets that you establish, whatever. I just want to control the experience." Still, in my conversations with Dick's lawyer, he still believes the networks will walk away. They're simply not ready or willing to go there with content creators.

So back to your question, I think the best way forward is to separate digital rights into two separate issues: one is control over the online brand experience and the other is online streaming rights. Those issues are just two fundamentally different things to me. I think we understand the latter much better than we do the former.

Why do you think networks don't value the digital space as an important site to build content brands?

Well, the truth is, the digital space just hasn't played out well for the networks. No one remembers who the networks are anymore. They just remember the shows. In fact, the more access to content we can get online, the less we know about the network that broadcasts the content. In other words, loyalty to a brand had not translated into loyalty to a network. Can you guys think of an example where someone said, "I love this show so much that I'm going to watch everything that ABC, NBC, and CBS does"?

Discovery has been incredibly good at leveraging its identity across a lot of its programming—ESPN, Bravo, Food Network.

Well you are hitting on something, right? That's more niche-based television. For the networks, and even some cable channels, it's much harder for them. It's niche programming where the brand translates to network identification. That's a good point.

If we are thinking about a transition away from television consumption into a world where online digital streaming is a principal mode through which to consume, then for AMC to invest in the Mad Men *brand and to manage that brand at AMC.com pays off for AMC because it's about building that space where people come to watch the program.*

I think you are right. But here is the other distinction. There is AMC.com and there is Twitter and Facebook, right? Where the conversation really happens is actually not where the network controls the experience. Twitter is actually analyzing a bunch of *Law & Order* data right now because they think it's a unique opportunity to see how Twitter impacts television ratings. I can't really share the specifics, but I can tell you anecdotally from having watched *Law & Order* conversations ad nauseam and in great detail that trending on Twitter during the first half of the show absolutely brings a higher second-half rating. I can tell you that trending on Twitter consistently on both coasts for a show will result in higher ratings for that show, for that week. Now we just want to really prove it, quantitatively.

But the networks don't fully understand that distinction. In fact, I have a great example: *Law & Order: Criminal Intent*. It plays on USA. It has a rabid fan base. *Criminal Intent* had a different set of detectives who were on the show for a certain period of time, but for the final season it brought back the original detectives. There was so much excitement. It was crazy town, just crazy! We're talking about three-point ratings on a cable network for scripted drama.

I spoke to Vince [D'Onofrio], who played one of the original detectives, and I asked if he might be interested in live tweeting during the show's second episode when it aired on the East Coast. He agreed. The result? Larger ratings! USA did smart things leading up to that episode. They advertised that it was going to happen, on air and online. They did everything right, and everyone from the broadcast executives to the advertising team was happy.

Meanwhile, the digital team says, "We gave all the value to Twitter." What? "We gave all the value to Twitter when we have our own platform called Chatter that competes with Twitter." I think to myself, "Did you just tell me that you have a platform that competes with Twitter? No, you don't. Maybe in your dreams." They thank me for getting Vince to tweet but ask that we do it again using Chatter instead because they can monetize that platform. We're talking about a few banner ads around the page, but it's really that important to them. They say, "It's a directive from the higher-ups that next time Vince has to do it on Chatter." So I then have to explain the difference between Twitter and Chatter to Vince who doesn't get why we can't just use Twitter. I explain that Chatter is a USA platform and we want to try and create value for USA too because obviously we want them to pick the show up for another season, and so on.

So, fast-forward, Vince does the next live conversation on Chatter. The ratings don't soar as they did with Twitter. Also, it was less exciting for Vince because it was the same people over and over again for an hour asking questions. It didn't compare to Twitter, where we couldn't keep up because there were literally forty or fifty people who would come in almost every three or four seconds, and there were people from all parts of the world. With Chatter, we started recognizing the people's IDs, and they would repeat their question if you didn't answer it the first time. So, for Vince, it was less fulfilling. He didn't really want to upset anybody, but he didn't love the experience.

[The] USA online team fought with me, but we were allowed to do the rest of the live conversations on Twitter. Ratings went up each time. This example goes back to the networks' problem. They still think that by tweaking their own model, they eventually will strike oil and emerge as the next big player online. It's not going to happen, but they leverage and abuse various show brands to try and get there anyway.

What are some of the things you hope to achieve from the social media component?

Let me try to break that down. Let me start by saying very early on I was just learning. I didn't really know what these online fans were about. So it was just curiosity at first. I would just watch it and watch it just to see if anything started sticking with me that started to make sense. So a lot of it in the early days was just that.

As I've come to understand the community, I can say this is what we look for: On a week-by-week basis, we look for volumes of conversation. If the conversation is of a certain volume, then I know where we are headed for ratings that week. If the volume isn't at a certain level, we might want to think of doing other things, hence tweeting live or whatever. Unfortunately, because the networks don't move as quickly as I would like, I often can't respond to stuff as quickly as I would like. So I'll end up just watching the conversation and waiting to see what happens and gain knowledge about trends and relationships along the way. It helps to also schedule things on a regular basis so you're not overly hindered by slow responses. It's a good safety net, plus it is a productive boost to the online community.

In addition to volume, I also look for themes. I look first at the East Coast. The East Coast tends to represent a larger part of our ratings base. I look at what they are saying and if there are consistent themes that are popping up for more than a couple weeks. If so, it's very important to talk about that with Dick and the showrunners and writers. I do the same thing for the West Coast, but it has less weight. If there's an entirely different theme that emerges on the West Coast, I convey it differently in my conversations with Dick. He knows that, and understands why. He knows where the ratings come from and where the volumes of conversation come from. Every single night that a new episode airs, I send him a recap of what happened on each coast.

So I look for volumes and I look for themes. I also look to see what other television shows or what other things people are talking about that aren't related to *Law & Order* but are within the *Law & Order* conversation. I try to figure out what it means. I've learned that trending for a short period of time doesn't really translate into ratings. Trending's impact on ratings is much more a factor of velocity. As an example, John Stamos, who starred as Uncle Jesse in *Full House,* was on *SVU.* I'm watching and I'm thinking, my God, the volume of conversation is nuts, and I'm looking at Twitter trends and normally this volume and velocity results in trending. Why are we not trending? I realized what was trending wasn't *SVU* but Uncle Jesse. Freaking Uncle Jesse was trending for like two hours!

So I look for trending and I look for volume and velocity, especially on something like *Law & Order: Los Angeles* because it was a brand-new show. For an existing show like *SVU* or *CI [Criminal Intent],* I'm looking for how to drive ratings. For example, I have noticed *CI* fans forget when episodes are on because they have been stuck in front of the TV doing an *SVU* marathon and they are tired and they are about to go have dinner and it's 9 P.M. So twenty minutes before a new episode, I send out a tweet: "Don't forget: new *Criminal Intent* with Katie and Vince in twenty minutes." Thank God. If you don't remind them, they are literally going to die. They haven't had a thing to eat or drink for hours. They haven't moved from their couch. It's crazy. I don't think they pee. It's unbelievable. But they have to go, right? So I have to remind them that they have twenty minutes to come back, and they do.

But with a new show like *Law & Order: Los Angeles,* we looked for more input from the audience. We first identified the most influential fans—the fans who were re-tweeted the most, who had the most followers, who showed up the most often. We wanted to know what consistencies appeared in their comments about the show. And they were strikingly consistent. The very first week of that show, these fans said, "Where is the *Law & Order* stuff?" The show's creative team had removed the intro music by Mike Posner. They had also removed "the voice" that says, "And these are their stories." There were some "cha-chings," but they weren't consistent. And people were like, "What the hell is this? What the hell are they doing? It was bad enough they took away my New York show. This isn't even 'our' show. What is this?" Crazy! They didn't relate to the detectives from the very first episode. The fans wouldn't stop telling us that until it was announced that the cast would be changed. Some might say it was too late then.

But week over week, these trends became very consistent. Dick had all of these trends in mind when he made major changes to the show. In fact, the bringing back of "the voice" and the "cha-chings" happened almost immediately. Retooling the more substantial elements of the show took a bit more time. But I could really taste how upset everybody was, and how much they missed the original show. They missed New York, and we knew we couldn't do anything about that. Eventually they started asking us to at least bring back a character. Ultimately, we did. We brought back an original character from *Law & Order*. We brought back the graphics. We redid the intro with a version of the old song. Alfred [Molina] and Fred [Thompson] were on every single episode, and the detective that was resonating the least was gone.

How do you craft a voice for the show? You're not tweeting as Dick Wolf . . .

Every once in a while we'll send something out in Dick's name, but that's only if I have talked about it with Dick and he has something he wants to say and he says it. It's Wolf Films, and we've created a voice for Wolf Films that is all about nurturing community, providing information, being enthusiastic and authoritative. We don't actually participate much in the conversation as it's happening unless there is a recurring question. That sometimes can happen, where the fans will get really caught up in something and I can tell they are no longer watching the show. They are focused on some question. "Didn't I see that person in another episode, and didn't they play so-and-so?" And then they can't stop. So we have to fix it. We have to find someone who can answer the question, and if we can't, we'll chime in and say, "We'll let you know tomorrow." We do this so that people will focus back on the show. During the show, I might do little things to help spike a trend, but for the most part we are not in the conversation. We are watching it and listening to it.

Most of our work takes place leading up to the show. It's about making sure people know when the new episodes are on, and it's about providing them with cool content. It's a constant reminder that we are still around and that we care and we are giving them things that no one has given them in the past. A lot of this work is for my own knowledge. It helps me predict ratings and to figure out how much we need to do that week for tune-in awareness. Really, I want the conversation to focus on the next show coming up. If it's not, we will interject. We will send something out. We will send something with every hashtag we know of, to every conversation. We have worked hard to aggregate most *Law & Order* conversation to a few hashtags. This helps us communicate more effectively and allows fans to really enjoy robust and diverse conversation and interaction.

Are there instances when a marketing firm is enlisted to handle audience relationships?

Yes! And it's ineffective. If you look at most shows' online following numbers in social media, it doesn't work to be that disingenuous and distant from the audience. You can't be effective in social media unless you are genuine. It's like listening to a radio show and the person on the radio show is really just making things up. Fans know when they are making things up. If they don't feel it, don't love it, they are done.

Christian Mann, General Manager, Evil Angel Productions

As a thirty-year veteran of the adult entertainment industry, Christian Mann has worked in various capacities, including magazines, mail order, production, and sales and marketing. As owner of Video Team, he pioneered niche marketing with the popular all-girl series *No Man's Land* and the urban series *My Baby Got Back*. In 2008 Mann took a position as general manager of Evil Angel Video.

Mann is no stranger to the challenges inherent in marketing adult products for adult consumers. He was indicted in 1989, withstood a federal obscenity trial in Texas, and was eventually acquitted of all charges. Over twenty years later, as Evil Angel's founder John Stagliano was facing obscenity charges in Washington, D.C. (charges that were ultimately dismissed in July 2010), Mann was elected to the Free Speech Coalition (FSC) Board of Directors, where he is actively involved with FSC's anti-piracy efforts. AVN, one of the two leading trade journals for the adult entertainment industry, awarded Mann with its First Amendment Defense Award in 1991. He also received the FSC's Good Guy Award in 2000, and, most recently, was inducted into the "AVN Hall of Fame—Founder's Branch" in January 2010.

As a new generation of companies finds big fortunes on the Internet, Mann finds himself confronting another challenge. He worries that the industry's legacy is at stake: a broader, more conceptual sense of the audience and its relationship to sexually explicit material is displaced by dot-com entrepreneurs who approach the entire business as a matter of get-rich-quick schemes based on algorithms and analytics. He spoke to us about his concerns, as well as some provocative parallels with the music industry, when we sat down with him at the Evil Angel offices in North Hollywood.

MEDIA INDUSTRIES PROJECT: *Tell us a little about your history in the adult entertainment industry and what you do now at Evil Angel.*

CHRISTIAN MANN: I'm the general manager at Evil Angel. I oversee all of the business operations, and that includes liaisons with about twenty different directors. We don't own our movies. We distribute them exclusively for a group of directors. It's part of John Stagliano's vision, and as far as I know ours is the only successful implementation of the United Artists' approach. Where D. W. Griffith, Charlie Chaplin, Mary Pickford, and Douglas Fairbanks failed, John succeeded, which is to create an environment where the creative people could own their works and have some self-determination and profit from their sales.

John was a director who didn't like being a gun for hire: directing a movie, turning it into a company like VCA or Caballero, and then walking away from it. He thought with that model he was not properly incentivized to make the best movie possible. Instead it incentivized him to make a movie with the tightest budget possible, and that would require the least amount of work, so he could still claim his standard $2,000 rate for directing. He realized that business model was counterproductive to what he wanted to see happen, which was people caring about making better movies. So he started Evil Angel and he was clearly right because he became very, very successful. He was able to have his pick of the best directors because they saw the advantages of his model. It's been a model that has been copied a couple of times, but we are still the best at it, and as far as I know this is the only content distribution media company that operates this way. Certainly in the adult industry it was revolutionary, and it worked.

I have been in the adult entertainment business since 1979. I am a second-generation member. My father started in the adult entertainment business in 1964. He had been in the printing business and entertainment business in Hollywood and he wound up in jail for unrelated reasons. He was released from jail in 1964, and the only place that he could get a job was for a printing company that printed adult magazines, specifically London Press, which was owned by one of the pioneers of the adult industry, Milt Luros. So my dad worked at this printing company printing adult magazines and shortly thereafter went and started a printing company of his own. His business was strictly printing until one day he was forced into distribution by a customer who did not take a print run he had ordered.

So my father, stuck with 20,000 copies of one title, started trading with others so that he could wind up with 1,000 copies of twenty titles, and with that he got into magazine distribution. In 1979, while on summer break from college, I started interning with my father. I was eighteen years old, and before long the attraction of easy money lured me into the business. Instead of continuing on with my university studies, I studied under my father's tutelage for five years until I left his employ and went to work for a company called Catalina Video. I was really overwhelmed and over my head. I was only twenty-three years old at the time but willing to fake it, and after some time I wound up being the president of Catalina Video. I learned a lot, specifically about the gay business, because Catalina Video targets gay consumers. It was there that I first started understanding the value of niche marketing and the value of pandering, for a lack of a better word, to niche appeals. I guess, and I say this with some arrogance, I found it fun to market to demographics that did not include me. How would I appeal to not only the gay market but also to factions within the gay market? How would I change the copy? How would I change the graphics? What would I do to speak to the Tom of Finland market or to the cult market or to something more *GQ*-ish? I did that until I left Catalina Video in 1989. In 1994 I bought Video Team. We were located at South Normandie Avenue and West Adams Boulevard, near the flashpoint of the Rodney King riots in 1992. In the five years that transpired working at Normandie and Adams, I learned about yet another demographic that clearly does not include me: the African American market. I pandered to that market and started a subdivision of Video Team called AfroCentric Productions because I saw a niche that was not being catered to. I also focused a lot on all-girl productions. I had a series called *No Man's Land,* which bears no relation to the Oscar-nominated movie that came out sometime after ours, of course.

I did that up until the point that it became harder and harder for a boutique company that wasn't vertically integrated to survive. If you weren't a big guy, it was really difficult. So I sold Video Team in 2006. Some people would assert that I sold at the right time. I think I did; we all know what happened to DVD sales starting right about then.

I retired and I was just doing a little bit of consulting for a few months when I received a phone call from John [Stagliano]. He had been indicted on his first federal obscenity case that summer and he reached out to me to be the general manager of Evil Angel. John knew that with the trial coming up he had all the more reason to hire new help. I have been here ever since. That was the summer of 2008.

We are very interested in how the last ten years have treated the adult entertainment industry. What have been the key developments?

I use this analogy: When my father, who was born in 1921 in Austria, was a little boy, milk was delivered to their home on a horse and buggy. Obviously, that model doesn't exist anymore, but children still drink milk. Similarly, when my father started in this industry, adult content was distributed in print—magazines and dirty books sold in dirty little bookstores—or on 8 mm reels of film. Now those delivery methods are dead. There is still a market for print magazines, but it's changed drastically alongside the advent of new technologies. So here we are today—8 mm is gone, and VHS is gone. DVD is certainly not here to stay. Yet the thing that continues is the consumer's interest in sexually explicit content.

So we consume content differently, and the economic paradigm that funds that content is different. There's very little subscriber-funded or viewer-funded content today. It's really advertiser-funded. Ergo, this so-called "free" content on the Internet, someone is paying for it. There's a business there. It's just not the same paradigm as before. It's short clips surrounded by ads. More dramatically, the Internet has made decades of entrenched power, ownership, and control obsolete and brought in a whole new group of people who are younger, more technologically savvy, and yet uninterested in the history of this business and not necessarily even that interested in the content itself. It created a group of people who made the kind of money overnight that previous barons took twenty years to accumulate. It was wealth accumulation in hyper-drive, especially in the early days of the Internet.

Ironically, the workforce that's replacing the old guard knows a lot about technology but is, overall, less educated. They can't compose a cogent sentence much less a paragraph if their life depended on it. And yet they can look at a spreadsheet and balance infinite rows of variables and data and use analytics almost instinctively and turn it into money. How did they figure all of that out and have never even heard of Pearl Harbor? They're simply lured by the promise of easy money or a fascination with the sexual component of the business, and they've all been brought up in the age of instant gratification. So what we have now are very young people with a desire for fast money being put in charge of companies that are more and more complicated to manage.

You're speaking about distribution, right? You are saying they are able to create platforms and to monetize those platforms and target their audience and do all of those sorts of things, and yet they lack a more conceptual sense of the business, its history, and its audiences?

That's exactly what I'm saying, and the proof is evidenced by the fact that they refer to it as "content." They might as well be referring to it as widgets. They are not that interested in why something is good or bad, or even the psychological basis for the appeal of certain content, prurient or whatnot, other than to the degree that they can use analytics to figure out buy rates and join rates. That said, I want to be careful before sending arrows in their direction, because if it's about the bottom line, then they are not so stupid. The new guys came in first and foremost fueled by an understanding of commerce, specifically new commerce and how that's done.

Who are these guys? Which companies?

Razor, Reality Kings, for a time, Cyberotica. A lot of them started in the "audio sex industry," or phone sex. They understood early on that if you can get content to somebody's phone or computer with the advent of broadband, you can reach a lot more people for a lot less cost almost instantaneously. Digital distribution—it was as significant as the invention of gunpowder or the steam engine.

All of a sudden these companies just blew the rest of the industry out of the water. Suddenly you had guys in their twenties, guys like Facebook's Mark Zuckerberg, who weren't even into pornography per se but who came out of college and found a way into this industry by making a series of quick deals with content owners. They were willing to acquire content from anyone! They didn't care if it came from Vivid Video or Caballero or Reuben Sturman. And, of course, the content owners didn't understand what they were giving away—they sold their content for well below market value. They simply didn't understand that what seemed like a quick and easy dollar earned from licensing their content on this ancillary platform was really going to mortgage their entire future. Imagine being in the movie business at the advent of television and getting a little bit of extra cash by selling a movie, selling perpetuity television rights to I don't know, *Citizen Kane*? Actually, those deals did happen, and they're just tragic. People didn't realize what they were signing away, at least partly because they couldn't predict the future and understand how things would be distributed tomorrow. And the parallel exists today in the adult business and the mainstream industry.

It's one of the reasons here at Evil Angel we don't sell perpetuity rights, and it's one of the reasons that we don't sell content for use on so-called "all-you-can-eat" platforms.

We do have a relationship with one such company only because they were able to (a) offer our content not as part of the regular all-you-can-eat model but as an up-sell so that there is a quantifiable financial transaction that happens as a result of a consumer paying to access our content, and

(b) within that, they were able to give us information about the percentage of use for our content: what was viewed and in what percentages so that we can take our monthly money and distribute it to the directors. So on this particular platform, we are more like a premium channel. We are the HBO.

Why HBO and not ESPN? Why be a premium upgrade instead of charging a higher subscriber carriage fee?

We didn't want our content aggregated with 100,000 movies that we feel are of lesser quality. We wanted the world to be told, "Okay, this is what you get on free TV, but to get the good quality stuff, HBO stuff, you have to pay extra."

It also doesn't make sense for the platform or service. They have 100,000 people giving them fifteen bucks a month. The only part they want to share with us is the part where revenue was created for our two hundred movies, the part where additional revenue was created as a result of our presence.

Our content is something closer to a fight: the special event, the boxing match, the fifty-dollar upgrade, or the pay-per-view event. It's just more specific accounting, and it makes it possible for the platforms or services to up-sell. We feel we bring something to the table that makes subscribers want to double their money.

You have a lot of experience marketing to niche audiences. How has digital distribution affected your ability to market your goods?

Digital technologies have made the cost of distribution low. In the days of DVD or VHS, if one made a product for a very specific niche, the question was, how do you make it so that your product is easily accessible to them and yet doesn't cost so much to make and market that it threatens your profits? In that situation, my video really has to maintain some appeal to every possible interest in order to get the most amount of purchase activity. That changed with digital distribution. Now I can make something targeted to a very specific market segment and know that the Internet offers significant cost savings to market that product. It really united the buyer and the seller and took the expensive middleman out of the equation.

Digital distribution also has changed the nature of competition. It's no longer about competing with one hundred titles on a shelf but 100,000 titles in a platform. Now the question is how to make your title jump out, how to make your title land on the front page. Some of it is a matter of sales-manship and connection to whomever it is that runs that platform. It's what the beer salesman used to do: go to the grocery store and pay the guy off so he places your product at eye-level on the shelf. But it's also very much about graphics and trying to make one's product stand out. For example, previously it was accepted practice to show as much as one can on the front cover. But now your front cover is reduced to the size of a thumbnail in a gallery where a consumer is looking at twenty images on a single page. It's best to use a single picture on that cover and make sure it's one that grabs. Make yours outrageous, over the top. Make it noteworthy.

If you are going to be marketing something that is aimed at fans of black male, white female pornography and you know that you are appealing to a certain taboo for shock value, then maybe you are going to call yours, "Oh, my God! My mother is fucking an 'N word'." You know? Something that is shocking and outrageous. Remember that in this kind of competition for space and eyes, any publicity is good publicity. You see it in the mainstream and you see it in adult entertainment.

What parallels do you see between the adult entertainment industry and the mainstream industry? What challenges do you share?

Pornography is not like the movie business. Pornography is like the music business. Nobody wants to watch the middle ten minutes of *The Godfather* or *The Hunger Games;* viewers want the whole thing. But with music, not so. You want the track. It might be the fourth cut that really appeals to you.

Well, pornography movies are really about the scene. Pornography is consumed in a five- or ten- minute experience. And because of that, it became something that people wanted to chop up and put out in clip form, and broadband technology was such that it was very easy to take a five-minute segment and put it out there for free, or even a forty-minute clip from a movie, a scene, as opposed to the whole three-hour movie. So contrary to what the movie business was facing at that time, people weren't really pirating entire pornography movies and putting them online. Actually, that did happen, but the effort it took to upload it and download it to a computer ruined the experience for the viewer. Once they figured out how to upload a clip, we were ravaged by piracy.

The solution ended up being a three-pronged approach that I learned from Disney. They said, "The answer here is technological, it's legislative, and it's marketing. If you are only going to use one or two of these, you are not going to win this war. You have to be prepared to bring all three to bear."

Let's discuss those three solutions. First, technology. It's called "spidering." Spider technology makes it possible for us to fingerprint our content, so to speak. We no longer have to go online and do manual searches for our content by title, by director, by star. We no longer have to look around and say, "I recognize that! Out of these four hundred scenes with Bella-donna, these three hundred belong to us!" Now, with spidering, we can go online and in one simple search identify our products. With that, it's be-come harder for the tube operators to claim ignorance, to defend them-selves by saying it's all "user-generated content." We can give them notice, tell them to take it down, and then go a step further with the technology to say, "Use this code to filter your site. Everything that comes up is ours. You have to take that down too."

The next step is in the legislative side. Lawsuits. I tell people, "When you pirate our movies, you are not stealing that movie, you are stealing from our company. You are not shoplifting from the store; you are picking up the entire store and taking it away from the owner."

And then the third approach, which hadn't occurred to me until the guys at Disney showed me how, was the marketing side—in other words, beat-ing the tube operators and pirates to the punch. We did studies and found that a huge jump in piracy happens right after the DVD of that product hits the streets. They are not really lifting it from other websites; they are ripping the DVD. Well now we can actually embed things in the DVD that lead consumers back to us. We can embed little trailers in there and say, "Like what you see? Click here." Then it takes them back to our website.

We also upload our own titles on tube sites with key phrases: "The new Jonnie Darkko scene featuring Belladonna and Mike Adriano." We upload that to the tube sites, but instead of uploading the fifty- or sixty-minute scene, we upload a three-minute trailer of that scene with a live link that says, "Love it? Want to see the cum shot? Go to EvilAngel.com." We take the traffic that these tube sites are getting and redirect it back to us. And if we upload the trailer one day before the DVD hits the street—if we are first to get it online—for everybody that searches the tube site, our trailer is going to be the first listing in the search results.

What's the tube site operator going to say to us? "You are stealing the customers that I was getting by stealing your content?" We became so ob-noxious to the tube sites that it gave us leverage to say, "Okay, would you like to work with us or against us? Tell you what—instead of stealing from us, how about you become our partner?" We started approaching tube sites as a pusher approached new customers in the 1960s. Pushers give you that first reefer for free. So we said, "Okay, instead of allowing you to steal case after case of cigarettes out of our place and give them to people for free, we'll give you some samples, but if they want more of this particular brand of cigarette, they have to come back to us and buy it."

Those are the three basic prongs of our approach. We've added a fourth one that we've borrowed from the music business. It's the iTunes model. If you're a member of our site, for example, you don't have to waste your time or money paying forty bucks for a DVD with six scenes on it when you really only want one scene. So on our site you can select scenes from different DVDs like you can select tracks from different CDs. You basically create your own anthology. You become your own editor, which gives you (a) a much better value for your money, and (b) it makes the online experience sticky and interactive.

What else have you learned from the mainstream industry?

I'm going to reference the music industry again. We've observed them turn their business model upside down and find themselves in another lucrative situation. It used to be that a band made an album and in interest of selling those albums, they toured. But the reality is, albums don't make money anymore. Record stores are gone, right? So the saving grace for the music industry has been concert tickets. People still love to go see a live show. For some reason, they'll complain about a $15 CD but don't mind paying $50 or $60 to see a concert. Today the prices are up to $250! They'll pay for the experience. That's become the core of the industry's business.

Now, of course, we can't take our sex acts on the road. But we can look for other revenue streams in similar ways. We're also much more financially efficient, I think. We don't frivolously spend money on production like Hollywood does. Look, I live in downtown LA. I've seen them shut down an entire block to film a car turning the corner during a chase scene. With the amount of crew, lighting, trucks, wardrobe trailers, and so on, you can just see them throwing money away. Our highest budgets sometimes equal the catering budget on those studio movies. Ironically, as those traditional models start to waiver, the mainstream industry is becoming more and more interested in our guerilla style.

Let's talk about policy. Do you have any alliances with the mainstream industry when it comes to policy on piracy, freedom of speech? Or do certain tensions prohibit those alliances?

A lot of the top guys in our industry recently found themselves sitting down with some top executives from the mainstream movie business to discuss our shared challenges, which is the piracy thing, and the amount of free content available on the web. Even though our content might be pirated in different ways, broadband speeds have improved to such an extent that virtually anyone can find entire films and television series online. So these executives all wanted to hear more about the solutions we have identified over the years. It was one of the most fascinating things from my point of view to find out that these guys were studying very carefully what's happening to the content in the adult industry, hoping they might learn some best practices from us.

I won't tell you who or what mainstream companies were involved because it isn't in their best interest to have this association, but they recognized two things: one, they could learn something from us, and two, if they can help us put a stop to the tube sites as a viable model for people who want to steal content, it would impact them in a beneficial way as well, because what has to be stopped isn't just the piracy itself but the existence of a business model for the piracy that starts with us and then morphs its way to them.

This reciprocity isn't entirely novel. There have been a lot of people in our business who have made it by doing some things in the mainstream. There are several directors who have directed some nonadult stuff under different names with various levels of success. And there are some people in the mainstream industry who have come to moonlight with us. Often it is a matter of financial need—the mainstream industry, especially the television industry, has had a lot of technicians become unemployed thanks to the huge success of reality television that replaced hour-long dramas and their huge film crews. It just devastated an entire industry. Now you can do a very successful TV show with just a couple of cameras following around some dumb celebrity. Others moonlight with us simply because they are fascinated or interested in the subject matter.

What do we need to know about the future of the adult entertainment industry?

Regulating obscenity always has been tricky. And the presiding logic says it has to be patently offensive to the average member of a particular community, and that it has to have absolutely no social value, that it only appeals to prurient interest. Digital distribution is going to cause significant problems here. Simply, how does one define "community" anymore? Originally, if I shipped something from my warehouse in Los Angeles to a theater in Oshkosh, Wisconsin, Dubuque, Iowa, or Santa Barbara, California, the communities under question are quite literally drawn. If I ship something to Santa Barbara, it doesn't affect the community in San Francisco.

But what about the person who accesses content hosted on a server in Los Angeles from the privacy of his own home in Oshkosh? I didn't ship it. That person brought it to Oshkosh. Obscenity laws no longer work in an era of digital distribution. My prediction is that *Miller v. California*, which established the current status quo in 1973, will fall apart. I worry about what the future will look like when that happens.

If it goes away, will somebody start saying, "Okay, this is what's okay and that's what isn't?" Because right now there is no such differentiation except for easily identifiable unacceptable content, like child porn. If the community standard won't hold court anymore, what are you going to say then?

Ted Sarandos, Chief Content Officer, Netflix

With more than 36 million subscribers in forty different countries, Netflix is one of the leading subscription streaming services in the world, especially in the United States (HBO, for comparison's sake, only boasts 27.8 million subscribers). In the past few years, it's also emerged as a potentially serious player in the game for original content, shelling out $100 million for its first outing, a two-season commitment for an adaptation of the BBC miniseries *House of Cards*, which premiered to critical praise on February 1, 2013. Original series *Hemlock Grove, Arrested Development,* and *Orange Is the New Black* have followed with equally impressive hype, even if the company remains mum on the exact returns.

Ted Sarandos, who has served as Netflix's chief content officer since 2000, deserves notice in this context for two reasons. First, he's the man behind the content, overseeing an acquisition budget reportedly worth nearly $4 billion. This makes him the chief negotiator when it comes to licensing content from major studios whose executives remain leery about the service's potential to cannibalize more lucrative revenue streams. Second, Sarandos has an unabashed disregard for the traditional television business model. He says audience content development is flawed, metrics are outdated, marketing is too costly, and the future of television is one made up of taste-based algorithms. He mapped out some alternatives for us when we met with him at his office in Netflix's Los Angeles headquarters.

MEDIA INDUSTRIES PROJECT: *I read that you signed 3.9 billion dollars' worth of licensing contracts in 2011. Is that true?*
TED SARANDOS: We don't release public numbers on our individual contracts. The number you're referencing is a cumulative figure over the next

several years. It is the impact of long-range deals as they continue to flow product through Netflix.

How does that compare to contract totals made by other licensers, such as cable networks?

HBO is at the high end of that number, but we're still slightly larger on a domestic basis. But, remember, we're now licensing content for Canada, the United Kingdom, and all of Latin America.

Can you talk about some of the challenges you face when licensing content?

I started with the company almost thirteen years ago when we were focused exclusively on our DVD business. In the United States the "first sale" doctrine enables a company, with little friction, to acquire a large library of movies and television shows and then distribute those titles because the original copyright holder does not have a perpetual license. In other words, a company can buy a DVD from the content provider and rent or resell that DVD until it breaks. As long as the physical media holds up, you don't have to keep paying for your right to rent or resell it.

As you move to the streaming business, however, the "first sale" doctrine doesn't apply. Instead, you have to secure a subscription video-on-demand [SVOD] television right to distribute the content. And that license has to be renewed constantly in competition with other SVOD players. Right now, every network is interested in holding, withholding, buying, or blocking SVOD rights as a way to create an atmosphere for their own VOD services, like the TV Everywhere initiative.

Windowing also posed a challenge to us when we first entered the streaming business. Every major studio had a pay-TV deal, which typically grants premium channels and cable networks exclusive rights to major releases for a period of nine years following the DVD release. For us, that blocked every major movie release from our business for nine years. We were forced to license titles that were in theaters ten years earlier.

So, as classic innovators, we started out with a product—our streaming business—that addressed the needs of only a few consumers. It was just an add-on to our DVD business. It didn't cost extra; at the time, it wasn't worth paying extra. But because we offered it, people started developing the habit of watching it. Then the content improved, delivery improved—no more buffering—and the licensing environment opened up. We shared a licensing agreement with Starz, which helped shrink that nine-year window down to six months. We made direct deals with producers like Relativity Media, Open Roads, and New Image. This helped secure some exclusive rights to keep content from going into pay-TV deals with HBO and others. We also created new markets: acquiring the rights to distribute television content one year after broadcast didn't exist before we invested in it. It wasn't the day-after transaction on iTunes. It wasn't traditional syndication. It was a new window we created with broadcast networks and cable channels to license their shows in a season-after model. It's an especially great market for cable channels. They can't really syndicate their shows to other cable channels, and most of the content is so serialized that it's difficult to syndicate at all. We secured exclusive rights to *Mad Men* partially because we outbid everybody else, but mostly because nobody else wanted it. Because we can get more viewing for that show than anyone else, we can pay more for it than anyone else.

Simply put, we continued to invest in television, and grow our investment in television, because, as a company, we really believe the *digital* future of television is *the* future of television. I don't think it's controversial to say that the Internet will replace the cable box as the primary delivery mechanism for television within the next twenty years.

How has your relationship with content providers evolved? Some love you. Others see you as a threat.

I don't seek to be loved. I seek to be respected. The reason why a network or a studio loves you is because you make them money. If I don't make them money, then I don't expect them to love me. But I do make them money, and, more importantly, I make them money in unintuitive ways. We offer a really great economic sweetener: a buyer for highly serialized content, which is very expensive to produce and very hard to monetize. *Mad Men* is the perfect example: I not only gave AMC a very high license fee for that show, but the ability to binge on seasons 1–4 helped launched the biggest premiere [season 5] in the show's history. It's the same for *Sons of Anarchy*. People will stream the seasons we have before jumping to the network to watch the latest season premiere. I realize not everyone jumps. Some viewers will just wait for the next season to premiere on Netflix. But on a net basis I think most people migrate to the network after binging on Netflix. So FX grows their audience, and we derive value from the license fee. And then the network is able to produce more seasons of *Sons of Anarchy*. It's win-win for everyone, including viewers.

But what happens to the value of your content once a viewer makes the jump back to the network?

We think about the value of content differently. I think marketing has way too much influence in the current entertainment economy. It's the biggest item in this town on anyone's profit and loss statement. Fill the seats in the theater on opening night. Make sure everyone gathers at the same time on the same night in front of the television. And let's just hope everyone likes it so numbers don't drop 80 percent the next night or the next week.

For me, I'm doing the exact opposite. I want everyone who watches something to love it. And I'm willing to let the content take a lot longer to resonate with audiences because there is long-term value in doing so: you can't get as much content that really matters to you from anyone else for just eight bucks per month.

During the early days of the Internet, when everybody else was spending big money on Super Bowl ads, we were investing instead in technology, on taste-based algorithms, to make sure every single user had a personalized, highly effective matching tool to use when they visited our site. For us, that's why breadth matters. We are trying to match tastes, and tastes are really specific—even in your own household. So imagine trying to do it across the country. We have to have a lot of titles to produce the results our customers want.

But to answer your question, we've had *Mad Men* for a couple of years now. Last night, what was the most watched episode? Episode 1, season 1. There are new people coming to our shows every day. Plus we have thousands of titles. If you start watching *Mad Men* on AMC, you'll find something else on Netflix to watch. Our website, which is so personalized, will help you find something that you're going to love. What I really want you to do is find a show in which you'll just get lost, a show that makes you want to watch "just one more episode," even though you know you have to get up early tomorrow morning.

We are uniquely able to build our business model around that sort of behavior. If we pick the shows right and we invest heavily in the right kind of content, we'll make the viewers' dreams come true. We connect people to media in a way filmed entertainment has lost to video games and the web. We are restoring a sense of connection between consumers and content. I think audiences have lost that emotional investment in content because television can no longer provide them access in the way they want it, or in a way that matches current lifestyles. Restoring that sense of connection is the biggest shift in the economy of entertainment.

How have your metrics evolved with the launch of your streaming service?

Here is what the data from our DVD business tells us: We know what we shipped to you, and we know when you returned it. I have no idea if you watched it. I have no idea if you watched it twenty times.

With streaming, we have insight into every second of the viewing experience. I know what you have tried and what you have turned off. I know at what point you turned it off. If there's a glitch in the soundtrack or something wrong in the code, the data is so refined that it can detect mass quantities of people stopping at the same point and signal a red flag within hours of the content going live. That's a much more efficient quality assurance process. We don't have to wait for someone to complain. We don't have to go back to the file and watch every second of it to find and correct the problem. It's very sophisticated.

How do you use this data when negotiating licensing deals? Do you share any numbers with content providers?

We share some high-level viewing data—how many viewers and how frequently do subscribers view content. We don't really use the data to tell us what we should and shouldn't have on the site. We use it to indicate how much I should or shouldn't pay. In other words, if I can get an enormous amount of viewing, I'll pay an enormous amount of money.

We invest in a lot of content for really small audiences too, because it's still valuable for subscribers who are really engaged fans of a particular program, and, therefore, it's a valuable investment for us. We're fortunate because we have unlimited inventory space. It allows us to value content in more ways than just mass numbers.

For a lot of other buyers, the threshold is very high for what makes it on the air because they only have so much space they can allocate to programming—there are a finite number of hours in their schedules. In that world, new series usually succeed or fail because of marketing— did they get enough viewers in the right window to make it a success? Again, those windows are way too small. It has little to do with the actual quality of the content.

Our data draws from viewer behavior to bring a bit more science to that calculation. So, really, we can bring some equilibrium to a business that otherwise doesn't have it.

Does this logic apply to your original shows too?

Yes. I don't care if you watch our shows Wednesday night at 8 P.M. or Sunday morning at 10 A.M. Yet others will spend more money trying to get you to watch their shows at a particular time than they'll spend on the show itself. For us, we pick the shows by intuitive, data-driven hunches. The good example is our production *House of Cards*. David Fincher is directing. Beau Willimon is the showrunner. Kevin Spacey and Robin Wright are starring in it. It's based on a piece of intellectual property that we know very well. We can draw real data pools of people who love Kevin Spacey movies, David Fincher movies, the original *House of Cards*, political thrillers, and on and on. You wind up with a very predictable pool of viewers. If the show is executed well, we know how many people will watch it.

Does all this data make the current ratings system look suspect?

The current ratings model makes no sense whatsoever. It doesn't reflect human behavior at all. By design, I'm sure. If people really wanted to know who is watching what when, it's completely knowable. Digital cable boxes capture the data. It's all there. It's much better business for people not to know.

Can you elaborate on that critique?

My kids watch absolutely nothing on the linear grid. They watch everything on our DVR or on-demand. And there is no ratings credit for that behavior because they don't watch it live and they don't watch it three days after or even seven days after the original broadcast. Yet my daughter is the most engaged *Gossip Girl* fan on the planet. She should count for four viewers! But she doesn't count at all because she doesn't watch it in a way the current measurement system values. She likes to stack—to marathon on a Saturday afternoon—and that's the way the entire CW audience watches content.

Our own data supports this trend. For people watching television, especially younger viewers, they're no longer connected to a linear grid. They very much consume television on-demand: when they want it, where they want it, and how they want it. Also, the shows that work well for us, like *Mad Men*, don't necessarily draw the highest television ratings. Yet we know viewers of *Mad Men* on Netflix are much more engaged than viewers of the show on AMC. It's ridiculous to base the value of content on such a flawed measurement system.

What's your window to determine success?

Our economics are based on the length of the license—one to five years, depending on what the deal is. It's no more or less valuable for us if you watch it on either end of the deal.

It's the same for original content. It's no cheaper for me if you watch it all at once or watch it over the several-year license that we have the show for. It's more important to me that if you're someone who is going to love it, you watch it eventually. And if we think you're going to hate it, we don't even show it to you.

What are your primary policy concerns?

Privacy is in our blood. We are a Silicon Valley–based intellectual property company that was born on the Internet. We will not have credit card leaks or data leaks. We know the importance of protecting privacy; it's what we do.

We are actively lobbying to change the Video Privacy Protection Act. Congress passed this law in the eighties when a Supreme Court nominee's [Robert Bork] video store rental records were leaked to the press during his confirmation hearings. Your rental history is now legally protected, but it's such an antiquated law written at a time before Facebook popularized the idea of sharing. I have two teenagers at home, and they share everything. We're living in a culture of sharing, recommending, and curating. You can share the music you listen to on Spotify. You can share the books you're reading from Amazon. You can share the news you're reading from the *Washington Post*. But this law makes it impossible to do the same for the videos you watch on Netflix. Yet we can do it in every other country in the world. We connect Facebook accounts to Netflix accounts, and people love it! Of course, if you don't want to do it, you just tick a box. It's simple.

It's a fixable problem, and we're working with Hollywood and the MPAA [Motion Picture Association of America] and with Congress to address privacy in a commonsense way that doesn't shut down the Internet or compromise free speech. We've done some amazing things in the world. I'm sure we can figure this one out too.

[*Editor's Note:* In January 2013 the U.S. government amended the 1988 Video Privacy Protection Act to allow social-media sharing of video-viewing histories from sites like Netflix when users consent to such disclosures.]

What do you see as the key sources of tension and/or misunderstanding in the relationship between Hollywood and Silicon Valley?

Hollywood believes Silicon Valley wants to commoditize all content, and Silicon Valley thinks Hollywood is their grandfather who doesn't understand how the world works. Both of those things are untrue.

Silicon Valley is trying to monetize content in the same way as all other distributors. But they also understand the more friction you add to transactions, the less frequently transactions happen. Critics of Silicon Valley argue Google wants to monetize everything, so it's all just a search result and the company won't support piracy initiatives because they will slow down Google's ability to accomplish these goals. But when you carefully consider the process of DNS [domain name system] blocking, you realize that it's a flawed process. You want to block "*Black Swan* Free Download" from appearing in a search result. Fine. But what about the kid who is performing in a local production somewhere called *Black Swan?* You get a poor search result in your hometown, because of the mechanism in place to block one thing also blocks this other thing. I'm not saying there isn't a solution—it can be done—but there isn't anything sinister at work in Silicon Valley either. It just wants to ensure the process produces the right results with as little friction as possible. There has been a bunch of work done to hide kiddie porn and illegal gambling, but those terms are pretty straightforward, whereas movie titles and the words "bit" and "torrent" in any combination prove more difficult to block effectively.

I hate to say it, because it has an economic impact, but a lot of anti-piracy efforts are just sport. Technology is great because it constantly evolves. But it also means that for every successful technological solution to piracy, a countertechnology will emerge. Look, the things we license from the studios—the content we spend millions and millions of dollars to protect—no one is stealing it. Most piracy happens in the theatrical window, and yet the studios continually focus heavily on content online. It's also much easier and cheaper to rip a DVD than it is to try to steal a file from us or from anyone else online. Focusing so much attention on the Internet is like nailing the upstairs windows shut but leaving the front door open.

Can you talk a little bit more about the unique challenges you face in different territories?

The biggest thing country to country is trying to address different windows. Remember, the United States is the only place with the funky pay-TV block where a movie is licensed for nine years. Everywhere else has just one pay-TV window. It's eighteen months, and then it's open buying. So we'll bid for titles when they come up, and we'll bid competitively. We'll even bid in the first window and pick a few titles off here and there.

Already we are pretty serious competition in the U.K. television market. We've been able to secure exclusive rights to some television series from the United States, making us the premiere window in the United Kingdom for *It's Always Sunny in Philadelphia* and for *Breaking Bad*. We are the only place U.K. viewers can access those shows.

In Canada we are the premiere window for *90210*, *Damages*, and the BBC show called *The Hour*. We have a number of similar deals where we bring foreign content into different markets around the world, including the United States. It's been an interesting sweet spot for us. As we expand internationally, people get a little less nervous about us in the market place. They increasingly see us as another opportunity to distribute content globally and less like a regional threat.

Who are your key competitors?

It's a little bit of everybody, honestly. We compete for consumers' time and attention. Comcast wants to make us obsolete by improving TV Everywhere. That's fine. They just shouldn't be able to do it for free. We pay a very large fee for streaming rights, and if they're willing to pay for them too, then we're just straight competitors. I'll still bet on us over them.

Obviously we also compete with HBO for content and subscribers. They're probably our strongest competitor because their product is so similar to our own. People say our investment in original content makes us more and more like HBO. I think it's the other way around. HBO is becoming more and more like us by making their content available on-demand and on mobile platforms. Our current challenge is to make better originals more quickly than they can perfect what we already do so well.

Actually there's a flaw in that logic. Bundling constrains the market for premium television. You can't have HBO if you don't have 125 dollars' worth of cable. Netflix is direct to consumer. For eight bucks a month, you can have the content you want when and where you want it. I would argue that makes us far superior. We're not behind a big, expensive cable pay wall. How many more people would have HBO today if bundling was out of the equation? Of course, there's the argument that bundling actually works in HBO's favor, but I really don't believe that's true.

I don't know what to think of Amazon as a competitor. We're real competition—for content and subscribers—in the United Kingdom, where they own LoveFilm. But they have this funky product here where they are adding streaming to freight, which risks contradicting their core business. I wonder if they're just trying something new? I wonder if they're dabbling? I wonder if they're thinking about the loss of revenue over time from physical media? I wonder if they see the streaming service as a way to feed content to the Kindle? Right now, they are hard to read because they do so many things. But they also are really smart about e-commerce and interface design.

We have set the bar very high for competitors in terms of content costs. I don't think you can get in on the cheap anymore.

What's your brand? If it's not TV, it's HBO, but what is Netflix?

What is HBO anymore? What does that mean to you? Quality? What kind of quality? PBS quality? Something trendier, more cutting edge? I'm wrestling with this all the time because so many other channels now do it better than HBO. FX is better at it. AMC is better at it. By better, I mean the shows are better. I really loved *The Sopranos,* and I really, really like Bill Maher, but that's what, two in twenty years? HBO no longer has an exclusive grip on "quality" television.

So you're saying its moment has passed?

It's a very risky business to put all of your chips in a handful of baskets. You have to be really good at it. You have to spend a lot of money on it. HBO spends a lot of money on development, but the shows are fewer and farther between. I think *Luck* is an example of how things can go wrong. I think *Girls* and *Veep* can go either way. It's hard to continue to say HBO is not TV when FX and AMC have become just like HBO.

Why venture into original programming?

There are a few reasons. If services like TV Everywhere and HBO GO gain traction, then they will start to attack us on the things we believe we do better than anyone else. Subscription. Personalization. Encoding. Multiplatform delivery. We need to differentiate ourselves on all fronts.

Our data and algorithms help us perfect personalization. Likewise, we manage that data, including credit cards, more safely than anyone else. We deliver content on more devices than anyone else. We give access to full seasons. TV Everywhere only provides the last five episodes. Hulu is completely random and differs from show to show.

Ultimately we want to produce original content, because it's time we have more control over the shows that matter most to our costumers. We've really come to appreciate the value serialized shows provide. So many people watch them and love them. Our data supports the trend, and that's why you see such an explicit investment in television on Netflix. We've been able to grow the audience for serialized content by recognizing their behavior and securing more and more highly serialized, well-produced, one-hour dramas.

Yet you discover pretty quickly that networks don't make very many of these shows anymore because they're expensive and they're perceived as difficult to monetize. HBO, Showtime, and Starz are making them, but they're also the people who least want to sell to us in the season-after model because we are direct competitors. So at a certain point I said, "Are we going to remain dependent on everybody else making good shows, or are we going to try to develop some of them ourselves?"

It would be much easier for us if HBO, Showtime, and Starz would just sell us previous seasons of their shows because they're proven and they're good at it and we would pay for them. But the truth is that they don't want to open that door. So it's time to figure out if we can become good at it ourselves.

Also, I think it's the direction the entire entertainment industry is heading—networks and cable channels will evolve into something like web channels, just like radio networks evolved into TV networks, and TV networks evolved into cable channels. Look at the widgets on a Samsung Smart TV. You see Netflix. You see Hulu Plus. You see MLB. It gives you a sense of things to come. Currently the problem is that network brands don't really mean anything. If they want to survive, broadcasters need to figure out how to make their brands more meaningful. Cable is better at this. Comedy Central, for example, will be very powerful in this new world.

When a creative comes in here and pitches a program idea, how is it different, or is it different, from them going to a network or a cable channel?

It's different today than it will be in a couple years. Right now, I'm trying *not* to build a big development infrastructure. The existing development departments in networks and cable channels are typically risk management. If a show doesn't work out, it's *not* because they didn't invest millions of dollars into development. They spend $8–$10 million on a pilot that they screen to sixteen people and decide not to make it because of how it tested. It's not a good investment, but people do it.

What I said I would do early on is vet the projects better. Let's shift the development burden to the producer. If they'll invest a little more in the project and bring it to us better developed, a couple of scripts, talent attached, a bible, then we can make a bigger commitment to them, meaning I won't give them anything short of a full-season commitment. It's how we got David Fincher to jump in with us. We gave him a two-season commitment for *House of Cards.* Nobody else would do that, and they all thought we were nuts when we did. But I feel much better spending what we did knowing that I'm going to end up with twenty-six hours of content that at worst is going to be mediocre, and I highly doubt David Fincher would create a mediocre product. So that was the bet. That's as far as I wanted to bet creatively. It had the stars attached. It had scripts written. It had a showrunner. It had a bible. It had executive producers with great track records. We could have done the same thing as networks and literally spent $8–$14 million just to shoot that pilot. HBO did that with *Newsroom*. It had the most expensive pilot in history. I wasn't going to take the risk of spending all that money and ending up with nothing to watch.

So that's how we're different: If producers are willing to develop a little bit more, we're willing to make a much bigger commitment.

Why do you stick to the formula of a season being thirteen episodes?

No reason, and we won't always. *Arrested Development* is only ten. *Lilyhammer* was only eight. We have flexibility with running times too. Remember how long the negotiations between AMC, Lionsgate, and [Matthew] Weiner delayed the season 5 premier of *Mad Men* because, among other things, they disagreed over two minutes of run time? I don't care about that. I want the show to be really great. If it runs over, or if it runs short, it's fine, as long as it's just enough time to tell the story perfectly.

How much of your business do you see original content becoming?

It's a very small percent now in terms of total spending.

Do you want to talk about that percent?

No. *[Laughter]* It's single-digit though. But with success, there's no reason why the number won't grow dramatically, especially if we're good at it and people watch. Then it's a good use of our money.

I think *Lilyhammer* is a really good example of what we can accomplish. *Lilyhammer* was not a mainstream project. Half of the dialogue is in Norwegian and subtitled in English. But with a fraction of the marketing budget and using our own tools on the website, we built a really nice-sized audience for the show. We're definitely doing a second season, and its success is indicative of what we can do on the site with other original content.

Can you tell us a little more about the algorithms you use?

Our algorithms are incredibly precise and draw from multiple data points. The star rating is a dependable indicator. You watched this show, and you rated it five stars. If you rated the show but didn't stream it because you saw it in a theater, on a DVD, or you just rated it because you like a particular actor it features, the algorithm weighs the rating slightly less. Similarly, if you only partially watch something and rate it, the algorithm degrades the ratings value too. We account for all of those behaviors. Star ratings also are one of our internal metrics. How closely can we predict the rating you give a film or television show? We can predict within half of a star or quarter of a star.

We also have implemented a lot of predictive mechanisms: People who love X, Y, and Z also love these films but hate those films. We've made really incredible strides to predict what people watch right after they finish something else. Basically, it's a statistical push based on what other people have watched and really enjoyed immediately after viewing the same program you just finished. There are some really wonky results here too, like right after somebody watches *Thelma and Louise* they are much more likely to watch a Geena Davis movie than a Susan Sarandon movie.

Algorithms drive our entire website—there isn't an inch of uncalculated editorial space.

How are you promoting your original content if algorithms run the site?

We treat it the same way you might promote a lesser-known movie. First we identify attributes of the production that we think best matches the taste preferences of a large population of customers. We call it a "cold start." Then we immediately replace our attributes with attributes culled from the first couple hundred people who rate the program. So our marketing improves.

You will get a more prominent presentation for *House of Cards* if you're in a group of people the data indicates as likely viewers. But if you never watch anything but *Dukes of Hazzard,* you probably won't see an ad for *House of Cards. [Laughter]* We love that you love *Dukes of Hazzard.* It's not a personal judgment. *[Laughter]*

Are you dabbling in these various genres based on what your data suggests about your audiences, or are you trying to test what will really stick, a sweet spot of sorts?

I don't want our brand to influence our programs, and I don't want the programs to influence our brand. Netflix is about personalization. Making our brand about one thing over another risks polarizing our costumers. Tastes are just way too broad for us to even consider it. If you ask five people what they love about Netflix, they will give you five dramatically different answers. So we have to be really careful to ensure our brand is really about the shows *you* love, not about the shows we tell you about. If you've seen any of our external marketing for *Lilyhammer*, for example, it's mostly about the show. Netflix is downplayed.

Anders Sjöman, Vice President, Communication, Voddler

Anders Sjöman is head of corporate and consumer communication at Voddler, the Swedish-based video-on-demand (VOD) provider, which he joined in 2010. He has experience in public relations, as a researcher for the Harvard Business School in Paris, and as head of production for Englishtown. com, an online language school.

But Sjöman says his current post at Voddler provides him special satisfaction. Having been raised in a family where all members were and are active in the cultural and entertainment business (his father is the legendary Swedish film auteur Vilgot Sjöman), he was excited to return to film and television, especially in times of disruption. Indeed, that renegade spirit underpins Voddler's entire business model: a VOD solution that distributes licensed entertainment content over a peer-to-peer network. Pitching the service to major studios, he recalls, was not easy. Nevertheless, the company has expanded its services from Scandinavia to Spain and Italy and includes content from five of the six major media conglomerates.

Sjöman offers an important perspective to this section, and not only because of his company's unique business model. He shares insights into the particular challenges that VOD services face in Europe, bringing an important international dimension to debates about regulation, piracy, and consumer desires.

MEDIA INDUSTRIES PROJECT: *Tell us about the origins of Voddler.*

ANDERS SJÖMAN: As a company, Voddler was founded in 2006, but it was launched as a video-on-demand service in the fall of 2009. It's been fully operational since the summer of 2010. Like all good start-up stories, Voddler began with three guys in a basement. In our particular story, they were trying to figure out how to deliver large data files online. They were simply interested in how to do online distribution more efficiently. In practical terms, they asked, "How could you make video streaming more efficient? Video is one of the largest data files out there. How can you do that more efficiently?" So they came up with an idea that we now use for our streaming. It's something we patented and that we've called "VoddlerNet."

In a world of online streaming, there are two ways to transfer large files. There is the traditional central-server streaming solution that you get from a content delivery network [CDN]—typical ones are Akamai and Level 3, for example. If you're a streaming service today, you probably buy your streaming capacity from them. The other way is very decentralized, builds on some sort of torrent or other peer-to-peer solution, and is most associated with online piracy. The technical beauty of that solution is that it doesn't need a central server to survive or distribute content. It just makes use of all the participating computers for storage and bandwidth.

The beauty of the CDN solution is central control; you can decide which content gets distributed where, for how long, and under which business terms. The traditional peer-to-peer solution doesn't give you any control—it is just chaos. Whatever content you put online, you can never take away. And everybody who is part of the network can put content on it. The beauty of the decentralized solution, though, is that it scales phenomenally. The more people who participate, the stronger it becomes, which is the opposite to a central-server solution, where the more people who connect, the more servers you have to run during peak hours. And most of the time you actually end up with unused capacity, because you have to scale your server farms to work with peak hours, and peak hours only happen a few times a week.

So the VoddlerNet solution combines these two approaches. Fast-forward to where we are today. When you watch a movie on Voddler, that movie does not come to you from a central server but instead comes to you from everybody else who has seen that movie on Voddler and are keeping parts of that movie on their computer. As a user, you have given us permission to use parts of your hard drive and your broadband connectivity to stream to you and to others. Now that movie didn't just land on everybody's computer; we centrally decided that this movie is now available, for which geographies, for how long, and under which business model so we can still live up to our obligations to content owners. So VoddlerNet lets us keep central control when it comes to geographies, times, and revenue models but allows for decentralized distribution, so we can save on distribution and storage costs.

A popular movie, like *The Dark Knight*, is so well distributed and so well watched that we actually have no streaming costs for them at all. Instead, it's streaming from everybody in our network who is a Voddler user. We save on streaming and save on storage, and the more people who want to watch the movie, the better and stronger the network becomes because the movie keeps spreading.

But our history is a technological one. These three guys came up with the idea, they found some investors, and although the idea was still unproven around 2008–9, they took it on the road and tried to find content owners or distributors, broadcasters, what have you, to see if they were interested in licensing the technology. Everybody said yes in theory but no in practice, since this was still only an on-paper product. So these guys went back to the drawing board, and to their investors said, "Let's build our own VOD service on top of this technology, as proof our concept will work." And that's how Voddler was born.

In a way, isn't it a classically elegant Swedish redesign of a CDN? It's an original, simple kind of design, but it still functions in some ways like a traditional CDN.

It functions like a streaming solution. If you're a viewer, you really can't tell the difference, except that we ask you to share your bandwidth and hard-drive space. Of course, that's a hurdle. If you are one of our local competitors here, or if you're Netflix, you don't ask customers for that. So we make sure to offer something back to our customers, like cheaper rentals and better picture quality. We're soon going to offer true surround sound through a web-based browser, which we think we're the first in the world to do. We're working with Dolby to do that, and it's not going to cost costumers anything extra. We're offering high-definition [HD] at the same price as standard-definition [SD], for example. HD doesn't cost any more to stream for us than SD, since we don't have any streaming costs to talk about. We pass those savings on to the consumer. We always try to find things that our technology allows us to offer that our competitors cannot, and we pass those benefits on to our customers.

How do the content providers feel about their content being delivered in this way? Are they tolerant or resistant?

Back when we started building Voddler, we decided to involve the studios early on. We asked around, "Who is the most difficult major to work with?" Disney came back more than others as a suggestion. So we went to

Disney first. We thought, if we can get Disney on board, it would send a signal to everybody else that this is a technology they can trust.

Of course, you can imagine when you go to a major and say, "Hey, we have a peer-to-peer-based technology, give us your content," you're pretty much shown the door. It took a lot of demonstrations and explanations, a lot of just showing how the technology works so that they felt secure. We also had to learn how to implement digital rights management [DRM] through VoddlerNet, which we did. A key security benefit of VoddlerNet is that the full movie is never stored on a single device—just slices of the movie on different users' computers. And on top of that, each slice has its own copy-protection wrapper. Once we had the DRM systems in place, we were able to get most of the majors on board. Now we have five of the six majors, plus we have all the major Scandinavian players. They feel very comfortable with the solution.

Is Disney included in the five?

It does include Disney. Disney was the first one to sign on. Their reputation was true. They *are* tough, but we love doing business with them.

So who is not on board?

20th Century Fox is holding out.

Why are they holding out?

We can't figure out why. It's not a technology issue, from what we can tell, but they have been reluctant to sign. We think they might be following the strategy where they only sign with one VOD player per region. They have already signed with one here in Sweden. But that's just guesswork on our part.

How much broadband capacity and storage do users provide?

It varies. Each slice is about 4 megabytes. Right now we have it set in Scandinavia so we can take up to 1 gigabyte of your hard drive, but it's dynamic so if you need more of your hard-drive space, we'll decrease what we're using. We're actually running a separate VoddlerNet in Spain. Our markets right now are Sweden, Norway, Denmark, Finland, and Spain. I will come back to why we chose Spain, but one of the reasons was that we wanted to set up a new VoddlerNet installation in a country that does not have as good of a broadband penetration as Scandinavia does, and just to test run the system once more. There I think we set the quota at 200 megabytes.

If I were a consumer, I think my main concern would be about my firewall and being online all the time. How do you deal with those issues?

Our tech guys are working with all the major firewall providers to have our traffic whitelisted, which is time-consuming but doable. You simply contact Symantec, or whoever the big firewall providers of the world are, and you say, "This is our traffic. You can recognize it via these identifications. You don't have to worry about traffic that's carrying these identifications because it's coming from us. And we always travel through these ports on the firewall." That's how you get approved. A lot of times when a firewall doesn't recognize traffic, they block it. Now that we are whitelisted, however, they recognize our traffic as safe traffic.

Also, VoddlerNet goes active only when you go online, but you can turn it off if you don't want to share. The only time you really need to have it on is when you're watching a movie. We have nodes going on and off at all times. At any given moment we have about 400,000 nodes in Scandinavia and I think about 80,000 nodes in Spain. But it differs exactly who those 400,000 are. Some turn on their computer and leave it on; some will just have it on for a while and then turn it off; some turn it off overnight; some will always have it on.

We have built-in controls in the software too. It turns off, for instance, if you leave your country, so you won't get international roaming charges, which is a common situation in Europe.

Who are your key competitors?

On the technology side, all the big streaming solutions. We are basically trying to say that we are a better way to do your streaming. We have, however, built VoddlerNet to integrate nicely with an existing CDN solution, so from that perspective we're more additional and complemental than competitive with CDNs. On the content side, we're competing with all regular VOD services. But, above all, we're even more in competition with physical DVDs and traditional broadcasters, be they pay-TV or free-to-air TV. And then, of course, the biggest competitor for any online entertainment provider is piracy.

When we talk about competition for our VOD business, we talk internally about two types of customers. One type is already online. They already switched their movie consumption to digital solutions. There we are in competition with piracy but also legal VOD alternatives.

But for the other type of customers that are not online yet, our goal is to bring them online. In other words, our goal is to get what we call the

"DVD Dad" to start using us. There are almost no DVD chains in Sweden anymore, but it is very common to rent DVDs at your local gas station, which will always be fully stocked with the latest arrivals. So the typical DVD Dad drives home from work on a Friday night, he stops at a gas station, fills up the tank, buys a pack of cigarettes, and picks up three DVDs for the family, hoping they'll all agree on at least one to watch. Once he gets home, though, the family doesn't want to watch any of the DVDs, so he'll set them aside and forget about them, he'll have late fees, and so on. We want to be his best friend. We want to get those guys to move online and take their DVD rentals with them, just as we want to get pay-TV customers to cut the cord and go straight online to VOD services.

Do you plan to continue with all three business models: video on demand, subscription, and ad supported? Do you plan to keep those all going or shift in one direction?

For the time we have all three. We have transactional video on demand [TVOD], subscription video on demand [SVOD], and ad-supported video on demand [AVOD]. We are probably going to shift a little bit away from AVOD, for a time at least, until the ad market for online video picks up more in our current markets, so our focus is going to be on TVOD and SVOD. We're also adding a fourth model, which is EST [electronic sell-through]. We're launching that in two weeks. EST in our world is going to allow you to purchase your movie but as a cloud purchase. Wherever you find Voddler, your purchases are going to be there. If you do want to download it, you can. But you don't have to. That will be our interpretation of electronic sell-through.

As we built the technology and when we started negotiating with studios, we quickly understood that, depending on which of the three distinct business models, TVOD, AVOD, and SVOD, that you choose, we'll end up with different parts of their libraries. So if you choose TVOD, you get the freshest material, titles that are four months out of cinematic release. If you choose SVOD, you get titles that are six months to a year older than the TVODs. And if you choose AVOD, you get even older titles.

We decided to keep all business models so we can manage titles over their life cycle. But we still keep it all within Voddler. In my view of the world, there are four traditional windows: cinematic first, then DVD, third is pay TV, and fourth is free-to-air TV. When we talk to some content owners, they say, "You guys at Voddler, you're funny. Normally, when a movie is four months out of theatrical, we take it as a TVOD and give it to Amazon Prime, and when it has run its course there, we give it to Netflix for a while, and when it has run its course there, we might give it back to Amazon as a cheaper TVOD, or we might give it to Hulu. But with you guys, we can do that life-cycle management all within one player."

Are you able to leverage the fact that you have these four different business models in your license agreements with content providers?

We haven't been able to do that so far, but I think we will now that we are no longer the newcomers.

Are there any policies that have either helped or hindered the expansion of your service?

There are a couple of clouds on the horizon, and one is a data cap on your Internet service and mobile broadband. People don't have fixed broadband anymore in Scandinavia. It's mobile broadband. It's 4G. All over-the-top [OTT] services that use the Internet are concerned with data caps. And we're even more concerned with data caps than other OTTs that don't have the data volumes that video streamers have. That said, I don't think we're going to see caps implemented that heavily. People are going to pay for the bandwidth, but I don't think it's going to be at price levels that would be that prohibitive. That cloud is there, and we keep an eye on it, but it hasn't grown recently.

The other cloud we keep an eye on is net neutrality. Most of the revenue telecommunications companies receive right now is from phone calls, but most of the traffic on their network is data, which they're not getting paid for, since they painted themselves into a corner with flat fees. From that perspective, I can see why they want to get rid of flat fees and uncapped data programs. They are trying to figure out how to make money on all those video streams and other heavy data traveling through the network.

Many of the telcos are building their own video solutions, or VOD services. In Sweden we have TeliaSonera, which is the big incumbent, a giant in the telecommunications market here. They have their own IPTV [Internet Protocol TV] and VOD service. The equivalent in Norway is Telenor. They are building their own VOD service and starting to negotiate with studios directly themselves. We're worried OTT services like ourselves will become second-rate data in their system. They will always prioritize their own data for their own services and customers. Net neutrality is a big potential issue for us or, rather, violating net neutrality. It hasn't become one, but we're keeping an eye on it.

The third thing that is hindering our growth is the old tradition of rights handling that is locked down by geographic territories. If you're a fan of liberal, open markets like I am, of course it's up to the content owner, the creator, to decide how they want to license the material. If they want to license on a territory-by-territory basis, that's their prerogative and their business then is to find people that want to buy it that way. Obviously that is how the current content market worldwide has evolved, but it does hinder us a little bit because we have to pay for the same content over and over again in each market. That makes it very cumbersome to open up in new markets. We have the technology to easily offer our services to the world tomorrow, but we wouldn't have any content to show because of the various licensing agreements we'd need to secure for each territory.

That said, I do not want to take away the right of the content holders to deal with the content how they wish. But we do see these market dynamics changing, as more content owners are ready to question the practice of territorial and window licensing and look for new deal structures. And to allow those dynamics to play out fully, we need to get rid of state subsidies that cement the existing structure. Those can be both national and international regulations. Given that we work and operate entirely in the European Union, we are concerned with things like collecting societies, which are really strong in each geographic region. So on top of having to pay content owners for their movies, we also have to deal with each market and whatever collecting society happens to be there. The traditional one has an extra fee for the music that plays in the movie. We would have to pay that. And that fee differs for the same movie between countries, depending on how strong their collecting society is.

What we would love to have is one collecting society that controls all of Europe. There are initiatives in the European Parliament in Brussels to make this happen, but it will take time before the current system goes away.

Another thing we would like to see go away is legislation that favors one distribution method over another. In France and Portugal, theatrical release is actually legally obligated. You can't open a movie anywhere else but in the theater. They have found a way to really guard that first window. There is no such legislation in other European countries, but instead there are softer forms of locks. For instance, most state subsidy programs, those where a filmmaker can apply for support from a state fund, only give subsidies to movies made for cinematic release. Some even stipulate that you have to have a cinematic chain guarantee distribution before you get your funds. We'd like to see those type of subsidies removed. State funds should be for filmmaking, and then it's up to the filmmaker to decide how they want to distribute it. If they want to go to cinema first, they should. If they want to go to VOD first and then cinema, they should be able to do that. We're not kidding ourselves, of course. Filmmakers will always want to have their movies shown in cinema, and they should, but it should not be the state deciding that.

What about the rights of consumers? It seems they share many of the same frustrations about current windowing strategies.

Absolutely. That's the consumer side. On the one hand, you have the content owners, and the distribution value chain. The content owners would like to sell their content over and over again, and they would like to do it market by market. This has resulted in the current distribution systems and value chains set up in each market. The content owners like to have windows, and within each window, they like to have several players that can fight for that content. That becomes the dynamic that goes against what consumers want—they want to have content here and now.

And the frustration of the consumer is connected to the problems of piracy. Since I started at Voddler, I've had to become an enormous pirate myself, simply because I have to see and understand what's on the various piracy sites. The big piracy site in Sweden is The Pirate Bay. I'm there daily to see how quickly content is posted, if it's good quality, and how popular it is. That's actually a good indicator for us in our own decisions to license content, especially American television. Right now I am a huge fan of *Mad Men,* and it's fun to follow how quickly it appears on The Pirate Bay compared to when it's broadcast in America. It's on AMC on Sunday nights in the United States at 8 P.M., I believe. Approximately twenty-five minutes after airing has finished, it's available on The Pirate Bay for the world to download.

Does that provide you with leverage when you're negotiating with studios like Lionsgate or Time Warner?

It doesn't. We've tried to make that an argument, but they say, if you allow the paraphrase, "Yeah, whatever, we're going to kill piracy anyway, so let's not involve that."

What has happened, at least for TV series right now, is that they're being translated much more quickly and rebroadcast on the pay-TV or free-to-air channels here in Sweden much more quickly. I think *Grey's Anatomy* is on Sweden Channel 5 just one week after its American broadcast. I think, in part, piracy has made that happen.

HBO Nordic is a joint venture between HBO in the United States and the Parsifal VOD platform. Their marketing pitch has been that whatever they're showing in HBO America, they'll have the next day on HBO Nordic. Interestingly, HBO Nordic is just a VOD service here. HBO is not big on our pay-TV systems, so there's no cord-cutting worry. I guess they want to go straight online in one test territory and see how that works.

In terms of the content that you offer, what's the ratio between foreign and domestic content? Film to TV?

Our origin is with feature films, so I'd say it's 80:20. We're looking to beef up our TV service. We need to strike a couple of new deals with the more TV series-focused people.

Given how licensing works, and for a relatively small company like ours that prefers to go to someone with a big catalog when we negotiate, I would say 90 percent of our catalog is American, simply because there are six players to go to and then you've basically covered what's there. Nine percent of our content is then Swedish, from the leading Swedish content provider. One percent is the rest of Europe with the odd Asian content thrown in there. We wish we could obtain more European content, but it's not a simple process, since on a European level, there are no European majors. There is no mass to be found unless you create one, and nobody has seen the commercial need to do that. You have Cannes and MIPCOM and film festivals where you buy all the American movies or you find the odd film from another country. I'd love to show Romanian movies or Greek movies but to get those we'd have to travel to Greece and negotiate with the content providers in Greece, and then repeat that for each other country, and that's just too time-consuming. There's simply a lack of infrastructure to facilitate face-to-face interactions with folks outside of America to make those content deals.

Can you talk about why you decided to expand to Spain first?

We started out in Stockholm. The major studios have lumped all of Scandinavia into one region, so we actually secured Scandinavian rights right away when we looked for Swedish rights. That opened up the other countries. We ran it for two years in Scandinavia first and thought, "Now we know how to do this. Let's try it properly in a new territory."

We set a couple of guidelines for what that territory should be. It should be a big country. It should be a country pretty far away from Scandinavia because we wanted to set up a whole new VoddlerNet. We wanted a country with a high piracy rate because that is an indication to us that people are moving online for their video consumption. In a country with huge piracy, there are fewer DVD dads. We looked around in Europe, and if you have those criteria, you end up with only a couple of markets: Germany, Poland, France, the United Kingdom, Italy, and Spain. We struck the United

Kingdom because that's the United States' backyard. We took away France because that's run through Paris by Vivendi. We decided against Germany, given its very decentralized nature as a country and the strong media players already at work there. We immediately struck Italy off the list because that was Berlusconi's turf. So then we were left with Poland and Spain. Poland was interesting, but they actually had too good of an infrastructure for what we wanted to do. Their broadband penetration is really good, and we wanted a country with more of an average broadband penetration and telecommunications infrastructure than what we were used to so we could road test VoddlerNet properly. So Spain it was. And Spain is huge on piracy. We opened up in Spain in March 2012 after running a beta test for six months.

The results so far have been that the technology performs extremely well. We're delivering a quality digital service. We are doing great on our AVOD business there. The SVOD is slowly picking up, but the TVOD is nonexistent. That's a really tough nut to crack in that market, especially now that Spain is going through one of the worst recessions ever.

It's interesting that this company has inherited the legacy of your father's tradition for pushing boundaries. For our readers who might not know, Vilgot Sjöman *was a legendary Swedish writer and director who made* I Am Curious (Yellow) *and* I Am Curious (Blue). *He is also famous for winning a case against TV 4 (Sweden's leading commercial TV channel) in which he argued that they damaged the artistic integrity of his work by inserting commercials into it. That kind of renegade spirit . . . it seems there is something about what he accomplished that filters through to this project.*

I don't know if it was an influence for Voddler. But Voddler was a disruptive agent looking to give consumers more access to movies much more easily than existing systems—and, of course, that's what drew me to Voddler. I opted to work for Voddler and not for a broadcaster, for instance. I suppose that my dad's perspectives and energy probably influence me—we both like to challenge existing systems. Just before he died [in 2005] he brought that court case against TV 4, arguing that they had no right to interfere with his work by inserting ads, a case that in the end went all the way up to the Supreme Court, where he won. So he liked a challenge, and maybe that rubbed off on me.

Creatives

EDITORS' INTRODUCTION

Discussions about digital distribution tend to focus on the challenges that media companies confront as they scramble to develop compelling new services. Another topic that draws lively speculation is the proliferating number of media choices enjoyed by consumers via cable, online, and mobile devices. Less attention has been paid, however, to the profound and pervasive changes experienced by creative talent at all levels. This section focuses especially on writers and directors, largely because they have been at the center of recent struggles between the major media companies and their employees. In 2007 these tensions erupted into a labor strike called by the West Coast branch of the Writers Guild of America (WGAW) that shut down much of the Los Angeles entertainment industry for over three months. The issues raised by the strike persist today, such that memories of the past significantly influence the ways in which creative talent thinks about the digital distribution revolution.

The conflict centered on compensation rates for the reuse of film and television content across new digital platforms. Patric Verrone, then president of the WGAW, observes in the following interview that residual royalties from broadcast, cable, and international syndication have been a crucial form of compensation, averaging a quarter of the total income that a writer earns in her or his career. As digital distribution grows increasingly important, writers, directors, actors, and craft employees want to ensure that they will share in new revenue streams, especially as digital media erode or displace broadcast and cable distribution. Yet the major media conglomerates, represented by the Association of Motion Picture and

Television Producers, balked at the writers' demands, claiming it was too early in the digital revolution to establish viable compensation formulas.

Money wasn't the only issue, however; writers also complain about increasing demands for supplementary content. In the television business, it begins with the pitch process, says Felicia Henderson, whose credits include *Moesha* and *Gossip Girl*. Producers are looking for compelling story ideas that will earn high ratings, but they also want writers to develop product placements, web content, and social media buzz. Similarly, in the movie business, Scott Frank observes that the major studios now pay closest attention to event films with sequel potential that can be spun out across media platforms, theme park rides, and branded merchandise. Most high-profile studio films are adaptations of novels, comics, or other source material. Writers are therefore paid to adapt, rewrite, or "doctor" existing material on a salaried basis. Only a small elite among the screenwriting community can get an original script produced and have a chance of earning residuals. As a result, many screenwriters have migrated from film to television, drawn by the success of shows with complex narratives and mature themes, shows where writers exercise greater creative authority.

Both film and television today require that writers and directors envision their material across a range of media, and that they play an active role in the promotional campaigns. Director Paris Barclay, who is also co-executive producer of *Sons of Anarchy*, claims that he spends 10 percent of his time cultivating viewers on social media. He estimates that colleague Kurt Sutter devotes close to 20 percent of his time engaging the fan base on Twitter. Due to the emergence of new delivery platforms and the fragmentation of audiences, the pressure to promote becomes ever more intense, while the tools of promotion grow increasingly sophisticated. In his interview, Barclay offers an inside look at the multimedia campaign deployed by Fox Studios to promote a special episode of *Glee* that rode the wave of popular remorse following Whitney Houston's unexpected death in 2012.

Yet not everyone is enamored of social media, as revealed in our interview with Dick Wolf, writer and executive producer of *Law & Order*. Wolf contends that the success of a television series still rides on the quality of scriptwriting and the ongoing management of series production. So far Wolf has been able to resist the growing demands of studio executives for ancillary digital content, both a testament to his enduring success and an indication of how much things have changed in the television industry since the original *Law & Order* series premiered in 1990, followed by *Special Victims Unit* (1999) and *Criminal Intent* (2001). Unlike recent dramas that rely on DVD, streaming, and other forms of digital distribution, Wolf's NBC/Universal shows are the darlings of the syndication world, generating up to $1 million per episode on broadcast and cable channels, with more than one hundred episodes appearing in any given week. Each show offers a self-contained short story that can be rerun in any order and programmed at various times of day on a variety of channels. Wolf contends that each *Law & Order* series has a distinctive identity, but because they are part of a well-established brand the shows are less dependent on transmedia linkages and social media promotion.

On the other hand, most television shows struggle for attention, and executive producers fret about relentless shifts in audience tastes and preferences. Consequently, writers such as Henderson find themselves confronted by new demands for social media chatter, vlog postings, and supplementary content to boost ratings. Writers are furthermore asked to consider potential product placements in order to boost revenues. Most of this extra labor goes uncompensated, but writers are loath to say no, given the intense competition for audience attention. Even worse, studio executives are constantly searching for ways to trim the size of writing staffs. In many cases, assistant staffers pick up part of the extra workload, posting online diaries of a show's characters or monitoring Facebook pages and fan postings. For them, it's better than fetching coffee or running the copy machine, since it provides new opportunities for training and creative engagement. Yet in the end Henderson says even the most gifted assistants have a tough time landing a full-time job in the writers' room or the director's chair. This is especially the case for talent from diverse backgrounds. Women, blacks, Latinos, and lesbian, gay, bisexual, and transgender talent find it difficult to make their way into the inner circle, despite the industry's putative commitment to diversity and the seeming explosion of new film and television content. Barclay says that producers often defend their choices by claiming that the stakes are too high to take risks on untested talent. Others recall, however, their early days in the business, and advocates such as Barclay and Henderson tap those memories when they're trying to mobilize support for diversity initiatives.

The culture of risk aversion and cost containment extends beyond debates over hiring practices. Most creatives contend that a new form of corporatization has taken hold in the entertainment industry, much of it driven by media mergers that began in the 1980s and culminated with the formation of huge conglomerates—Fox, Sony, Disney, Viacom, CBS, NBC/Universal, and Time Warner—that today dominate the film and television business. Throughout this period of consolidation, attorney Larry Stein has represented the interests of creative talent in courtroom litigation against the majors. He contends that the federal government failed to enforce anti-trust principles that used to keep the interests of producers and distributors apart. For example, in 1970, the Federal Communications Commission (FCC) formulated the Financial Interest and Syndication Rules (known as Fin-Syn Rules) in an effort to separate the operations of television distributors (the networks) from those of the Hollywood studios and independent producers. During the early 1990s, the FCC signaled that it would allow Fin-Syn Rules to lapse at the very moment when the U.S. Justice Department was relaxing its prosecution of anti-trust cases against the movie studios. In the merger mania that ensued, all of the major studios became aligned with television networks and cable channels under the umbrella of a major conglomerate.

The result, says Stein, is a culture of "self-dealing," whereby networks and cable channels most commonly fill their schedules with shows produced by the studios they own. So, for example, Fox Television produces for the Fox Network, the FX cable channel, and other Fox outlets. It's difficult for unaligned studios to sell a show to Fox and even harder for an independent producer, since most have either been bought up or driven out of business. Stein contends that producers and talent used to be on the same side. Today, studio and network interests are closely aligned, which means that talent has a difficult time negotiating contracts and deciphering the logic of conglomerate accounting practices. Consequently, Stein spends much of his time in court arguing their interests, as they feel they have not received their fair share.

Another source of anxiety for talent comes from the rising tide of piracy and authorized use of copyrighted content. Frank lives with the fear that the movie business could decline as quickly as the music business did during the early 2000s. With that in mind, most creative talent supports proactive attempts to provide quality product in a timely fashion across a range of platforms. It's now widely agreed that piracy thrives when audiences feel frustrated about access to their favorite films and television shows. Yet both the media companies and their employees are moving into the digital distribution era with some trepidation. One of the major concerns, according to Wolf, is the possibility of cannibalizing existing services in order to feed new digital distribution pipelines. If a program is available on Netflix without commercials, why would a viewer tune in to the network or the cable showing? And why, then, would a sponsor pay to advertise with the telecast version?

This set of concerns fanned the flames of discontent leading up to the 2007–8 Writers' Strike, and most of these concerns remain today. Indeed, they will again inform the deliberations of writers, directors, and actors when their union contracts expire in June 2014. Yet Verrone, who led the WGAW during its last contract negotiation, says he's optimistic about the future of film and television writers. Like most of the talent represented in this section, Verrone believes that digital technologies provide new distribution opportunities for writers to showcase their work, and that social media offer new opportunities for low-cost promotion. In order to realize those opportunities, however, digital distribution channels have to remain open and unbiased in their delivery of services. Therefore, says Verrone, "Net Neutrality" may be the best way to restore a balance between the interests of media companies and creative talent.

Scott Frank, Screenwriter-Director

Scott Frank moved onto the A-list of Hollywood screenwriters with *Little Man Tate,* a 1991 film starring Jodie Foster that earned critical praise and scored solidly at the box office for Orion Pictures. Four years later, *Get Shorty* was Frank's first film to crack the $100 million mark at the box office, and he has scored solid hits with features such as *Out of Sight, The Interpreter,* and *Marley & Me. Out of Sight* won awards for "Best Adapted Screenplay" from the Writers Guild of America and the National Society of Film Critics. It was also nominated for an Academy Award in the same category.

Frank wrote the screenplay for *Minority Report,* a high-concept futuristic thriller, adapted from a Philip K. Dick novel. Directed by Steven Spielberg and starring Tom Cruise, the film scored a resounding success at the summer box office in 2002, earning more than $350 million and lavish critical praise. Most recently, Frank scripted and directed *A Walk Among the Tombstones,* adapted from a crime thriller novel by Lawrence Block.

Despite such success, screenwriting in the commercial film business remains one of the toughest jobs in Hollywood these days, since the major studios are turning away from original screenplays in favor of franchise films. Consequently, successful screenwriters such as Frank spend much of their time "doctoring" scripts that are already in production, a lucrative but an uncredited and creatively less satisfying form of authorship. As it will become apparent in the following interview, Hollywood has changed dramatically in the digital distribution era. We spoke with Frank at the Carsey-Wolf Center about these issues.

MEDIA INDUSTRIES PROJECT: *How have changes in distribution affected your work as a creative professional?*

SCOTT FRANK: The answer really has two parts. Part one is that the changes in distribution reflect dramatic changes in technology, rapid changes in delivery systems, and radical shifts in the ways audiences are consuming media. In the last ten years I have been overwhelmed by the degree to which technology has evolved. I can't keep up, and sometimes I just cry "uncle" because there is so much of it.

But technological change is only half of the conversation about distribution. The bigger thing that *isn't* talked about is that distribution has become the driving creative force in determining what gets produced. These two points are obviously connected, but the biggest factor determining whether a movie gets green-lit is whether or not the studios can sell it. In the last ten to fifteen years the studios' marketing and distribution departments have had an increasingly louder voice with regard to what gets made, how many movies get made, and how much is spent on what gets made.

One topic of concern is the decline in the DVD home video market. It used to be that there was a formula you could count on when you were green-lighting a movie. When you went into a negotiating room you would talk with the studio's head of creative, the head of distribution and marketing, and the DVD guy. The DVD guy knew that if he had a certain actor, say Brad Pitt, in a certain type of movie, the gross would be X number of dollars. It was a given, and the studios could count on that money all the time. That was money they didn't really have to share. The amount they had to pay to talent in terms of residuals was basically negligible. It was less than the amount you paid per package on the DVD. It was pure profit. Studios knew that you could make that money.

Those formulas no longer apply. Today, movies with a certain actor or a certain genre can't deliver guaranteed DVD revenues. There are very few guarantees. The DVD market isn't the investment it used to be. The studios just aren't making fewer films; they're making fewer kinds of films. For example, it is very hard today to get a straight-up drama made, because the audience isn't there and the numbers aren't there. Even though I'm a creative person, if I were running a studio I would have to agree—I don't think I could sell a certain kind of film today. It would be very, very difficult because of the changing nature of the delivery systems.

This has a huge impact on me as a writer. I know that unless I want to work on a big-budget, 3-D event film, the opportunities have shrunk. If I want to develop a movie from scratch, I am now forced to finance my own development rather than go to the studio to give them my pitch and ask them to pay me to write the script. Because of this, I choose to do rewrites because I see the uphill struggle to make the kinds of movies I want to make. Instead of developing my own scripts, I rewrite the kinds of movies I know they want to make. I rewrite them because the opportunities to do what I want to do are few and far between.

The same thing is happening to quality directors. Sam Mendes wins an Oscar for *American Beauty* [and] then directs *Road to Perdition* and *Revolutionary Road*. His most recent film is a James Bond film. Brad Bird, arguably one of the finest animation directors we have, directed *The Incredibles* and *Ratatouille* and then spent the last two years working on his dream live-action project, a film for Warner Bros. called *1906*. He was having trouble, for whatever reason, and now he is directing *Mission Impossible 4*. Matthew Vaughn does *Kick-Ass,* and now he is directing yet another *X-Men* film. Maybe these are passion projects—maybe. I'm not passing judgment on any of these, but these are arguably three auteurs with incredible vision. They are avoiding the uphill movie and jumping on the downhill movie, the movie that is already being made, and locating their artistic self somewhere in that movie.

Changes in marketing and distribution are having a big impact on the kinds of movies we are going to see. People vote with their pocketbooks, and they have voted against a certain kind of movie, at least at the movie theater. They may be renting it, and may continue to rent it down the road. They may watch it on TV or pay cable, but they are not going to go to the theater. And that has had a huge effect on the creative professions.

Could you talk more specifically about changes in the financing and development of movies?

Let's focus on independent movies. In the independent realm you can still get certain kinds of movies produced, particularly if they have a genre hook to them. Films for adult audiences can be made, but only if they are thrillers, cop films, or have action elements. The magic number these days seems to be around $25 million or less for a *Michael Clayton*-type independent. Everyone who invested in *Michael Clayton* got paid. Today, lots of companies are working with this model. Media Rights Capital and Lionsgate, for example, are both keeping budgets down. Summit, a foreign sales company, made *The Beaver* with a friend of mine. They partnered with Participant and a group out of Abu Dhabi—Imagination, I think—to get some extra equity and cover the predicted shortfall on foreign sales, because apparently Mel Gibson and Jodie Foster weren't going to cut it overseas. Those three companies were partnering on an $18 million movie—$18 million! We are not talking about an $80 million movie. In the independent world, even with much lower levels of risk, you nevertheless have people scrambling to find money.

The money is there, though, because there are lots of guys with cash and a surprisingly large number of equity people. Ryan Kavanaugh is a good example; his company, Relativity, is the biggest of them all right now. Summit, another big company, made money hand over fist on *Twilight*. Media Rights Capital, which has *The Adjustment Bureau* coming out, is also plugged into the independent financing model. Graham King, who won a Best Picture Oscar for *The Departed*, has placed independent pictures at a couple of studios. His company paid $100 million to fund *The Tourist*, with Angelina Jolie and Johnny Depp. Yet even with that star power, it still took Graham King to get that movie made.

Today, money is available for some things, but not for others. Take *Moneyball*, for example. Columbia Pictures didn't want to roll the dice on Steven Soderbergh's version because they didn't think it was commercial enough, so they brought the budget down and rewrote the script. A few years ago they probably would have let Soderbergh make his film. Instead, they brought on a new producer and are going forward with a different director—Bennett Miller, the director of *Capote*. Aaron Sorkin rewrote the script, and off they go.

Brad Pitt is still in *Moneyball*, but Steven's version is not going to be made. The risks are so high now, whether it's an $18 million or a $150 million movie, and the net result is that everyone is looking for the same movie; no one is looking for the outlier. Even so, outliers do become hits. Alcon came along with *The Blind Side*, which made money. They produced the movie, kept their costs down, distributed it through a deal they had with Warner Bros., and have done rather well, but no one else wanted to make that movie. Fox wanted them to turn it into a father-and-son story rather than a mother-and-son story, and they wanted more football.

When studios do take risks, like Universal does, it can cost them. Universal had a long list of films, like *State of Play* and *Duplicity*, that, on paper, looked as if they would excite adult filmgoers. Movies like these have to be good to get adult audiences to attend, and I don't think those movies hit their targets, but at least Universal was betting on them. Now their big hope for next year is a movie based on the board game Battleship. They're putting a lot of effort into it because they don't feel they have a big summer movie, like a *Spider-Man* or a *Batman*.

As for Sony, it's going back to the well and making another *Spider-Man*. Today the catchword is "prequel" or "reinvention." Sony is reinventing *Spider-Man*—they'll cast a younger lead and go back to his high school years. Warner Bros. will certainly make another *Batman*. Paramount is producing their third *Transformers* film. Someone is developing a *Barbie* movie somewhere; someone else has the rights to the Ouija board game; and for a while Ridley Scott was going to develop *Monopoly* into a movie. The common denominator here is fear: Whenever you make a decision out of fear, the odds are that it will turn out badly. And it's easy for me to say this because my butt isn't on the line—I'm not running a studio.

A friend of mine who has been nominated twice for Academy Awards and has written and directed some great movies tried to convince me to write *The Jungle Cruise* with him, a movie based on the ride at Disneyland. He is an amazing screenwriter who has enjoyed a twenty-five-year career. He was serious and told me there is a strong case to be made that the business is changing and if we don't change with it . . .

I'm fifty and have lots of close friends who are screenwriters, who have been doing well at a very high level. They are all trying to locate themselves in the industry—trying to figure out where they fit into the movie business of the future. If we are really honest about it, the movies we want to make today generally aren't being made for the cinema; they are being made on television. The things we once would have written as movies are now being realized as TV series. The kinds of dramas that we really respect are almost all happening on cable.

Do you ever consider writing for television?

Sure, but you have to have an idea and you have to be ready to commit. I would love to do TV, but I don't know that I have the right idea right now. The bigger thing that people are trying to figure out is transmedia storytelling. People are trying to create viral experiences, but you really can't create "viral" experiences; they just happen. People can smell if you are trying to sell them something. It feels uncool and uninteresting. I don't know that getting a character's messages on my cell phone is that interesting.

Maybe I am wrong and just old, but it doesn't seem that selling a viral campaign will be successful without a great story and without content that people want to discover. I think people have to discover content on their own. I don't think storytelling online has really been that successful. There is certainly a lot of content being watched online, via Hulu and Netflix and iTunes. Consumers are buying things, but they aren't really watching a lot of made-for-Internet content. As a delivery system, the Internet is very interesting, but I'm not sure about the success of using the web as another place to tell stories. It's a great delivery system, however, because you can have hundreds of thousands of choices instantly.

Have you ever been asked to script something that could potentially become a StoryWorld—to write a movie that could become much bigger than the theatrical experience itself, an interactive, multiplatform media property?

I've never been approached, and I won't be, because I'm the wrong guy to ask. Most screenwriters are wrong because we cost too much for this. Transmedia storytelling in the movies isn't a good fit; gaming is where it's at. At release, *Grand Theft Auto: San Andreas* made far more money than any movie in release at the time. The game outsold everything. *Red Dead Redemption,* which we call "Grand Theft Horse" in my house, is also doing quite well. Gaming is where all the money is being made right now. Games are huge, just huge. They do way more business than movies do, and if a movie lends itself to a game, so much the better.

The studios have tried, and they continue to try, to make all sorts of games into movies. None have been particularly good. It has been very, very hard to succeed, and there are some good games that would make very good candidates—*Bio-shock* feels like a movie world, but it doesn't have a story. It has characters and useful elements but not quite a story. The interactive feeling that transmedia storytelling strives for is already offered in games, and that model is already working. They are already making a fortune, so it feels like a horse and a dog to me. I don't think you can mate those two things because the movie experience is such a different experience. It is a storytelling medium, whereas a gaming is experiential. You are in that world, and it is different from watching a movie. The tension and release you feel when playing a game is different from the tension and release you feel in a movie theater. I think to make a story work in one medium costs you something in the other.

I don't know about the added value of transmedia. It is designed so that you get e-mails and phone calls from characters. That sounds lame to me and to my eighteen-year-old. Maybe it is great for someone that wants to live in the fantasy world of the movie. I don't know if you can build and create that experience except in a game, because there you are already role-playing in a fantasy world.

As for the viral component, that has to occur organically. *Blair Witch* was a great idea because nobody knew they were being sold an experience. People arrived at the website and thought film footage had actually been discovered. It became viral and then everybody tried to copy that use of the Internet, and the vast majority failed. I would love to know the success rate of viral video.

Do you feel that your point of view is representative of a lot of scriptwriters in the feature film business?

I'm sure there are a lot of younger screenwriters who love games and feel differently. They might want to create exactly what you are talking about—a world that is game-like. 3-D addresses that experiential aspect, though I do wonder whether 3-D will get annoying really fast. I certainly liked *Avatar* in 3-D and I liked *How to Train Your Dragon* in 3-D. I thought they were fun. I don't know, however, that there is much added value.

I was in a theater in Hollywood not too long ago watching *Sherlock Holmes,* and some of the seats rumbled. They had a thing on the seat that was like a tingler. I thought, "Really? The seats are vibrating? The film is already a headache and it's too loud, and now the seats are moving?" On the other hand, I just saw *Harry Brown,* a very old-fashioned yet contemporary movie about a seventy-year-old guy that loses his temper. That movie is shot in an incredibly hip way. It is gorgeous. It looks good and is not showing off. The whole movie is extraordinarily powerful without 3-D. It worked and it was intense. I don't know what you are getting for your extra ten bucks with 3-D. Maybe it's a slightly better experience than the vibrating chair.

Doesn't this take us back to our discussion about the industry being driven by fear? Essentially, exhibitors are concerned about keeping people coming to their theaters. For many people the home theater experience is just fine. What do you think will keep attracting people to theaters?

I am going to say something blasphemous—people should go to theaters to see 3-D movies and giant spectacle movies. But if I were at a studio, I would be thinking about what to do for the people at home. That's what TV dramas are doing these days. I was glad I saw *Harry Brown* on the big screen because it had a huge impact, but if I can't have that, I am just as blown away by *The Sopranos* or *The Wire* or *Mad Men.*

If I were at the studios I would be figuring out home theater. Studios are currently trying to get thirty bucks from people who want to see a movie at home on the same day it opens in a theater. People will pay a premium if they can get movies at home and the quality is great. They can invite friends over for dinner or pizza or whatever. You spend thirty dollars but split it between eight people, who cares? It is still better than movies disappearing. It is better than movies being stolen. People don't necessarily need the whole Roman Coliseum theater experience. They may be just as willing to watch a more serious drama or something a little more interesting at home than in the cinema. That doesn't break my heart at all. The theatergoing experience that we are all trying to protect may just be fucked up right now. People talk at the movies, they text, they tweet, so maybe it's not such a good experience anymore.

For a lot of folks in the creative community, and even for executives at major studios, there is a feeling of disenchantment with the effects of conglomeration on Hollywood. I wonder if the adverse changes you've described are largely caused by corporate conglomeration rather than changes in technology?

Absolutely. When Comcast took over NBC, their executives looked hard at the way Universal spent money. I'm not so sure I think that is wrong. I don't blame them for making the safe stuff, and I don't blame them for trying to cut costs. I think movies cost too much and there is a lot of waste. I wish the big movies were delivering not just on the bigness but also on the small stuff within the bigness, like story and character. I like those movies. I grew up liking those movies, and I want them to make those movies. I understand that they are trying to be safe, and to cut costs. I understand that they have to answer to a corporate parent. I don't think that is bad. I just wish they would diversify. I wish they had a little more in their portfolio for the other types of films. They should make a couple of movies that are just gambles, that are made because they love them. Maybe they do, and they will probably tell you that they do, but their definition of a gamble is something like *Inception,* which is the Chris Nolan film with Leonardo DiCaprio. Maybe they consider that risky. I don't know how you couldn't make that movie.

I am going to say another blasphemous thing. I want conglomerates running the movie companies because conglomerates don't go out of business all that often. The money is with the conglomerates. The stability is with the conglomerates. What it costs me in terms of creative capital, I make up because conglomerates are the only ones that have the money to stay alive in this environment. The guys who come in as individuals, who knows? Hollywood is littered with guys who can't last.

We don't have the Medici family; there is no one just sponsoring us. We need the conglomerates as much as they need us. I believe that taking away the conglomerate structure will take away creative income. You cannot have all these little companies; it just won't work. They will go away because they can't bear the risk. They can't bear it at all. They are in for a while, and then one bad movie and they are off the board.

I can't believe I just said all that.

It makes sense in a certain way. Entertainment is such a high-risk business that the number of successful projects is microscopic compared to all the failures, so you really have to have some durable companies. But how did we get to the point where studio executives seem to have forgotten that the outlier or the sleeper can occasionally generate huge profits and in the process offer audiences some interesting films?

No one has figured out how to make the development chain for the outlier profitable. That is a problem. In other words, the studios know that the money and effort it takes to go look for the outlier is not worth it.

If we were sitting here with Tom Rothman [CEO of Fox Filmed Entertainment], we could have the best conversation about movies. He is an extremely kind, decent, and intelligent man who knows movies. He loves movies. Loves them! He is very well versed in film history and cohosts a movie show on Fox. That is who he is as an individual.

None of that factors into his decision-making matrix as head of the studio, however. In other words, if the studio decided they could make money on outliers, he would love it. He would be happy to do that. But right now, there is a limited way they make money. Blaming the studios is only part of it.

The people we tend to talk to are people who love movies, who read a lot, or are looking to be challenged by entertainment. The people that fund the movies want to go see what everybody else is seeing. They don't go to the theater that often. They want to see a movie that is being seen because they don't want to miss out. If they know a movie is mediocre but everybody at work saw it, they want to go to be part of the conversation. Despite this trend, there is no reason that movies can't be better than they are now. Just because you are making a genre action movie for the masses, there is no reason why it can't also be good.

The studios will tell you that sometimes the best way to make a movie is to just start making a movie. Once that train leaves the station, making it good is not the priority; finishing it is the priority. Fox is maniacal about release dates. Once they announce the release date, they own that date. Sometimes that takes precedent over the quality of the movie. On the other hand, if the studios just let filmmakers make what they want to make, we would have the same percentage of crap.

If any of my friends heard me say that I would be thrown out of a window, but it's true. We assume that everything would be better if we just let filmmakers create, but the worst thing you can say to any artist is "just do what you want to do." Limits like budget and release date are not such a bad thing for us creatively, but quality still needs to be a top priority.

Of course, studio blockbusters aren't the only films that Fox handles. Why hasn't Fox Searchlight, their specialty shingle, grown? It's a very low-risk investment, and if they're smart, they can have decent grosses and great quality. Why isn't more money invested in that?

The system is working just fine for them. They don't need to put more money into Fox Searchlight because there isn't that much good product available in the marketplace. They develop some stuff on their own, but they buy most of their films. *Slumdog Millionaire*, for instance, which won everything for them, was a negative pickup. That's the story with most of their movies.

From Searchlight's point of view, there just aren't that many movies at that scale that are worth distributing. They are not going to make money on them. I don't know that they need to expand, and I wonder even if they did if they could make money. I think Searchlight is doing it exactly right, as is Sony Classics, who just picked up a couple of movies in Cannes this year.

Another aspect of the distribution revolution is the rise in film piracy. How does that affect your work as a writer?

Everyone in my business worries about piracy because there are so many ways to steal content, and we will only be able to hold people off for so long. The music business was greedy—they were charging eighteen or twenty dollars for a CD that cost them a few dollars to make. The movie business has wisely brought down the price point of DVD and EST [electronic sell-through], but people steal content anyway. I talk to college-age kids regularly and they tell me they go onto Mojo and other websites to share movies. They don't care. You can't un-ring a bell once it has been rung—once content is available for free, it is very hard to get people to pay for it.

I don't worry about my work; I worry about my career. I worry that my career will go away, literally that it will just suddenly change overnight. Look at what happened in the music business. Things changed very rapidly.

Piracy is worldwide. On the one hand, we need to start delivering movies digitally, but on the other hand, that leaves them vulnerable to piracy. The conversation with the studios is a very scary one. Even they don't know what to do about it. The guilds are trying to deal with it, but the Writers Guild is not that effective. The Directors Guild is more effective, and they're trying their best.

Piracy doesn't affect what I'm writing, but it does make me think I should just make money, just do rewrites, and bank as much money as I can, because the whole business is going to crash in the next three to five years, and everything will be a free-for-all. People will be stealing content, and the whole model will adjust. I don't know how, but I'm very nervous about it. My wife keeps telling me I'm insane, but that is the thing that I worry about. There is this train coming.

Do you think other kinds of creative models could break through and improve the situation? That digital distribution could inspire things like day-and-date release in the home theater market? What do you think the opportunities might be?

I would imagine that could be the case, but not knowing doesn't make me feel much better.

What do you think about the new financing and compensation models we're seeing? We see stars being asked to take less per film and to trade for options or points that are indexed against the performance of the film.

I see that happening all the time. It is unbelievably common right now for people to invest in their movies. I don't think that is bad, actually. What I think is tricky, though, is that if you spend a year writing a script and it doesn't get made, you spent a year writing a script. If an actor is investing in a movie that has been green-lighted, they are investing in a movie that is already being made. As a screenwriter, you are essentially always doing things on spec, or for a very nominal fee. The upside is that the movie could get made, and that's terrific, but if the studios are making fewer kinds of movies, it becomes difficult.

As I mentioned earlier, I am approaching things from a very specific place in the business. I will also add that I tend to worry. I look back at Napster and see that someone came out of nowhere and took an entire income stream off the table. And that could happen again today. There is something about the Internet that makes that freak occurrence more likely to happen. And I worry because, given wide exposure to visual stimuli, people's appetites for certain kinds of movies have disappeared. Those things make me worried. Maybe I am worried about nothing; maybe I don't know enough to not be worried, but that is where I am coming from.

Paris Barclay, Director-Producer

Paris Barclay has been directing and producing television shows for over twenty years, earning two Emmy Awards for his work on *NYPD Blue* and a host of other distinctions along the way. He started his career composing musicals during his college days. He then landed a job as an advertising copywriter, before working his way into the director's seat making commercials for leading national agencies. He moved on in 1989 to music videos, where he caught the eye of such top performers as Janet Jackson, Bob Dylan, and LL Cool J.

Barclay's first big break in television came with two seasons of regular work on *NYPD Blue*, followed by episodes of such leadings shows as *Lost, CSI, ER, Law & Order, House, The Shield, Numb3rs, Huff, Glee, Cold Case,* and *In Treatment*. In 2008 he joined the *Sons of Anarchy*, where he serves as principal director and coexecutive producer.

Barclay has long been committed to diversity issues in the creative community. In 2000 he worked on *City of Angels*, the first television hospital drama with an all-minority cast. The same year he was named cochair of the African American Steering Committee of the Directors Guild of America (DGA). Then in 2005 he was elected first vice president of the DGA's board of directors and in 2013 was named president of the guild. We met with Barclay early one morning at the production offices of *Sons of Anarchy* in North Hollywood.

MEDIA INDUSTRIES PROJECT: *Audience engagement with film and television has changed substantially with the explosion of social media over the past few years. How have social media affected your work as a director and producer?*

PARIS BARCLAY: Social media consumes about 10 percent of my time as executive producer of *Sons of Anarchy*. That is a big chunk, considering that time is incredibly valuable. I have a Twitter account, but I also have to monitor Kurt Sutter's [Sutter is an executive producer and writer] Twitter account. Every once in a while his tweets stir things up—both online and off—always exciting for the media. But that's part of the show's promotion. I don't think it would be as successful if he didn't do that. He probably spends 20 percent of his time actually dealing with social media.

Fox and other networks have very cleverly figured out that social media campaigns need to be more than just commercials running during other shows. Our campaigns have to use every aspect of social media, from Facebook to YouTube to Twitter. A great example is the episode of *Glee* that paid tribute to Whitney Houston that I directed. I was awed by Fox's promotion in the two weeks leading up to the episode. The network started tweeting about a promo on YouTube two weeks prior to the show. It started with behind-the-scenes clips that got a lot of hits right away. Then they just continued to ramp it up as the broadcast date approached. Every hour some information or a photo from the set was tweeted. Then Fox started releasing songs on Whitney Houston's website, where it knew it could reach Whitney's fan base. So on Fox.com, it would say, "If you want to listen to the songs from the upcoming Whitney Houston episode, you can go to Whitney Houston's website." Fox cross-pollinated, and the response from Whitney's fans was huge.

Then the *Glee* versions of the songs were released—very methodically. I think one day Fox released a song every hour, on the hour, just to keep people engaged and keep them listening. Then people started commenting about the songs. Hundreds of comments rolled in, and people started linking them to their Facebook pages. Then Fox released a clip of the first musical number, which was "How Will I Know," sung a cappella by the girls, a few days before the show. Views of that clip went through the roof. All of that was building up to the show.

We also did interviews on set that the promotional team sprinkled around the Internet. The promotion was beautifully orchestrated, and the episode aired to much higher ratings than normal. It was extremely clever. Producers are now expected to build that sort of promotion into their shows. That includes every aspect of social media they can touch.

The downside is the back end of social media. Social media still plays a role after your show airs, and that has a huge impact on our work, because now everyone is a critic. Everyone has an opinion and either immediately likes or dislikes the show and writes about it. Obviously it's not everyone, but it's quite a few people. Some people build romances with your story that go on forever. Some people ravage it. It's something you can't manage, but it's now part of the rise and demise of the show.

Creators of *The Killing* discovered that social media can also play a role in a show's decline, after they disappointed viewers by not revealing the murderer at the end of last season. Social media users and the traditional media joined forces and took the creators to task relentlessly. The new season has much lower ratings than the previous season. Viewers felt let down and were not going back there again. The creators discovered the downside of social media and weren't able to control it.

Was Fox's "Whitney" campaign done by the studios, or was it the network?

It was both.

It sounds very coordinated. We've heard that promotional campaigns for shows can sometimes be very uncoordinated.

Promotional campaigns are extremely well coordinated in the Fox world. Different people are in charge of each aspect of the brand, but they work very much in concert. Fox also has a head of promotion that supervises and plans the brand's overall promotional profile. It's a lot like the Obama campaign, where tweets get logged in immediately from all different quarters after going through a central point. Communications are mapped out meticulously. They have the materials in advance and know what shows they have as assets. Then they figure out how to stoke interest in each episode as they build toward the air date. It's very coordinated.

Interesting. When did Fox's promotion become so effective?

It began around 2010. It has been that recent. A couple years ago people started to say, "Wow, *Modern Family* has a real presence in social media, and it seems to be helping it build."

Kurt Sutter has been able to increase *Sons of Anarchy*'s viewership each season by being an outspoken Twitter presence and saying some provocative things. Those comments have gotten a lot of people curious about the show. People are starting to see social media as a way to separate themselves from the pack. Movie divisions have also figured this out: "Hmm, if Paramount can open *Paranormal Activity* without any expensive promotion and just use a lot of social media, why aren't we doing the same thing?" Social media is cheaper than traditional media. We just have to use it properly and smartly.

Is audience trust, and engagement, more important to directors now than it was five or ten years ago?

It's absolutely more important. Show creators, writers, and directors are now extremely sensitive to what the blogosphere is saying about their shows. Sometimes creators take comments too seriously. Some shows have become increasingly dull because taking risks with the show is discouraged. Audiences generally want to see a different version of the show that they love. They don't really want to see it become something else.

I'd be killed if I did a musical version of *Sons of Anarchy*, even though it might be a cool idea and would surprise people. Before social media, Joss Whedon would do strange things with *Buffy*. No one knew they were going to happen until they aired. He did an episode without any dialogue; he did an episode that was a musical. He got away with these things. I don't know if he could get away with them right now because of the way that social media has changed the television landscape. The urge to criticize would be too great. Even someone as brilliant as Joss Whedon would end up getting slammed.

Do you think increased viewer feedback and social media require a different sort of showrunner than ten years ago?

The characteristics of a successful showrunner have definitely changed. For instance, I don't think David Milch is a great showrunner in the era of the Internet. I do still think he's the finest writer in television, though. I just don't think this is something that interests him, or that he would be able to jump into full bore. He's from an era when just writing well was enough. Maybe that's part of the reason why some of his shows aren't quite as popular nowadays. Writing well is still enough, but you also have to figure out how to promote that show, and you have to be able to create things that are promotable.

Ryan Murphy is excellent at that. Obviously he did not think of doing a "Whitney" episode until a day or two after Whitney died. It just happened that the *Glee* character Mercedes was singing "I Will Always Love You" two days after Houston's death. Ryan said, "This is really strange. We should do something." It struck a chord with the blogosphere, and that's when the episode was born. We were in production four weeks later. He knew it was something that was going to be promotable. He also knew that it may have been controversial to a certain extent, so he also had an idea of how to do it in a way that wasn't salacious and manipulative. I thought his idea was wonderful because it became about the kids' loss and the teacher's loss and not so much about Whitney. The topic was the trigger for the characters' feelings about not being together anymore. It was a brilliant way of doing it. Plus we knew we had social media to support the project all along. We could develop, present, and push this idea forward because of that support.

Do social media also affect the way you shoot things? Do you ever think about what kind of viral life a scene might have if it's filmed one way as opposed to another?

We realize now that our shows have to fit a shorter attention span, that you can't really get away with building a story the way you used to, because viewers just won't stay with you long enough for the payoff. There is a new adrenalized storytelling as a result of Internet clips and the ability for viewers to multitask on their iPads or their phones while watching. Television is telling stories in shorter bursts. Even dramatic shows have adapted. We rarely will go longer than three pages with a scene. It used to be quite common. Will they ever again sit there for three entire pages of people talking with no one getting killed? Rarely. I often find myself thinking about how we can pace up the three-page scene so we don't lose viewers.

When you're working on episodes of Sons of Anarchy, *on what size screen do you assume people are watching? How does that affect your creative decisions?*

It's interesting. Every show is different. *Sons of Anarchy* has decided that it's not going to pay attention to that concern. We are just going to make the movie for the Cinerama Dome. That's the way we do it. We don't use a lot of extreme close-ups, and we use a lot of bigger expansive shots. You're just going to have to look closer if you're watching on your phone. I'm sorry. It should be watched on a larger screen, because it's an intrinsically big outdoor show.

In Treatment was designed for a smaller screen. It's a very small thing, and it's really about the minute twitch of an eye, in some cases. It focuses on how people display their discomfort when they're dissembling. I don't see a lot of producers saying we have to make this show for whatever screen people use. People are more inclined to think that the show looks how it is supposed to look and accept that it's in the scale it should be. Television is getting bigger, even though the screens are getting smaller.

Even a show like *Touch*—which is a fantastically big show that goes all around the world—is not being designed for a little screen. I don't think the creators care. I think they are telling the story the way they want to tell it. They are telling it big. That's what it is.

Regarding some of the financial issues raised by new modes of distribution, as a board member of the Directors Guild, you've had a front-row seat during discussions about the ways in which creative talent is—or is not— being compensated for their work. Can you tell us about some of DGA's discussions concerning these issues?

I cannot.

Nothing?

There are a lot of them, though.

Could you talk about them in an abstract way?

Yes, I can talk about some of the major trends. For example, studios often super-sell the growth of new media to help investors see their company as progressive and worth the investment, but that growth is actually going to be much slower than they say. Television and DVDs are not going to be dead in five years. It's not like everything will be new media five years from now. It's going to take some real time and creativity to figure out the best models. Just like back in the earlier days of television, it's going to take a few very successful programs to show the way: *American Bandstand, Ed Sullivan, All in the Family.* The transition will require the development of creative products that are done primarily for the Internet and that show it is a model that can work. That's going to take some time. Slowly but surely the money will flow and the balance will start to shift. Right now, advertisers spend the lion's share of their money on network television, but that will change.

The challenge for the guilds is to anticipate these changes when they nego- tiate compensation issues with the studios, to make sure that their members get a fair share of the back-end revenues. What is your strategy for ensur- ing that you're positioned well when new business models appear?

I can only speak for myself, but my answer is to act sooner rather than later. You cannot wait until it's a big business to ask for your fair share. You have to do it on a dollar-for-dollar basis. You have to get your fair percent- age when dollars start coming in. Then you'll already have a percentage when those dollars increase. You can't wait until it becomes huge. You can't take a penny on the dollar now and then say you want five pennies when things begin to take off. It's too late. The ship has sailed. That's what I think we learned with VHS and DVD. You have to make your claim clear, and you have to show the producers [the Alliance of Motion Picture and Television Producers] that they don't have anything without the creative content. They just have the commercials. We need to be compensated for the value that we provide.

Has the AMPTP been responsive to that approach?

They are looking at history, too, and saying, "Hmm, we'll make a killing if we can keep a cap on this and keep everything as low as we did with DVD and VHS. We recognize we didn't compensate people fairly for what they created. We got away with it, though. Why should we do anything different this time?" I think the Writers Guild would agree with me when I say that we learned from that. I think the next couple rounds of negotiations are going to be very interesting.

Do you think the next round of negotiations could head in the same direction?

I think in their heart of hearts, producers recognize that without writers and directors and actors, they are screwed. What are they going to do? In the long run, the Internet is proving that we need them less than they need us. The ground is shifting, and distribution is becoming much easier.

Can you give me an example?

An example is the independent filmmaker who makes something like *Martha Marcy May Marlene* or *Paranormal Activity* for a dime. *Chronicle* is a film about kids who all get super powers and start to destroy each other. That was made for maybe $10–12 million. They ended up grossing over $125 million. I think there are great ideas for properties that can be created using digital technologies at much less cost. These are projects that can be financed by your dentist or your mom's savings. It's the cost of a few dresses for Ann Romney, and suddenly you have a movie. That's something new. And these movies can work. They can be distributed independently or over the Internet.

Some people would turn around and say that Paranormal Activity *was a very well-calculated campaign by Paramount's distribution apparatus that went viral because it was strategically deployed.*

You don't have anything to promote if you don't have a property that delivers. You can have a terrific viral campaign, but then people get there and think it's shit. You are out of luck. Paramount has to have the asset to promote. That's what we provide.

You sound kind of optimistic about independent distribution.

I'm absolutely optimistic about it.

Why? Many creative folks would disagree.

Look at the trends. It's becoming easier and easier to sell your music over the Internet if you are a songwriter or performer. Prince is making quite a good living without a record deal. It's much easier to build a direct relationship with the consumer these days when you have PayPal, so there are ways to ensure that people will pay you for your content. Then there are new modes of delivery. I think it's going to be wonderful as streaming becomes more accessible. A couple years ago people couldn't stream anything because the bandwidth was so narrow. Now we have Netflix, and as that technology becomes a little bit more accessible, even to a fourteen-year-old, you are going to see great movies from fourteen-year-olds that are going to become hits. It's going to cost you $3.99 to see that fourteen-year-old's movie, but that teen is going to be able to pay for college.

But the pessimists wonder how an independently distributed property is going to break through that clutter without a $60–$70 million marketing campaign behind it.

Quality plus social media. Social media is where people are going to go. Directors are going to start with a group of people, like friends of friends on Facebook. They will have their clips, they will have their little promotional trailer, they'll connect to each other, and they'll continue to tweet. If it's really good, it will start to trend. They will figure out different ways to reference the content on YouTube and in different places on other sites. Before long a clever person will be able to put together the same kind of things that Fox was able to do for the "Whitney" episode. He or she will be able to do it on his or her own home computer. It's not that complicated.

And then there will be channels that will be dedicated to innovative new movies and television series for people who are interested. Amazon, Netflix, and YouTube are trying to do something like that. They know that's the next thing. These channels will create a stage for young talent. People will say, "Wow, that's where I first saw blank, and that's cool. I'm going back there to see what they have that's cool now." *Funny or Die* is like that, and it's extremely successful.

Do you think there are more opportunities now for young talent than in the past?

Definitely. My assistant made a short film over a weekend with some friends, and he showed it to me. It was one of the best short films I have ever seen. It was a five-minute fistfight set in the 1920s. The costumes were impeccable, and the actors were great. It was incredibly well edited, and the music was very original. They made it for zero money. It's going to be submitted to all of these festivals, and it will do very well.

These sorts of films can become calling cards for the creator's future presentations. It's like what I did in music videos. I was still using film for that, but now you can do HD [high-definition] and Final Cut Pro. You can have your friends do the music. New technologies and distribution models are going to provide even more access. I always tell the young filmmakers I teach to think up an original idea and make something that compels me to take out my computer and show it to someone else.

That gets your foot in the door, but what about access to the inner circle of well-compensated jobs? Are those jobs still as difficult to obtain?

Well, sadly, there is a squeeze from the top. Fewer motion pictures are being made, and motion picture directors are moving into television. TV is now very cool and often better than motion pictures, at least when it comes to the writing. A lot of motion picture directors have invaded television and taken away a lot of the top-tier jobs, so some television directors are being pushed down and are fighting for the lower-tier jobs. That doesn't leave much room for younger talent.

But we are seeing the middle spread out a bit, as more shows are produced. Not all of the shows are of the highest quality, but there is some growth. The DGA and many studios are trying to figure out specific ways to make it easier for young people to break through in the beginning of their careers. These things become more essential in a world where the jobs are being squeezed out.

As the number of shows increases, are we seeing a greater variety of viewpoints among the shows that have strong resources and promotional backing?

No.

Are we seeing more diverse talent?

No.

It sounds like the more things change, the more they stay the same. Why is that?

There aren't enough powerful people that care about diversity. I have discussed diversity with showrunners, executives, and virtually all the studios. As cochair of the Directors Guild's diversity committee, I have discussed these issues with showrunners and studio executives, and I am almost always startled by what I hear. One showrunner said diversity was not his concern, and that he only cared about getting the best director. He asked why he shouldn't hire his friends, who are good directors, for all of the episodes. He said, "Who are you to tell me who I should hire? I just won't hear it." After I picked my jaw up off the floor I said, "You were the second writer from the left on a small, bad CBS show before you wrote this show and became not quite a household name, but the show became a household name. You were nobody, really. You had very little money. You were lucky to get a couple of scripts a season. That's where you were. You invented an idea that became a business and became huge. Do you think you have any responsibility to give a hand up to the next person who is probably just like you were or maybe even lower?" He said, "No."

I was startled. Fortunately, Shonda Rhimes, another showrunner, was in the room. She said, "I do feel that. I absolutely do feel that. I recognize I was nobody before *Grey's Anatomy*. I built Shonda Land on the back of this show. Providing opportunity is a really, really important part of what I do. Maybe I feel that way because I'm an African American woman, and maybe because it's been particularly difficult for me to break through. I make a concerted effort to have a diverse group of writers and directors." Different people can respond to their own success in different ways.

Piracy is another major issue that generates debates about access as well as compensation. How did you feel about the controversy that arose around the Stop Online Piracy Act (SOPA)?

It wasn't the perfect legislation, in my opinion. I would have tried to target the legislation at very specific problems and would have avoided the broad sweep of SOPA. But I think the bigger problem was that some groups consciously lied about the legislation.

Google played a major role in that legislation because it had a huge vested interest. Literally 26 percent of Google's traffic is illegal. *[Laughter]* Materials go through Google, facilitating piracy in all forms. I would not underestimate Google's willingness to do evil when pushed against the wall. It's so strange that the company has this "do no evil" tagline. When they live up to it, I'll be happy to get off Bing and get back to Google. It has very few employees (relative to its size), billions of dollars, a corporate culture of greed, and a history of invading personal privacy. You should never underestimate the bad guys, but that's what we probably did in this case.

In the future, there will be another proposal for piracy legislation. There has to be. The problem is that I probably lose 20 percent of my income to piracy. When Vice President Biden was in town a few weeks ago, I told him that I would love to give him some money but that I don't have that money to give anymore due to piracy." *[Laughter]* I said, "I'm sorry. That was my money to give to you. It's gone." He didn't like that.

Major legislation such as SOPA usually involves discussion and negotiation among all interested parties. Why did this issue blow up into a pitched battle?

The tech companies created a groundswell against the legislation from late December up until the day of blackness in late January. At first they were just working in their traditional manner. They have a very powerful lobby, and they went to the legislators in a concerted effort to influence them, and then when their usual tactics didn't work, they totally lied and put the issue out there as broadly as possible to get everyone all shook up about freedom of expression on the Internet. And it succeeded. What it demonstrates to me is their willingness to do whatever they need to do to get done what they need to get done.

Rather than just walking away from the table, they walked away from the table and tossed a grenade over their shoulders?

Exactly, and it blew up. It's really interesting to see which people in Congress said the misinformation didn't make any sense and which people said, "Ooh, everyone is calling me. I need to get off this issue. I need to jump." We could clearly see which people were really thinking about this deeply and which people thought that stopping piracy would break the Internet and ruin lives.

Many complicated issues are at stake for the creative community these days. Do you think the guilds are coming together around some of these issues? If not, what keeps them apart?

Infighting among the guilds has prevented us from seeing that we have much more in common than we think. Our differences have been exploited in some cases and utilized by the producers to keep the masses down. It helps them if the Directors Guild is fighting with the Writers Guild and everybody's fighting with SAG [Screen Actors Guild]. Our fighting helps them stir up trouble and to give different things to the different guilds during contract negotiations. That's the game producers play. Our goal for the future is to see through that. We have to say, "Yo, yo, yo, which side are we on?" The guilds need to make a list of all the things that we agree on and look at how long it is. Perhaps we'll agree that content really should be protected, and that maybe [the] mega-conglomeration of companies is actually doing our members a disservice. We can look at all the stuff on which we agree and then work out the stuff on which we differ. We shouldn't let producers exploit those differences to get a better deal.

Do you think the mega-conglomeration of media industries is doing your guild members a disservice?

Yes, it's absolutely doing a disservice. That's one of the things on which we agree. I think the writers are more passionate about it than the directors, but we are all in the same camp.

How does conglomeration affect what you do?

Everything is worse, because there are fewer companies to purchase productions. When I was growing up I could watch *All in the Family* or *Maude*, which were made by independent companies that then sold them to the networks. Today those companies no longer exist due to the demise of the Fin-Syn [Financial Interest and Syndication] Rules. As a result, fewer and fewer original, provocative, thoughtful productions are being created. Today networks control the sources that produce their products. There are no independents.

Does that mean the networks are now reaching directly into the creative process?

Yes, it does. Networks are afraid of anything that might startle, surprise, irritate, or challenge their viewers. They don't want to do that. Those characteristics are good for HBO because it is a subscription service. The networks are advertiser-driven. Anything shocking, like Maude being raped or Archie Bunker calling his gay friend a fag, would be stopped cold in network land. Too many letters, e-mails, protests . . .

Do you think the conglomerates are going to have to recalibrate?

I think the conglomerates and the networks will probably die before they truly become innovative providers of a product. I am sadly not optimistic on this topic. I don't think they will be able to make that transition. I just don't think networks have any kind of a system in place that would actually reward the kind of original thinking that Brandon Tartikoff and Grant Tinker brought to NBC. You would have to change the whole way a conglomerate operates. [The conglomerate] would have to say, "Okay NBC, you are an independent company, I'm going to leave you alone for five years. I swear to God. I'm not going to even talk to you. Go and do what you think is great." It simply won't happen.

Is there any hope for change?

I think a new model will emerge as the networks continue to decline and distributors like Netflix and Amazon take up the slack. These distributors will start providing more original programming, and newer independent channels will siphon off the audiences from the networks as well.

The network television audience will shrink by half, I would say, in the next five years. It will be dramatic. Everyone will panic. The networks will try some desperate measures, but I think audiences will continue to decline, and finally the advertisers will wake up and say, "Why are we spending so much money? There are only two people watching this show." Advertisers will eventually move over to the other guys, and this will probably provide a little more room for creativity.

Where does Sons of Anarchy *fit into the world of conglomeration?*

We are fortunately in the beautiful world of basic cable with both advertiser and subscriber support, so we are not expected to draw huge audiences. Four million viewers is okay. It's a sweet spot. And we are now regularly beating the networks in our time slot in viewers 18–49, so what? Me, worry?

It's a conglomerate division, though, isn't it?

Yes, it's a conglomerate division. It's true. It's also a conglomerate's division that represents or likes to represent the feeling of outlaws. *Sons of Anarchy* is an outlaw show. Rupert Murdoch thinks of himself as an outlaw. Fox started as an outlaw network. We are in the long tradition of shows from Fox. The show couldn't exist at another network like NBC.

Do you think that the show has gotten more interesting and more provocative over time? How has the show changed to grow its audience?

It's so interesting. Kurt discovered how to grow the audience by going deeper instead of trying to be more extreme. You go deeper into the characters and showcase the Shakespearean entanglements among them. That's what our viewer is going to enjoy, because our viewer is a little different from the network viewer. Then you turbocharge that depth with action. You keep it exciting and blow things up at fairly regular intervals. But we still stay focused on this inter-nestled lore about families and the idea of a family of choice versus a blood family. The closer, the darker, and the deeper you get into that, the more audiences seem to be intrigued.

Felicia D. Henderson, Writer-Producer

First and foremost, Felicia Henderson considers herself a writer with a diverse skill set who has worked successfully on television sitcoms and dramas as well as feature films, comic books, and stage productions. She also has succeeded as a television producer, showrunner, and executive producer, and most recently she has taken turns in the director's chair.

Henderson began her television career with television comedies such as *The Fresh Prince of Bel Air, Family Matters,* and *Moesha.* In 2001 she developed, wrote, and served as executive producer for the Showtime drama *Soul Food,* which during its four seasons earned the distinction of being the longest-running TV drama with a predominantly black cast. Henderson also earned writing and producer credits on *Fringe, Gossip Girl,* and *Everybody Hates Chris.* A lifelong comic book fan, in 2009 she signed with DC Comics to author installments of *Teen Titans, Justice League,* and *Static Shock.*

Henderson's commitment to diversity issues is manifested both in her writing and service activities. She has helped found programs for at-risk teen girls and establish scholarships for young filmmakers. Deeply concerned about changes in the film and television industries, Henderson served as a strike captain during the Writers Guild of America walkout in 2007. Somehow in her spare time, Henderson earned an MFA and a PhD in the UCLA School of Film, Theater, and Television. We caught up with her at her home in Pasadena, the city where she grew up in a family of eight children.

MEDIA INDUSTRIES PROJECT: *Let's start with your role as a TV writer. How has that been affected by the revolution in digital distribution, such as the way you think about developing a project, the way you think about your contract, and the way you experience compensation?*

FELICIA HENDERSON: The changes to compensation are most interesting to me. I think that you know compensation for talent is always a tricky thing; it's always the trickiest part in my negotiations. I'm paid episodically. That means I have a salary per episode, and that number usually is very easy to agree on because it's mostly based on precedent. So if you were paid a dollar per episode on your last show, they'll offer to increase that dollar by 20 percent. That is the easy part. After that it depends on how good your team [agent, attorney, etc.] is at representing and negotiating for your services.

But the part that is always more ambiguous is the idea of being a profit participant in what I create. As part of that process, they are asking, "What is your value? How much do we value what you are bringing to the table?" It's nearly impossible to define. Really, it is about how badly they want you and, to some extent, how powerful your representatives are.

Then you include the digital revolution, and nobody knows how to define the value of all of that. You now have negotiations with the producers who have an interest in making sure it has no value, or that the value is so far off in the distance that we can't possibly determine what that value is. It's illogical the way they approach it, because it's like, "We don't know how much it is, so how can we possibly know how to value it?" Or they say it doesn't have any value. If that's true, why do they fight so hard to deny us profit participation in something that has no value? Why is it important for producers to keep 100 percent of this thing that has no value?

The whole conversation is around "Is there value there or not?" For producers/studios, the primary owners of the content, there is value. But they behave as if there isn't for fear of sharing with creatives, so it gets very complicated and very frustrating for those of us who create content.

Let's say you have a development deal and it's time to pitch your ideas. This means you've made a deal with a studio or network and they've said, "Yes, we like this idea, we want to do business with you. Here's a bunch of money, now go off and write a great script that we'll decide if we want to shoot it as a pilot, and then if we shoot that pilot, we will decide if it's good enough to launch as a new series."

At the beginning of this process, when you're coming up with the ideas you are passionate about, it's a good idea to at least consider thinking about what studios and networks are thinking about—dwindling audiences on traditional television platforms; how to monetize the investment in your project; how they are going to create value for your show idea in the marketplace. Five to ten years ago, writers used to be able to simply ask themselves, "What's in my heart?" "What story do I want to tell on a week-to-week basis?" "What idea do I have that I think lends itself to a hundred episodes of great television, or around fifty to seventy episodes for cable?" Ten years ago, that really was it. It was a great deal of work, but it was the extent of the work. But now, as you prepare your pitch, particularly if you are not pitching a relationship-driven idea, you know that your ideas have to lend themselves to a website presence, possible video game presence, and how your series idea can be advertised and marketed on iTunes.

Those who are still purists about their television ideas are having a harder time, because if the network can't see how your series idea works in a variety of platforms, then you'd better be Steven Spielberg or J. J. Abrams. The primary way something like Smash gets sold is because it has Steven Spielberg's name on it. Of course it helps if the new network president recently produced theater in New York and therefore is open to a show about what happens behind the scenes of a big Broadway musical. Without the new network president's recent theater experience and a behemoth producer with Spielberg's pedigree, a show like this probably doesn't get on the air.

I was one of the coexecutive producers on the inaugural season of *Gossip Girl* and responsible for running the writers' room, managing the process of breaking stories with the rest of the writing staff for each episode, etc. I remember generically writing in scripts that a character was using his or her cell phone. But pretty early in the season, the writing staff was told by the network that we needed to meet with Verizon because the carrier would be providing phones and product placement monies to the show. Verizon representatives flew in and met with the writers and walked us through each mobile phone model they wanted us to use and which character they thought was perfect for each phone. We'd then refer to the reference sheet for each phone to make sure a particular character's phone was capable of the function we wrote into the script. But if you get it wrong, suddenly you get a call from Verizon, who now gets to review scripts, telling you that a particular phone doesn't have the feature you referred to in your script.

Now I have been writing television and film for seventeen years. I am a freaking dinosaur, and for me the last conversation I want to have when deciding the creative direction of a show is one in which a phone carrier is now an element in my writers' room. That's sacrilege to me. But I have learned to go with the flow because I have to if I want to continue to work, and I do want to continue to work. The trick is to make sure that issues like product placement aren't driving storytelling. The challenge is to allow product placement to complement storytelling without causing your show to look like an advertisement for a particular product.

It almost makes you yearn for the Golden Age of television in the '60s when GM would interrupt the show to sell their product and then it was done, and you'd then go back to telling your story. Now the idea of product placement is really product integration, and with product integration, you find that Verizon is now one of the writers on your writing staff.

I was also on the writing staff on Fox's *Fringe*. Literally an alphabet was created to run as interstitials between commercial breaks—bloggers and fan boys and girls were asking, "What do these symbols mean?" There was a rush to decipher these symbols. So now you have a writer for whom part of his job, in addition to coming up with episodic stories, is to create these interstitials. In some ways, creating these "Easter eggs" becomes more important than writing the show. We're now servicing all of this stuff instead of that stuff servicing the storytelling.

How has this affected the size of the writers' room? Is managing it as an executive producer more complicated, more difficult? Or are people just working longer hours?

People are working longer hours. If there is a positive, it's that writers' assistants and executive assistants, in general, are aspiring writers, and they are getting more exposure to writing because they are enlisted to write this additional content, that is, online characters' diaries, comic books based on the series, etc. So that's a good thing—that the support staff is getting an opportunity to be more included in the creative process. Then when they get on the writing staff of that particular show, which is usually how it works, they are even more prepared to be on that staff because they understand the characters even better than they would if they were just answering phones, getting coffee, or whatever.

The need for webisodes based on a series, the network's website content, creating comic book ideas, etc., all equal great opportunities for aspiring young writers. Historically, as an aspiring writer working as a production assistant [PA] or writer's assistant, you would kill yourself doing a great job in the position for which you were hired, hoping that someone would one day notice what a good job you were doing and ask what your goals were beyond that position. Finally, you'd be able to share your spec script, and then you'd pray they'd like it. Now, with the additional opportunities as a result of the multiplatform approach to television series production, if you're smart, you are listening and paying close attention to what the writing staff is discussing beyond the episodes. Then one day you might get the opportunity to say, "Oh, I understand you guys are going to be starting a secret blog that nobody knows is coming from the show. I would like to write that."

How has the job of the showrunner changed? In addition to navigating these relationships between the writers and sponsors, what else has been added to the role?

Well everything we just discussed is still part of your job. It still, in some way, has to come across your desk, because you are still very concerned about how the characters that you created are being depicted. Sometimes you have to let go of some of it. You can convince yourself that it's okay if it's inconsistent, or not quite how you would've done it, because you can't do everything. Actually, it almost always is inconsistent.

When I was executive producing *Soul Food*, the studio decided that its popularity warranted novelization. I remember that being so difficult for me, because I had to pick the writer. I wasn't familiar with novelists who specialized in such books. So now I've got to read all the samples of all the writers, or else I can leave it in the hands of the network. Really, are you kidding me? So I read samples of ten writers. I read ten entire novels, and then interviewed five of the novelists to determine who seemed to best understand the voices of the characters. Even though the writers would be coming up with unique stories for the characters, I still wanted to be sure that this new and complementary direction for the show's characters would not be inconsistent with what I was doing on the television show. And then I have to read the first draft, the first manuscript, and all of that was being added to my very full plate while I'm writing episodes of the show, shooting episodes of the show, and editing episodes of the show. It's just more work. You do it because it's becoming more and more of the norm.

Also, social media! For example, I just signed on to retool a sitcom on BET. It's an abbreviated second season with only eight episodes. I believe they produced twenty-five episodes the first season, and it was one of the network's premiere shows and was proof that BET had entered the world of scripted programming in a major way. Unfortunately, it wasn't as successful as the network hoped, and so they ordered this abbreviated second season to see if relaunching it with changes in the cast and writing staff might lead to success. My goal, along with my partner-in-crime, Mara Brock Akil, who is also an executive producer on the show, is to do a great job and put the show in the best position possible in hopes of getting a season-three order.

Mara's company, Akil Productions, has a very active Twitter account, and she asked when I was going to start tweeting about the fact that I'm going to be running the show. And what did I plan to post on my Facebook page? I only recently got a Twitter account, and I did it to support a friend who was on *Dancing with the Stars.* How's that for multiplatform irony? I'm not on Facebook, and I really have no interest in it. More than one person has said to me that given that *Reed Between the Lines* is on BET, I need to do everything I can to help with marketing because the network doesn't have big dollars to market the show. Suddenly, I feel like a slacker if I don't participate in marketing the show through social media. Simply making myself available for publicity interviews is not enough. I have several friends who have someone tweet, blog, [and] post for them because they're too busy to do it themselves but know how important this presence is.

Additionally, there has been a "behind-the-scenes" crew on the set on at least three separate occasions. The sole reason for this crew has been to collect content for BET.com. When I conducted my interview with the crew, they asked that I end the interview by thanking the BET.com audience for tuning in. I was happy to do it because my job is to do whatever I can to bring as many eyeballs as possible to the show. Simply writing the best show that I can is no longer enough. It's where the job begins, not where it begins and ends. So my point is, the deal isn't even technically closed; it's supposed to close today. But already—and it's a comedy—I've gotten a call asking me what is my Twitter name because they want to know if I don't have time to do it myself, then do I want them to assign someone to tweet for me. Okay, where can I jump from?

Now this is all very personal. Whereas you used to fight to have input on how your show was marketed and advertised, now you're actually very much a part of that process because of social media. You are an integral part of the marketing team through your social media presence. At BET, the network is very much aware of and wants to capitalize on my standing in the black community. Although *Soul Food* ended in 2004, it is still remembered fondly as an important show in my community. Because we live in a time of showrunner celebrity, it's important for me to support this show as a showrunner celebrity—someone who consciously builds a public persona and participation, in an effort to garner interest in my show. I have input in the marketing, but I am also an entity to be marketed.

Does this mean that the show bible also has expanded? One would imagine that all of this social media marketing has to be thought through in addition to the characters, the narrative arc, and so on. Now you have to think through Twitter personas?

Yeah. You have more documents, and then there are some producers who are freaks about security and secrecy because their shows' success depends on the element of surprise, given their serialized nature. For example, for some productions, scripts are all watermarked, so there are ways to tell if someone photocopied an individual script. Again, it is not only the show-runner's job that has changed. It is the assistants who do all that water-marking. Of course they are still responsible for proofing scripts, making sure there are no typos, there isn't a day slug line when it should have been a night slug line, etc. So everyone's job changes.

If I may transition a bit to traditional barriers of entry, even though there are all kinds of ways the digital revolution changes barriers to entry, on that most basic level the PA who gets your lunch now also has a better opportunity to get to the next step, which is a writer's assistant, [and] that then leads to a staff position. That's because these weird and interesting ideas of how to give the show life on other platforms can come from any-where. You don't even have to have a spec script. If you are just a creative person who creates an interesting way to incorporate Easter eggs into a show that can benefit from such creative ideas, you have created an opportunity for yourself.

BET is the biggest game in town for African American–themed con-tent. Networks have basically turned their back on this audience. So where else are these projects going to be seen? The audience is there. Any re-search report you read tells us that blacks and Latinos watch more televi-sion than anybody. So that's wonderful to me that there are now all of these other places where people can do what they love to do. Their stories wouldn't be told if these other platforms didn't exist.

Do you think differently as a writer than as a showrunner about DVD, EST (electronic sell-through), and SVOD (subscription video on demand)?

I think two things. First, I think that some of those are the kind of issues you think about more in the feature world. Second, for writers and I guess others, DVDs will always be a political issue, because it just reminds us of what we lost in earlier contract negotiations with the AMPTP [Alliance of Motion Picture and Television Producers]. That absolutely influences ev-ery negotiation with the producers, and it will for eternity.

Can you talk for a moment about what you lost?

Yes. It sounds like a loved one. *[Laughter]* We'll start by talking about the 2007 strike. That strike was emotionally and politically about what we did not get in the previous rounds, including the 2001 negotiation of DVD rental fees. It's the history of this business, right? Because we never know the value or think something is going to be valuable until it is, we settled for 1.2 percent of distributors' gross for VHS/DVD rentals. Then there was this explosion of DVD sales, but we weren't participating or were barely participating because we didn't realize that this would become a very lucrative revenue stream. Now we are obviously on the downside of that curve in terms of the value of DVD residuals because sales are declining, but we're still trying to fight the fight for this thing that now has much less value.

What we lost was the opportunity to significantly participate in the profit stream from DVD rentals and electronic sell-through. It's particularly a difficult subject for television writers because as that boom was happening, reality shows came of age and severely crippled the demand for scripted programming during the summer rerun season. Primetime television writers depended on those residuals for many years, and suddenly they were drying up.

Those summer repeats played and you could literally live off of the residuals for a year. That's why my friends who haven't worked consistently are struggling. I have been so fortunate. In seventeen years I have only been on one show that wasn't a hit. That first half of my career bought my house. My down payment was paid with my residuals on really big hit shows, multicamera comedies that were syndicated. So I was very lucky to be in sitcoms at the time when sitcoms were king, and residuals were still king too. Then we come to this period where reality shows—which should have gone away by now, in my humble opinion—take up programming slots where repeats would have aired.

Then there are the DVDs. During the big boom, writers did not participate in profits as we should have. So every negotiation after that you try to go back and get what you already lost. "We want more of that." "Well, it's making a lot of money, why would we give you more of that?" Finally, we did strike, but everything about digital and where we stood was influenced by the fear that we didn't want this to be another DVD situation where we lose out on a revenue stream that may be substantial in the future. No one has quite figured out how to monetize digital play in a significant way yet, but it will happen.

So many people understand the value of content, but no one has come up with a model that is going to make everybody happy. Is that something you think about?

Obviously as a writer you are very interested in creative freedom and the freedom of people to access content, yet, on the other hand, it's your intellectual property. As a writer, how do you think about this problem?

I'm always a person that feels that the more there is, the more there will be to share. When you are holding onto zero, that is all you are holding onto.

A lot of showrunners will take unnecessary ownership stands with their casts: "You are on this show, and you can't do anything else because you belong to this show." But I have always bent over backwards to change and arrange schedules for actors to do additional work, films, etc. Isn't it just as good for me as it is for them if they become bigger stars? Yes. Because then I have the bigger star on my show.

So I have always thought about creativity in this way—it is for sharing. Or at least I used to think of it until I saw my work reappropriated in a way that was offensive to me. Suddenly I wasn't so open. Suddenly I felt that no one has the right to use your work without your permission or without compensating you. I've relaxed again lately, but I'm sure I'll be up in arms again when I see my work reappropriated in a way that I feel is in bad taste. *[Laughter]*

And in some ways we do look differently now at compensation, because there are certain revenue streams that don't exist anymore. You already know you won't have that great syndication money like we did in the past. In the past I was less concerned with my episodic salary—what I was paid per episode for a show. But, in some way, the changes in revenue streams have made me less entrepreneurial. Ten years ago I would be less concerned with my weekly/episodic salary. I'd rather bet on myself. In other words, I was willing to negotiate a lower episodic salary for a higher profit participation in the syndication of the series. I figured, "This is going to be such a huge success, that it will syndicate well and I will have a big payday because I negotiated a bigger profit participation."

I used to make those kinds of deals regularly. None of us were starving, regardless if they paid me the least amount they could; I was still making more money than 90 percent of the folks in this country. So I never looked at what, episodically, I needed to make. But now because of the cable space, which I love working in, those kinds of back-end opportunities don't necessarily exist. I guess I shouldn't say they don't exist—from a negotiations standpoint, they do. But cable shows, for the most part, have no syndication value, so even if you do negotiate a large back-end profit participation, you're very unlikely to ever benefit from that deal because cable shows don't syndicate well, if at all.

Today there are fewer possible revenue streams, although there are various platforms. The digital revolution has not been a monetization revolution, as of yet. Therefore, I find that I care much more about what I'm paid up front now because I'm less sure about tomorrow's profit potential. So, on one hand, I'm less entrepreneurial and I'm willing to gamble a lot less—I want to be paid a high episodic fee now. However, on the other hand, I'm more entrepreneurial, creatively—I'm willing to try new things—web series, indie comic books, etc.—that don't necessarily promise any profitability but are, creatively, very fulfilling.

What's your opinion of Shonda Rhimes's strategy of color-blind casting on her shows? Or someone like Issa Rae, who has attracted a strong following with The Mis-Adventures of Awkward Black Girl?

The most beautiful thing that something like that does is you start to hear, "Oh, my God! I have to see it and hear it!" It creates buzz. That's almost the only way that kind of diverse voice can be heard or thought of as possibly mainstream, because then it isn't only black people or black women who are interested in it. So I love these as examples of ways to lower the barriers of entry.

I think that, on the other side, if there is a lesson to be learned, it is the lesson for always, which is whatever the true voice is that you have, that's what you should be trying to express, not what is commercial, not what you think will sell. What is that true and special something that no one can do the way you do? That is what you should be pursuing.

I think color-blind casting is good and it is bad. The goodness is always that you see diverse faces in front of the camera. However, color-blind casting is also a way to "denormalize" cultural specificity.

I think it's important for America to see people who look like each other, loving each other. That doesn't mean I'm against interracial relationships— far from it. But in terms of what images are normalized through their depiction on television, I wouldn't want to see color-blind casting come at the expense of seeing black characters in love with black characters, a Japanese American in love with another Japanese American. I also think that cultural specificity in characters normalizes this specificity for mainstream America. Difference isn't the enemy. A lack of knowledge of difference is troubling for me and problematic for viewers if we are to ever be comfortable with how we are different, and not just celebrate how we are alike.

Color-blind casting also concerns me because it allows people who don't really have a commitment to diversity to feel like they are diverse. Diversity isn't just a physical difference. Diversity in cultural attitudes and behaviors is important as well. Without such difference, you actually aren't diverse or multicultural at all.

Do you have any final thoughts on the ways in which digital distribution has changed your job?

This thing that I value and treasure so much, television writing, isn't really simply writing anymore. What it is in my head is what it was when my career started, but it isn't that anymore because it's about all these other elements now. Is this going to be a show worth tweeting about? Are you going to be able to gather a following from this content that you are pitching? Is there going to be something interesting that we are going to put on our website from this content that you are pitching? Are we going to be able to promote it? Is it a video game? Is this a series that will draw product integration deals from advertisers? Will recording artists want us to place their music in the show so that viewers log onto the website and buy it later?

So shows have become more elaborate, and so has the pitching process. It sounds very competitive.

Yes, very much so. It's a very different world now because it's like, "Oh, she's a veteran TV writer that we can pretty much go to anytime. Or we can get J. J. Abrams!" So you have to say, "I also have a big feature way of looking at this thing," and you have to help them to see it too. Just presenting your script doesn't do it anymore. With J. J. Abrams they can go, "Oh, we've seen five features and we know what he's going to do, we know what that looks like." If you don't have that, then you have to say, "Let me show you what it would look like." You have to make a very elaborate and multidimensional presentation. We didn't used to have to do that. But now if you're going to pitch a television drama that is big and splashy or for which you need to paint a picture of a unique world, it's not a bad idea to bring visual aids—including a trailer you create to sell the show.

Stanton "Larry" Stein, Partner, Liner Law

Successful writers and directors are represented by talent agencies that help them secure work and legal firms that oversee negotiations with their employers. Of the latter, transactional lawyers represent clients during contract negotiations, while litigators help ensure that the terms of the contract are honored. Larry Stein is recognized as one of the leading litigators in the field of entertainment law and is a senior partner in Liner, Grode, Stein, Yankelevitz, Sunshine, Regenstreif & Taylor, commonly know as Liner Law.

Early in his career, Stein showed interest in civil liberties cases, representing the little guys pitted against the system. From there it wasn't much of a leap to representing talent that had been victimized by the accounting practices of vertically integrated media conglomerates. Many of the cases that Stein takes on involve profit participation controversies that are rendered ever more complex by the expanding number of distribution channels and subsequent revenue streams. Moreover, the surge of media conglomeration has meant that producers are often selling their shows to buyers in other divisions of the conglomerate, a form of "self-dealing" that usually favors the interests of the conglomerate over those of the talent.

Stein has represented such high-profile clients as David Duchovny, Alan Alda, Michael Moore, and Timbaland. Stein also advised Frank Zappa when he was called before Congress to testify about obscenity complaints against musicians. Stein's continuing interest in civil liberties issues earned him the American Civil Liberties Union (ACLU) Pro Bono Civil Liberties Award. We interviewed him at Liner Law in the Westwood section of Los Angeles.

MEDIA INDUSTRIES PROJECT: *How has your job changed over the last decade?*

LARRY STEIN: It's changed drastically over the course of my career. I spend a tremendous amount of time—much more in the last five or ten years—on privacy, defamation, and intellectual property. Entertainers think more and more about their reputations, their brands, and their intellectual property.

Repealing the Financial Interest and Syndication Rules [Fin-Syn] has had a huge impact on my job. As part of the deregulation that occurred in the early to late 1990s, the Fin-Syn Rules were eliminated. Studios were no longer prohibited from owning networks or owning the shows they aired on their networks. I always thought the repeal would result in significant anti-trust issues, but it didn't. Nearly every studio acquired or merged with a network, or every network acquired or merged with a studio. It's difficult to discern who swallowed whom, but regardless, you now have production and distribution under the same roof, especially in the television industry.

When Fin-Syn was repealed, proponents argued that the proliferation of distribution outlets meant that it was no longer necessary to regulate network content production. Supposedly the network oligopoly had been killed off by new competitors from cable and the Internet.

I think that logic is fallacious. Studios will do everything in their power to own whatever distribution outlets emerge—cable channels, online channels, whatever—because that ensures their products generate income. The goal here is to have complete control over your intellectual property so you can exploit it in as many ancillary markets as possible.

Deregulation was part of the concept that free market systems work best, but the repeal of Fin-Syn demonstrates the exact opposite. In fact, I think there are *not enough* distribution channels available to counter the negative impact of what's happened. Everything that ABC broadcasts is produced by ABC. Everything that CBS broadcasts is produced by CBS. Everything NBC broadcasts is produced by NBC. It simply killed independent producers. The Carsey-Werners and Dick Wolfs of the world can't compete with something owned by a single entity.

Do you think the issue today is less about the ABC Network and more about the ways in which ABC is trying to colonize new distribution technologies? How do you put boundaries around the activities of a conglomerate in an era of such open technological innovation?

I look at it in two different ways. First, it is a general policy matter. It's incredibly dangerous to have consolidated the power that determines what the public will see, hear, and read among just a very few companies. But I think it can be regulated, even though I know that won't be easy given that we're now discussing a number of platforms rather than just three clearly defined television networks. Nevertheless, if policy did as much as possible to separate production from distribution and exhibition, we then could use various legislative techniques and court decisions to limit the influence of studios and their parent companies.

But it's also an incredibly complicated accounting matter. Profit participation is a great example. Some years ago production companies decided to give talent some share of the profits, thereby making creative personnel a partner in the production. They thought that participation would act as an incentive to ensure the production was as strong as possible. During Fin-Syn, production companies were on the same side as the talent—everyone wanted to get the most money from the distributor or exhibitor because it increased the income for everyone, the production company and the talent. In television, for example, a production company normally approaches a network for an increased license fee after a few successful years on television. Traditionally, the network agrees, and everyone who is a profit participant enjoys a larger income. After Fin-Syn, however, we started seeing networks decline to increase the license fee for the shows they made in-house. Additionally, we started seeing production companies make deals with other entities *within* the conglomerate as they tried to monetize intellectual property across various subsidies. Consolidated financial reports make the accounting very complicated, and invariably the conglomerates self-deal to keep the money within the consolidated financial report and out of the hands of the talent who are profit participants. I find myself initiating a lot of audits to find money that is due to my clients—I was the first one to bring what we now call "vertical integration" lawsuits. I have represented Wind Dancer Productions regarding *Home Improvement*, David Duchovny on *X-Files*, Alan Alda on *M.A.S.H*, and John Langley from COPS, among others.

But isn't it even more complicated today? Concepts like "market" and "content" are so diffuse. Is there a "home entertainment market" anymore? How do you respond to the fact that writers are being asked to create content for a web page that the conglomerate refers to as "promotion" rather than as additional labor that deserves compensation?

The shit is about to hit the fan. I'm involved in multiple audits right now. There hasn't been significant litigation in this area, but unquestionably it's going to happen very soon.

For example, what is video on demand? Studios say it is home video. My clients, then, are entitled to a 20 percent royalty. But let's say I am a profit participant in *Grey's Anatomy*. The network claims it has the right to put the show on its network website or Hulu or some other dot-com service. But to me that's an independent method of capitalizing on the creative content, and my client deserves additional recognition for his or her participation. Now I recognize the economics of online distribution are fuzzy. We're still figuring out the best way to monetize content online. But, clearly, audiences are watching shows on the computers and mobile devices. We have to figure it out.

Right now, people are trying to twist old contractual language to fit a new media environment, saying online distribution was an anticipated activity when the talent entered into the contract. Unfortunately, legislation is slow to act, and technology moves much more rapidly. The courts are going to start making these decisions, and that's where you can look to see change happen. That puts me right in the middle of it, which is wonderful.

I'm thrilled and excited about all of this because I think it's such a creative area—copyright, intellectual property, and compensating people for the content they create are newer, fascinating areas of the law. It's going to be the court system that resolves these disputes.

You say it's going to hit the fan. Can you put a time line on that?

This is going to be within the next six months. I'm involved in numerous audits right now and many of them focus on video on demand and SVOD [subscription video on demand]. How do we treat Hulu? How do we treat network websites? I'm even looking into television formats. How do we value the talent's participation when the studio takes the concept abroad and repurposes the script and set and films the show in a foreign language? How do we value the showrunner's original investment in making it a hit show in the first place? Networks have clearly said that the talent's participation is largely confined to the show's first run on the network. This is a big fight.

How do you protect intellectual property? How do you use copyright to protect the creative person and make sure that the creative person gets his or her fair share of the pie? That's what this is all about. We're in a different reality now, and we need different rules. Studios have a hard time accepting this fact.

How do you try to structure deals based on potential revenues?

It's very hard because there's so much unknown right now, and because of conglomeration, there are just so few buyers with such great power. Transactional lawyers are running into brick walls—conglomerates constantly adjust contractual language to protect their profits. For instance, contracts didn't originally deal with self-dealing after the repeal of Fin-Syn until I started bringing lawsuits against the studios. Then, the introduced language that allows for self-dealing that's "presumed fair and just and equitable." Now, it's our burden to prove otherwise. The studios just keep eviscerating the talent's rights. Each time something new happens, the transactional lawyers run to me and say, "Larry, Larry, what do we do about this because this is unfair?" I tell them, "Just negotiate as hard as you can to get the best deal for the client." It will take some time. First, we need a product that's sufficiently successful over a few years. Then, we'll need to launch an audit, which will take about another year. Once that's done, we can file a lawsuit, which will require another two years or so before a result comes in. And the truth is, studios work really hard to keep these cases quiet because they don't want these issues public.

Do you see the film industry responding any differently to these challenges?

It's affecting all of the businesses because it's consolidating the power in a very few number of buyers, and everybody is frightened about alienating those buyers. Therefore, transactional lawyers can only negotiate much more limited deals for their clients. Similar to television, you don't see too many independent productions anymore. There's so much focus on the bottom line that conglomerates are only interested in big-budget franchises, like *Twilight* or *The Hunger Games*. Studios want products with built-in audiences—book series, sequels, reboots.

Studios don't want to spend money on development anymore. Rather, the types of products they make are dictated by their other interests within the company. *Cars* made a significant amount of money, but they made a sequel because the first films sold so much merchandise that dwarfed anything they could do at the box office alone. A lot of these companies are launching projects for reasons unrelated to the quality of the product itself.

Do different types of talent face different challenges? Do directors face different problems than writers, who face different problems than musicians?

One thing I want to say is, it amazes me that all of these people don't get together and figure out a way to satisfy everyone's needs. Look at the music industry. I'm going to give you a perfect example of what's going to happen and how we should learn from history. The RIAA [Recording Industry Association of America] sees the proliferation of avenues of distribution and sees piracy going on, and they think, "We're going to stop this. We're going to start suing all of these college students and stop them from illegally downloading this stuff." If it didn't work with Prohibition, what makes you think it's going to work now? And they're going along that route, and none of the labels or the organizations representing them is doing anything creative. So a guy like Steve Jobs comes along and says, "Hey, I've got an idea. How about we charge people 99 cents and let them listen to a good product?" It worked. Nobody in the industry thought about this, just this guy out there in the Internet world, in the technology world, came up with this thing. The industry just has to look at it and go, "This is what people want. Can I create a system for delivering quality product on a timely basis to people?" Because if you give them what they want for a reasonable price, and something of good quality, they'll pay for it instead of stealing, they really will. But you must give them that product in a timely basis, and it must be of good quality, and at a reasonable price. When I teach my class at USC's law school, I ask, "How many of you illegally download?" Eight years ago the numbers were much larger. But now they can get everything. At the time, their view was, "The record companies deserve it." Why? Because they would want to own one song but had to buy a whole damn album, and albums were twenty dollars a pop. There was no flexibility.

It's the same thing that's happening with movies. All of the movies have very specific release windows. We've got domestic distribution for this length of time, then we're going foreign, then we're going to go to pay TV, and then we're going to go to video or CDs or whatever. You've got to change the way you're doing business based upon the change in technology and the changing desires of the people who are paying for your product. It is so institutionalized and so slow to change in the entertainment industry. We brought a lot of this on ourselves.

Do you see a context where you could get everybody to the table and start to hammer some of these things out? Can you give an idea of what it might look like and whether there's something like that on the horizon?

The most successful of the transactional lawyers have tried dealing with the guilds, and tried dealing with the studios, and tried dealing with the networks, all trying to get people together. It hasn't succeeded yet. But that's where we have to go. I think if the litigation becomes destructive and distracting enough, and I hate putting it in those terms, but that probably will be the agitation that gets people to do it. Either that or the economics become so horrendous that at some point the big media companies will have to say, "Maybe we have to go into this kind of system because we just aren't making it without it. So fighting against the tide probably doesn't make sense, and let's see if we can get in line with technology instead of trying to prevent it." I think the situation is going to have to get worse. The transactional lawyers probably have the best chance, because, as you probably know, there are probably ten or twelve transactional entertainment law firms with between ten or twenty lawyers who represent probably 85 to 90 percent of the creative people in this town. If those transactional entertainment lawyers and their counterparts at the studios, networks, and record companies start to cooperate with each other, some serious and significant change can be made. But it's going to take that kind of cooperation.

What are the things you think everybody should know if they are negotiating a deal in the digital age?

The key is to not rely upon the existing law but to recognize that it's going to change. You have to build into the contract a fair way of compensating the creative talent as platforms change or modes of distribution change and therefore revenue streams change. If you're attempting to obtain a percentage of a particular revenue stream and that revenue stream suddenly becomes less valuable or nonexistent and you haven't anticipated other revenue streams, then you've got a real problem. Most people would not have the power to negotiate the kinds of terms you need because there's too much consolidation on one side and not enough consolidation on the other. So you have disparate bargaining power. Every transactional entertainment lawyer knows now that they should be making sure that VOD [video on demand] is at 100 percent, not 20 percent, royalty. Every transactional entertainment lawyer knows that your client should be compensated whether it's given to Hulu or a dot-com or the networks. They all know they can't get that automatically in their negotiation. What you have to do is try to be creative and look ahead. At one point, merchandising was nothing, and people would give away merchandising for an extra couple of bucks up front. Now, recognizing that the industry has changed, merchandising can be for some sorts of product the most revenue-generating stream. So they're smart enough to say they want to participate in the merchandising. And if they're really smart, they'll say, "Not only do I want to participate in the merchandise, but I don't want self-dealing between you and a subsidiary of yours because I'm somehow getting cut out of my fair share." That's the sort of stuff they do in contracts, but it's going to be damn tough to get the studios to give talent the revenue talent deserves.

What do you think of the position of Netflix right now in terms of its power in the distribution space?

I have a view that I don't think is shared by a lot of people. A lot of people are really big on digital distribution. A lot of people that have digital distribution think they're going to control the industry. I don't think so. I think digital distribution is going to allow so much competition in the area of distribution and exhibition that I think that with all of those digital distributors, the people who are going to have real power are the content providers. As the digital distributors become more and more prevalent and dispersed, they are going to be the ones who are going to have to keep lowering their profitability and giving more and more to content providers. It kind of switched around. Content providers at one time were powerhouses. Now the distributors have a lot of power and are growing. But I think it's all going to come back to the content; I see everything in economics and in life as kind of a pendulum swing, and I think it's going to swing back. And if it doesn't, there are going to be lawsuits in order to help regulate.

How has your thinking about piracy and intellectual property changed in this digital environment?

I'm kind of an interesting case because I was an ACLU pro bono lawyer of the year, so obviously I care about the First Amendment and freedom of speech and information. At the same time, I represent creative people who create content and I don't like seeing stuff that my clients create being pirated and misused. I'm kind of in a strange place. My view is that piracy is not the result of an inherent flaw in human nature that wants something for nothing; rather, it has resulted from the inability of the industry to provide quality product for a reasonable price on a timely basis. I think that we have to learn to do that. It's more complicated on the international level because we're dealing with different cultures and different people. Different countries have to get together and realize that those countries that are now using our product or pirating our product will be creating their own product and will want to protect it at some point. And we have to do an educational process internationally about that. Piracy has always had the greatest impact on the music industry, but it will have a significant impact on the rest of the entertainment industry if we don't change the way we do things. This new technology requires us to have new ways of doing things.

What is the nature of the litigation you're doing with respect to piracy and intellectual property issues?

There are two kinds of piracy that I see. One is the kind when people really do just pirate other people's work and try to sell it as their own, or pretend that their product is the real product. I've always been involved in that kind of straightforward litigation. The other kind is where someone will rip off someone else's idea and get away with it. That's why we have what are called "idea submission cases" in California, which is different than copyright. Because copyright can only protect the *expression* of the idea, whereas the concept itself is an idea, and the courts consider [that] free as the air. But ideas, even if not developed into a script, can be valuable. The reason why we have idea submission cases is that Hollywood realized that when you enter into a contract with someone basically by saying, "I will tell you my idea," you should be able to get legal protection for that idea if the other person agrees to it by saying, "I'll compensate you for it." That's the concept of idea submission cases. The studios tried to kill idea protection by claiming copyright preempts, and therefore eliminates, idea submission lawsuits. But in the Miramax case the court decided that copyright does not preempt idea submission. So there are two very different types of "rip-off" cases going on now in Hollywood.

Patric Verrone, Writer-Producer and Former President, Writers Guild of America, West

A 1981 Harvard graduate, Patric Verrone was a history major and an editor of the *Harvard Lampoon,* one of the most prolific incubators of American comedy talent. Yet Verrone headed to law school instead of the comedy circuit, which was perhaps more amusing, at least for a while. In 1986 he landed a writing gig on the *Tonight Show,* where he cut his teeth in one of television's most distinguished writers' rooms. Subsequent work with the Jim Henson Company and the Cartoon Network earned him writing credits on such shows as *Rugrats, The Critic, Muppets Tonight,* and *Pinky and the Brain.*

In 1999 Verrone joined the premiere season of Matt Groening's animated, sci-fi comedy, *Futurama,* produced by Fox Television, and during season 5 he was named coexecutive producer. *Futurama* has earned widespread critical acclaim and a passionate fan following, but the production of new episodes has been intermittent, with seven seasons of production stretching out over the course of fourteen years. Nevertheless, the show has earned five Emmy Awards and seven Annie Awards and has spun off a tie-in comic book series, video game, and related merchandise.

Verrone is perhaps best known as president of the Writers Guild of America, West (WGAW), during its 2007-8 contract negotiations with the major media conglomerates, represented by the Alliance of Motion Picture and Television Producers (AMPTP). Digital distribution issues were at the very center of those negotiations, resulting in a bruising hundred-day strike that earned writers a share of the revenues from emerging digital delivery systems, a historic victory on issues that are still raising concern among Writers Guild members. We met with Verrone in the *Futurama* writers' room on the Fox lot.

MEDIA INDUSTRIES PROJECT: *Residual payments seemed to be the most important issue behind the Writers' Strike in 2007–8. Why was that such an important issue? What's the history behind that?*

PATRIC VERRONE: With the advent of television, people said it would be the end of the motion picture because you could broadcast and therefore get to a much bigger audience. But of course it wasn't the end of motion pictures; television ended up just being a new place for motion pictures to be rerun. Once television became a medium that was reliant on the ability to reuse content, AFTRA [American Federation of Television and Radio Artists] negotiated a contract in the 1950s that said if you put something on TV that is just a reuse of the original program, you are getting the full benefit of our members' talent for free, so pay us again. This was the invention of residuals. You pay us 100 percent of our initial compensation if you want to rerun that show. That didn't last very long because that was not the kind of marketplace that the early television networks wanted. They wanted to be able to show things over and over without paying much for them. The same thing happened again in the 1980s with the advent of cable and the advent of home video, where again you had a whole new marketplace where everybody said, "This is death of television, this is the death of movies!" Of course it wasn't. It just ended up being a whole new place to reuse.

The guilds were a little more compliant in those days when it came to negotiating collective bargaining agreements; they either weren't organized, or they just didn't have their eye on the ball. They believed management's assertion that cable television and home video have a start-up cost that made them expensive. With home video, the studios said, "We have to make the video box, the videotape, and there is a cost that an outside vendor is charging us, so we are only getting a very small portion of the licensing fee and therefore you should only get a much smaller portion of the residual base."

The argument in cable was, "Look, we at the big networks and studios are facing new competitors. You have to give us a break when we move into these arenas." And the upstarts were saying, "You have to give us a break in terms of residuals because we are trying to compete with the established entities." Of course what ended up happening is we had these new contracts for cable and home video that were hobbled versions of the broadcast contracts. They allowed the companies to develop these new platforms, and eventually the networks and studios bought up the competition and grew into huge conglomerates.

When I started in the business there were about thirty or forty production entities that you could shop your wares to, and they were independent of the networks. Now there are six. The major networks have all merged, so now you have ABC Disney, NBC/Universal/Comcast, CBS, Viacom, and News Corp. And then there are the two that don't have networks per se: Warner Bros., although it does have an interest in the CW, and Sony, which also has a lot of influence in the digital world. So you have these companies that bought up everything. For the guilds it's now a case of negotiating with consolidated media empires that very cleverly cooperate.

Back in 1988, when the issues of cable and video residuals were first boiling over, why did the unions get such a bad deal?

Short of boring you with the whole history, I will bore you with just some sort of anecdotal recollections of my own. The DVD formula, which was the VHS formula, was really the creature of a series of bungles on the part of the unions in 1984 by the Directors Guild and in 1985 by the Writers Guild. We had language in a previous contract that said that this kind of ancillary marketplace would be covered at 2 percent of the take, so that 2 percent would go to the writers, 2 percent would go to the directors, 6 percent would go to the actors, and then another 10 percent would be divided among the below-the-line unions. That added up to 20 percent, which was supposed to be the overall residual pie that the industry had been paying. It was the formula that was being used in cable.

In home video, however, there was a difference between the producer's fee and the distributor's fee. In those days if you were Disney, for example, you didn't own the entity that made the VHS box or the tape itself. There was another separate entity that manufactured, packaged, and distributed the physical product, and studios were allowed to offset these costs, which they claimed were 80 percent of the total revenue collected. They argued that they should be entitled to offset the up-front costs of production because they were not the distributors, they were the producers. There was a short strike by the writers in 1985, and ultimately the guilds agreed to let the studios cover their costs before the residuals were calculated. Now, in time, all of that exterior production became internalized, and the studio distributors put together everything: content, videotape, and packaging. That meant they could play with the cost structure to favor them and reduce the residuals they paid to the talent.

By 2007 it was no longer a VHS box and a cumbersome tape; it was this silver disk that was very cheap to produce. It was almost cost-free to make the physical medium. At the same time the market shifted from rentals to ownership, and people began to buy DVDs and collect them. And it was no longer just movies, it was television series as well. In 1985 TV writers, who are a large part of the WGA's membership, didn't see the advantage of VHS residuals because most TV series weren't being marketed on VHS, so they didn't think it was the way they were going to make any kind of money. Now remember that WGA strikes affect TV writers first and foremost because they are the ones who immediately have to stop working, since they tend to work on a salaried staff basis. They usually bear the brunt of any strike. As a result, TV writers weren't especially supportive of the '85 strike, and they were much more willing to settle in order to get it over with. That's the reason that strike fell apart after two weeks.

As VHS moved to DVD, and as the marketplace expanded to include television shows, TV writers realized that they were getting screwed just as readily as motion picture writers. So one of the issues that repeatedly surfaced in our negotiations in 1988, '92, '95, '98, and 2001 was that we needed to up the VHS and DVD residual base, but it never happened. We were never able to get that number increased, and the reason was pattern bargaining. You could never convince the Directors Guild to fight against the original deal, and neither SAG [Screen Actors Guild] nor the Writers Guild [was] ever organized well enough to be able to stand on that issue.

Now along comes digital, and with it the ability to not only distribute media without the physical costs but also to create new media with very low cost structures. That really got the writers' attention, because now the companies were basically saying, "This is just like DVD. We are going to apply those same formulas. We are going to offset that 80 percent of cost that didn't exist for DVD, much less for digital, but we are going to offset all that. On top of that, we are going to ask you to do additional digital content for existing shows that is derivative of those shows, things like *The Office* or *Lost*, or other hot commodities on television. We're asking you to do additional material for the Internet for free as part of your initial compensation, as part of your day-to-day duties on that show. You do a twenty-two-minute half-hour show, you do forty-four minutes for an hour-long show, and do an additional two or three minutes and we'll put that up on the web to get people to watch the show itself."

So they asked writers and showrunners to do that, and they also began rerunning the shows on the Internet, calling it "promotion" and refusing to pay any residuals on this digital streaming at all. They called it "promotion" because they told viewers, "You missed last week's episode. Now you can catch up. You can watch the episode of *Lost* that you missed and you can then watch it again on broadcast TV, which is where we are making all our money on advertising." Writers in particular, but I think the industry in general, sensed that this was an unfair and inequitable approach to how residuals had historically been treated.

When we went to negotiations in 2007, the companies proposed a complete change to the way residuals worked, so that they were based on neither the fixed formulas that we had nor the percentage of revenue but rather a percentage of profit. Anybody who knows anything about Hollywood or has been in this business for any length of time knows that one of the great oxymorons alongside "jumbo shrimp" is "Hollywood accounting." It's pandemic how many profit participants have had to sue to get their share of actual profits. So their proposal was no residuals in new media and also profit-base residuals everywhere else. And I think that, more than anything, was a galvanizing issue for writers in 2007 with the dawn of digital.

So you see new technologies as being the impetus behind these labor conflicts?

Yeah, looking back, technology tends to be the provocateur. And each time the technology changed, our residual shares got smaller. The broadcast TV residual was more than the cable residual, which was more than the DVD residual. Other than the negotiations over digital in 2007, the only time we were able to raise the percentage for a residual was in 1977, when we got residuals in perpetuity. Up until then there was a limit on the number of times that a show would run. If it ran more than thirteen times, there was no residual pay.

In 1977 we got it into the contract that residuals would be paid in perpetuity, and that was the result of having struck during every single negotiation going back to 1960. It was a case of the companies saying, "Okay, fine, we'll give you what you want, just don't strike." That was the last time the companies negotiated without an umbrella entity. The creation of the Alliance of Motion Picture and Television Producers, which came about after the 1977 negotiation, allowed for genuine consolidated strategic planning on the part of what was then several dozen companies and is now the big six or seven. Technology is, I think, the driving element of when any kind of change in the residual structure takes place, but that doesn't mean the media companies are driving the innovation. Technological innovation happens independently of these big companies, for the most part. They tend to see technological changes happen, wait for them to evolve, and then buy them up or buy the company that's developed them or merge with that company so they can take advantage of their business models.

On the other hand, content innovation tends to happen from the bottom up; it comes from the likes of Joss Whedon, who creates a *Dr. Horrible's Sing-Along Blog*. There hasn't been a successful new media property that I can think of offhand that started as an executive idea coming out of News Corp., say, that trickles down and goes to the creatives with the directive "Go out and do this." There have been examples, such as *Battlestar Galactica*, when they wanted the writing staff to do extra webisodes and put that on between the seasons of the cable show. The writers went along with it, but it was a case of making them do it for free. It wasn't the writers' inspiration to do it, and I don't think it was ultimately successful. It had several problems, including the fact that when NBC/Universal made them do the webisodes, Ron Moore (the showrunner) and the actors wanted to be paid for them, so they kept them on their editing machines. The NBC/Universal executives had to break in under cover of darkness to steal the webisodes away so they could actually use them. It was an unpleasant state of affairs.

There are real innovators out there trying to do direct-to-the-Internet digital series, but the business model isn't there. And when something does reach a sort of critical mass or does get an audience, then a conglomerate gets wind of it and buys it up.

So HBO moves in on Funny or Die.

Exactly. And Cartoon Network buys *Annoying Orange,* or whatever the thing *du jour* is. That's where technology allows change from the ground up, and that's what I see happening.

Are conglomerates truly the biggest problem these days? We've had oligopoly in the media industries going back a long, long time. Is it worse today? And what might be an alternative?

I tend to agree with Tim Wu's book, *The Master Switch*. He argues that media technologies tend to evolve toward corporate control and oligopoly. It happened with the telegraph, motion pictures, radio, television, cable, etc. We see it happening right now in the Internet, as the historic entertainment industry and the new Internet giants battle it out.

The role the guilds or any creative entity plays in that, well, it's the old adage about when the elephants fight, the grass gets trampled. I can't begin to predict how it will happen, but as the digital media economy consolidates, the dominant corporations will do their best to limit the cost of content production in order to raise their profit margins.

The specifics of the successful WGA contract in 1977 go exactly to my point, which is that the conglomerates didn't have their act together then.

But once they got it together, they not only consolidated their control over distribution (broadcasting and cable), they also took control of production by eliminating the Financial Interest and Syndication Rules, "Fin-Syn," which had previously prohibited them from owning both production and distribution.

In the mid '90s, during an otherwise progressive Democratic presidential administration, you had laws being passed that allowed major media to go from an era of having to buy from independent producers like Norman Lear or Carsey-Werner to an era in which the major companies could own production, distribution, and exhibition.

With the end of Fin-Syn, you had the end of independent production. For a creative like myself or an actor or anybody who has an idea for a TV show or a film, you no longer had a wide variety of places to shop your ideas. You couldn't go to the independent producer because they have either been bought up or run out of the business since the big conglomerates were now producing their own content in-house. There is a limited amount of shelf space in broadcast television, and if the ABC Network is owned by the Walt Disney Company and they have a production arm, ABC Productions, then that's from whom they tend to buy.

Is there a way to create firewalls?

We had firewalls with Fin-Syn, and that's why they busted them down.

Is there a way to restore the firewalls?

What the Writers Guild, West, has done, and what I was called upon to do when I was president, was to lobby the FCC [Federal Communications Commission]. We also lobbied the U.S. Senate Commerce Committee and we testified before hearings on media consolidation where we promulgated and advanced the idea that there needs to be minimum amounts of independent production. If you look at the landscape of broadcast and cable TV thirty years ago, about 15 percent was produced in-house by the networks. The rest came from outside. Now it's completely flipped. Today, of that 15 percent that's produced outside, it's all reality television. Those are the only independent producers who still exist, and the reason is because it has no foreign resale value and those shows don't rerun. Reality TV is low-cost, but it has no syndication value, and that's where the real money is made by TV producers. The networks and studios know that, so they try to develop a vertical chain of control over programming. To put up firewalls against that is like getting a genie back in the bottle, getting toothpaste back in the tube.

But where the firewalls need to remain, and they currently do exist, is online. On the Internet is where you have net neutrality or at least some form of it right now. If those firewalls come down, then we lose the battle. The Writers Guild, West, has been out front in terms of trying to maintain, trying to convince the FCC to maintain those levels. So an entity like Comcast that now owns NBC Universal has restrictions on their ability to promote their own creative product or speed it through the pipeline in advance of anybody else's. Enforcement, however, is another matter.

But, in fact, those restrictions aren't binding. The big media companies have been behaving as if there is net neutrality, but that could change any time. Moreover, there's a lot of dissension within the conglomerates. For example, the digital divisions would like a more open Internet, while others are focused on issues like piracy. How does the Guild deal with this split personality that's emerging?

I don't run that zoo anymore, but when I did, it was absolutely my intention and assertion that we needed to be able to have a very strong net neutrality-style firewall that prevented companies like Comcast from being able to control and squeeze the pipe.

Since then, through a strategic advance of its piracy arguments, the Motion Picture Association of America [MPAA] has been able to get an alliance with the Directors Guild, the Screen Actors Guild, and AFTRA to support SOPA, the Stop Online Piracy Act.

The Writers Guild, West, was, shall we say, more discreet, and it ultimately did not join the alliance. There was an internal division as to how we should play along in that realm, because I think there were some who felt it was important for us, for the Writers Guild, West, to be allied with the other unions. Also, it was important for us to develop the kind of relationship with the companies that employ us when it came to piracy, because piracy hurts us too. So there is no question about our opposition to piracy, but there was some division in the leadership of the Guild as to whether or not we should make a full-blown alliance with the other guilds on SOPA or take a different tack. As it ended up, I think we missed an opportunity when SOPA crashed and burned.

I think the MPAA now has to rethink its strategy as to how it's going to get better control over online distribution, because it seems like the advantage right now is being held by the Internet service providers [ISPs], with whom they have difficulties. It still comes down to a political balancing act on the part of the FCC to make sure they continue to do their job and enact the mission statement in their enabling language that says that they are supposed to protect the public good. There is something to be said for "As Google goes, so goes the world." We need to protect a free and open Internet. I think that is the ultimate primary concern for us as citizens of the world.

What were your biggest challenges as president of the Writers Guild, West? Were they the most obvious ones that everybody would think about, such as the Guild versus the conglomerates, or were there other challenges that the average industry observer might not know about?

You know, the very first thing that happened when I took office in 2005—and I ran with a slate of candidates for the Guild board and we ran the table—was that we immediately removed our former executive director who had been a CBS labor relations executive for years and with whom I served when I was secretary-treasurer. He was someone whose genuine belief was that the best the union could do was survive by building a relationship with the companies and being able to get whatever the best deal that was being offered. Whereas, we ran for office because we were seeing the Guild's jurisdiction in film and television eroding, and we needed to develop an organizing model that would allow us to bring in writers who weren't being covered, we needed to get them into the tent, but we also had to get the people who were already in the tent prepared for collective action and to develop an understanding of what was actually going on. The third thing we needed to do was to make sure that our alliances with the Writers Guild, East, the Screen Actors Guild, AFTRA, the Directors Guild, the below-the-line unions, and the American labor movement in general were put back together.

What was impressive was that there was an editorial in the *Los Angeles Times* the weekend when I was elected that said my challenge would be like wrangling cats, because the writers are a diverse group. It was more fun than work, though, because it gave me personally and the team we built a chance to work together in a collaborative way, the way we are typically used to working in TV. We would have meetings where we brought in all the showrunners on ABC. Now these people, they are all writers. Many of them knew each other from way back. They served on school committees together or they worked together years ago when they were entry-level writers, but they had not been in a room together to talk about what was going on. Steven Bochco was among them. He was running a show at the time, and one of the showrunners said, "ABC was trying to get me to do some web content for free, and they told me that you, Steven Bochco, were being asked to do it for your show, so why shouldn't I?" We turned to Bochco and asked if it was true. He said, "Oh, yes, absolutely. They asked me." "And what did you tell them?" "Fuck you" he said. *[Laughter]*

So it was a case of writers getting together and being able to comingle and commiserate and then coordinate. Because we tend to be somewhat competitive for jobs and for ratings when shows get to go on the air, and we tend to be critical of each other's craft and art, it was actually refreshing to get people together in a room where they could agree.

Once the negotiation started, we got 3,000 writers at the LA Convention Center downtown. There were some meetings that I wouldn't call a lovefest, but there was some pretty free and frank discussion of ideas that led to a uniform assessment of how to proceed. I said at the time that the companies didn't think we would strike, but we did, and then they didn't think we would hold out, but we did, and then they didn't think we would win, but we did. It was really a case of a lot of very intelligent people pulling together, because everyone understood what was at stake.

Management was saying, "Look, we're not making any money on the Internet. There are no residuals here, there is no money." And so we came back and said, "That's why we are asking for a percentage, so if you make nothing, we make nothing." How much more fair could that be? Their response: "No, no, you don't understand, we are not making any money. And that's why we can't pay you." You know, it was a complicated thing to have to convey to members who would be sacrificing their salaries for who knows how long. It ended up being a hundred days in exchange for the prospect of a percentage of something that might develop in the future in this new medium that no one really understood.

The only way you do that is to have a certain level of consciousness. That means you have to have a compelling narrative that explains what's going on and what needs to be done, correct?

Yes. And writers are good at coming up with narrative. At that time it was a matter of convincing writers of traditional union things, like we are standing on the shoulders of people who have come before and the idea that you have to sacrifice for your kindred and for the future of the Guild and for a situation that you may not be experiencing right now. That was actually easier than I expected, because so many writers have long memories about when they were struggling, even the most successful ones, with few exceptions. Especially in television: Even though you are a showrunner, very few showrunners are born there. You work your way up the ladder, so you remember the days when you were working as a story editor and then you didn't get a job the next season, so you lived off your residuals from the years that you did work. One of our statistics that was very provocative and very effective was that over a writer's career, 25 percent of their earnings is residuals which, if you look at it chronologically, means that in any given twenty-year career, which is a long one, five years of your work is just residuals. Some people would use the old saying of Lew Wasserman's: "When my plumber puts in a toilet, he doesn't get money every time I flush it, so why should you get money every time we rerun your shows?" And our answer was, "That's because you don't get money every time you use the toilet, but you do get money every time you rerun one of our shows. If you get paid, we get paid. If you get nothing, we get nothing."

This brings us back to our central concern about the ways in which digital distribution is affecting compensation and creativity. Is this a unique historical moment?

I think it is, and another thing that makes this environment different from the past is that the barriers to entry are exceptionally low for digital content creation. That means writers have an almost unprecedented chance to get back into the driver's seat and into the ownership seat, whereas that's not the case with film or TV. Even when you make the movie you still have to get one of the big six to distribute it and one of the same three theater chains to exhibit it. Broadcast TV: You have to go to those four or five places. Cable TV: It's the same four or five companies that own those five hundred channels. But online I can make the movie, I can make the web series, I can put it up there, I can sell it, I can get the advertiser to underwrite it, and I can get the sugar daddy venture capitalist to support it. The other big difference is that on the Internet you don't have the limited window of release that you do in TV and film. You can put something up today, and as long [as] my website doesn't get taken down by the ISP, it's there, and it's there forever. It isn't like a TV show that goes on a network and has to be successful in the first two, three, maybe four installments. A movie's got two days in a theater to prove itself. Whereas online, you can grow the commodity over a very long time. That's a profound difference that gives us a leg up in a way that we haven't had for a very long time.

Could you then talk about venture capital and the role it's playing? Are venture capitalists becoming a big part of the opportunity equation?

When I ran the zoo, we tried to make writers into entrepreneurs. I had less than a year left in my term after the strike, so it was a case of trying to develop these entrepreneurial relationships, not just with advertisers but also with the new distributors, namely Google, Yahoo, Amazon, and these other entities that were looking to make themselves into television studios.

I think that's now atrophied. Again, it was a combination of the fact that the money itself became harder to come by, and, you know, television and other entertainment production has always been a huge risk. So when you've got a world financial meltdown and an unproven business model through the Internet that wasn't evolving as quickly as people thought . . . it was a tough sell. It used to be that a writer would work for a season on *Seinfeld* and the studio would offer them a million dollars a year just to sit by their pool and to come up with the next idea. Now, because of media consolidation, that doesn't exist anymore. It's up to that writer to now go off and make their own way via self-promotion, self-production, and whatever else works. It's certainly not easy, and it takes a lot of time and energy. I'm not sure all writers are likely to do it. And, again, because you've still got broadcast TV and you've still got motion pictures—in my case, I work on a cable television show that takes up all of my time, so I'm going to continue to do this as long as I can. Whether I will end up trying another business model when this ends, well, I can't say. I may end up just painting figurines. But that's because that's what I prefer to do. *[Laughter]*

Dick Wolf, Executive Producer and Creator, *Law & Order*

It's fitting to conclude this section of interviews with Dick Wolf, for in many ways he is the exception that proves the rule—a writer/producer that continues to excel with series television, despite the significant changes wrought by the digital distribution revolution. As mentioned earlier, Wolf is creator and executive producer of three *Law & Order* series that have proven exceptionally lucrative in the world of network and cable broadcasting, especially in syndication. This has allowed him to establish Wolf Films, a production and development unit that overseas the company's current productions and cultivates new shows that it shops around to studios, allowing NBC/Universal—its home base—a first look at all projects. Wolf is therefore more than a writer and executive producer; he is also the owner/manager of a production unit, which means he brings the perspective of a studio boss to our discussion of creative labor in the digital era.

Born and raised in New York City, Wolf initially followed his father into the advertising business but saw it largely as a way to support his screenwriting aspirations. He broke into series television on the writing staff of *Hill Street Blues*, earning an Emmy nomination and enough professional credibility to land him a spot as a supervising producer of *Miami Vice*. In 1990 he launched *Law & Order*, a show that ran twenty seasons, tying *Gunsmoke* as the longest-running drama in television history. Along the way, Wolf won two Emmy Awards, was inducted into the Television Academy Hall of Fame, and earned a star on the Hollywood Walk of Fame. We interviewed Wolf during one of his visits to the Carsey-Wolf Center.

MEDIA INDUSTRIES PROJECT: *How would you describe your job and your professional identity?*

DICK WOLF: Ideally, I would hope that I am thought of and at some point remembered as a teller of great stories. I think that would be my lasting legacy rather than any specific concept or television series. As a story-teller, I have had a good run, in part because I know my limits and I know the limits of the media I've worked in. Although, as I have said for years, I know what's going on my headstone: Canceled. *[Laughter]*

You're also a showrunner and a businessperson. You see yourself as a sto-ryteller, but you still have to manage this vast apparatus.

If I was going to give myself an honest assessment, I'm probably not as good a writer as some of my peers, but I am a better businessman.

In what sense?

Our shows don't go over budget. We've never missed an airdate. It's just an attitude—it's show business. No show, no business; but in the end, it's a business. That's why I wore a tie every day up until five years ago. It was very deliberate, because I was physically demonstrating to people it's a business. This is not high school with money. Someone's not happy? Don't let the door hit you on the way out.

When you're launching a new show like Chicago Fire, *you need to think about the story line, the casting, and the competition, but you also need to get it out there, to get it recognized. Is it getting harder to launch a show these days?*

When I worked for Procter & Gamble almost forty years ago, they could project a product launch to the decimal point: If we spend 5 percent more in the C and D markets, we will have a 1 percent rise in the market share. How did we know that? Well, because there were algorithms that go back fifty years, and we knew what would happen. That's not true in show busi-ness. Market research can't tell you what's going to work. More than 90 percent of all the TV shows don't make money. What business in the world would take a 95 percent failure rate in R&D?

And nobody knows what's going to work, right?

Nobody sets out to make a flop.

So what are the essential ingredients of success?

If I knew that, I wouldn't have a string of failures along with my string of successes. You pay your money and take your chances and try to make the best show possible. The most important thing is the writing.

I hate to be Pollyannaish, but I still believe that quality will win out. It's a terrible admission, but I look back at a bunch of the shows that didn't work and they were much more flawed in retrospect than the ones that did work. It's relatively easy to make a pilot, but the challenge is doing it 109 more times and making them all good.

Look, I'm not saying that it's me that is making it good. You have to have showrunners that can sustain the quality of the scripts over time. That's their responsibility. Luckily, I honestly think I have two of the best five in the business right now. Warren Leight *[Law & Order: SVU]* is a world-class playwright. Matt Olmstead *[Chicago Fire]* has been thoroughly schooled. This is not new territory to them. These guys have people that can get stuff out the door every eight days for months at a time. People have no idea. I've had showrunners literally crack up. At any given moment, one episode is shooting, two are in post-production, and you're working on a draft for the one that's going into prep. Beyond that, there's nothing. You know that in ten days you're going to be in a world of hurt unless you can make something happen. It can be brutal.

What about the storytelling strategies? Are they different now than they were before?

Not really. The biggest difference is that you can get stuff on the air now that you never could have gotten on before. But there are still limits. You couldn't put *Breaking Bad* on broadcast television. You couldn't put *Dexter* on broadcast. You really couldn't put *Homeland* on broadcast; not the way they're doing it. There would be too many standards notes from the networks.

That's one of the reasons that I'm really happy that *Chicago Fire* is working, because literally, creatively, career-wise, this was going all in.

What do you mean by "going all in"?

Look, I wouldn't say this is a negative, just a reality. I'm sixty-six years old. If the forty-six-year-old head of the network gets hit with a turkey of a show that is hardly cutting edge, it's going to be messy. Let's say they were cautious at first. "What, a fire show?" I said, "I think this is going to work." If I was him and this hadn't worked, I wouldn't come back to me. That's the reality.

It seems like a real departure. It's more character driven, sort of like ER in the firehouse.

Excuse me, but that's how it was pitched. *[Laughter]*

If I was going to make a prediction, I'd say this show has the potential to be a ten-year show. I've said that all along. It will never be worth what the *Law & Orders* are worth because it's serialized. If you tune in and you've missed an episode, it's a challenge. The wonderful thing about *Law & Order* is it doesn't matter whether you didn't see it for a week, a month, a year, or three years—you come in and say, oh, it's *Law & Order*. It's a Catholic High Mass.

On the other hand, *Chicago Fire* is a radical departure for me. It wouldn't have been for Steven Bochco or David Kelley. They've been doing these kinds of shows for thirty years. Not me. I've been doing stand-alone, self-contained episodes with no arcs.

Your shows have done very well in the syndication world, but now you're doing a show that might lean more favorably to a Netflix or Hulu environment. Going into it, were you saying to yourself, this is a different animal?

From a business standpoint, it's actually a very exciting period if you have a patient attitude. I'm very fortunate that I don't have to worry about this week's or next week's ratings on cable. Everything has been sold for a long time. The shows are working off preexisting contracts. I'm very, very fortunate. But launching anything new, it doesn't matter. The audience doesn't care what you did before. The network will use my track record to sell the show, but the audience doesn't care. It's a fresh page every time. I'm very gratified that *Chicago Fire* is now catching on. It was very scary for the first three months, but now the hook's in. You can feel it with the numbers and the audience. It was close.

Do you have someone like Betsy Scolnik monitoring social media?

She's doing both *Chicago Fire* and *SVU*. They're on the same night. She follows the conversation. Tries to guide it a bit. And then gives us a recap on Thursdays.

Is there crossover between the audiences?

A bit. We're getting more now, but initially it was two discrete audiences.

How do you use the recap information that Betsy provides?

It's nice to have the information, but the problem with social media is that there doesn't seem to be any correlation between the amount of social media discussion, the amount of advertising on Yahoo, and the interstitial stuff that's circulated. I've never seen it move the dial. And sometimes when the conversation is at the highest, the ratings have actually gone down.

My fear is that if you go into any blog and you look at the comments, they're 95 percent negative no matter what the subject is. My initial reaction to everything online is, well, would you get a life? They ask things like, "What does it mean that his tie changed from green to red?" If any television show is even a tertiary centerpiece of your life, you've got a problem. This is entertainment. We're not curing cancer here. This is not a solution to your love life or your emotional life. It's entertainment. Very disposable. Expungeable.

Do you get anything out of the social media feedback?

Look, it's good to know the audience seems to be getting what we're trying to do, that they're following the story arcs and the characters, but it's not like they're coming up with new insights that we can put to use. The audience only knows what you tell them. So if you're getting the feedback and they're using the characters' names, that's great.

Does social media feedback ever affect your writing process?

Sure, but I've never seen anything that would cause me to pick up the phone and call Matt [Olmstead]. Warren [Leight] is much more concerned about it than Matt is. I keep telling Warren, it's eighteen people, don't worry about it. But he tweets, and he's massively involved. That's a double-edged sword.

I don't know if you were following the Mike Tyson thing, but it was a huge tempest in a teacup. We cast Mike Tyson as a death row inmate who was abused as a child. A whole bunch of survivors were outraged, and it was two weeks of Warren almost having a nervous breakdown because he responded on Twitter and they attacked him . . . and then it was back and forth. It was endless. I just don't engage. Social media chatter about television shows has limited positive impact.

How about market research?

Sure, the network does mid-season research. We recently got the report on *Chicago Fire*. They don't even bother doing *SVU* anymore; it's been the same thing for thirteen years. We love Mariska—you don't need additional research.

But on *Chicago Fire*, they're tracking it very closely. You're seeing exactly again what you hope to see. People are very involved with the stories. About a month ago we instituted an edict: Three-episode arcs are the limit on any story line. People had started complaining about what [Lieutenant Kelly Severide, played by Taylor Kinney] was going to do about his arm. Was he going to become a drug addict? It went on too long. That's something you can learn through market research.

What are the most useful aspects of market research?

When you hear negatives. I tell my kids this: Success teaches you nothing. You only learn through failure. If you think that, gee, this guy is really interesting and 70 percent of the audience thinks he's an obnoxious dick-head, then you have to pay attention. Research is never a decision-making tool. It's really never a gross surprise. It's a diagnostic tool. You go, well, I can see how people might feel that way. Then you can make adjustments, but it takes a while for the adjustments to take hold, because by the time you start making an adjustment on the character, there are three more episodes that are too far gone to change. But there are many people with helpful comments during the course of the first season.

Is market research better today than twenty years ago?

I think it's about the same. The major market research during pilots is the dial test. People sitting in a room responding to the show, minute by minute, by twisting a dial. That hasn't changed in fifty years. And if you've been working on shows long enough, there are ways to stack the deck and get the response you want. Still, you do learn things that can prove useful.

Back to the issue of creative authority. During our interviews, we've heard that producers and writers are getting swamped with feedback these days, that there's more feedback coming from more directions. Do you feel that way, or do you find yourself in a charmed position?

I'm not in a charmed position, but I am in a different position than a lot of producers, because—I'm trying to have this come out sounding right—at this stage, everybody knows I don't have to be doing this anymore. On a basic level, I've got mine. Somebody said, why are you still doing it?, and I said I've worked thirty-five years to get to a point where I can operate this way.

I spoke with Bob Greenblatt [chairman, NBC Entertainment] just before this interview. He called and wanted to talk, which is odd, because usually Bob doesn't want to talk to anybody. I think he feels comfortable talking to me because I'm kind of bulletproof. I'm not trying to pick his pocket. I'm not trying to sell him stuff. When we have differences, it's usually a productive exchange. I say, look, this is the way I feel. You're the head of the network. It's your decision. We both may express strong opinions, but we work it out. If we have a disagreement about casting, for example, we try to keep it as uncontentious as possible.

I did make one request when [*Chicago Fire*] was picked up. I said, look, we have a huge job here and we all know it. We've got to get this show up, so what I would request is that since the network and the studio are the same company, and the same people are basically in charge, [that we have] one set of notes. Luckily, I had the ammunition. On the first two scripts we got diametrically opposed notes from the studio and the network. I said, you guys should have that conversation and then come to us with an agreed-upon approach. They said okay, and it has made a big difference. It's much better than what some shows have to deal with.

Can you explain the nature of the relationship between Wolf Films and NBC Universal?

Sure: We're a pod.

Which means?

NBC Universal picks up most of the hard costs of personnel and offices for Wolf Films. In exchange, we have a "first-look" deal. They see every new show we develop. If they pass, we can go outside. For better or worse, they haven't passed on any.

In an earlier conversation, you took exception to the idea of talking about Law & Order *as a franchise versus a brand.*

I do feel strongly about that, but nobody gives a shit about it but me.

We care. Why a brand?

I'll give you an example: A franchise is McCormick & Schmick's. If you go to Chicago or you go to LA or you go to New York, you know if it says McCormick & Schmick's, it's going to be good seafood and steaks, cooked well, and it will be similar and very comfortable.

A brand is Mercedes. They make lots of different cars that offer different driving experiences, but if you buy one, you're going to be happy with the model you got, even though the experience is different. I do think it's a big difference because *CSI: NY* and *CSI: Miami* are exactly the same as the original. If *Law & Order* wasn't on the front of our shows, nobody would ever claim that *SVU* and *Criminal Intent* were the same show.

So your brand is actually Wolf Films?

I hope so. That's what I would like it to become with the Chicago shows [*Chicago Fire* and *Chicago P.D.*], and obviously with the half-hour comedy, *Girlfriend in a Coma*. That would be great.

This sounds like beating my own drum, but among agents and executives, there is that awareness—even with the stuff that hasn't garnered attention or high ratings. The stuff has been pretty good, and that's what distinguishes it. And that's what allows us to grow the brand.

David Kelley is hog-tied because he writes everything himself. What? Why are you doing that? He could foster new writers and mentor new showrunners, both of which are really important. When we were doing *Law & Order*, Rene Balcer and Michael Chernuchin started out as staff writers the first year, and they both ended up writing and producing a variety of shows for a long time. They knew what the system was. You didn't have to explain it.

Is the brand both a signature style and the production system itself?

Look, the thing that's scary is the number of people involved in the company over the past twenty years. Yes, there is a way we do things and we pay attention to all the details on all the shows. Arthur Forney has been there twenty-two years. People sometimes say to me that they've seen every episode, but in fact they really haven't. There are only two people who have seen every episode, and that's Arthur and me—every single one.

You're kind of like a studio.

I would like to think that's what we have been or will become, especially with shows that are not in the one brand cycle of *Law & Order*. Nothing would make me happier than if the company would end up as MTM. When I started there in 1984, it was the Harvard Business School of television. The writers' building had *Hill Street* on the second floor and *St. Elsewhere* on the first floor. Wayland Green. Tom Fontana. David Milch. It was pretty rare air.

Only in your case (Wolf Films), the writers are running the asylum. At MTM it was Grant Tinker.

I'll tell you something, and I love Grant, but he made such an amazingly bad decision when he formed his own company. The fatal flaw was he respected what writers did. He knew their importance. He respected the written word. He just didn't understand them. He had kind of an idiot savant relationship with them. Like MTM, ours is a writers-oriented company, but we're also a company that is run by writers, all the way to the top.

You have been associated with NBC since the 1980s. During that time, the business has changed quite a bit. In fact, some say the change has been revolutionary. In what way is today's NBC different from the network thirty years ago?

Probably not a great interview if I said exactly the same.

Really?

It doesn't matter whether it was Brandon or Bob or Les or the other Brandon—do you remember Brandon Stoddard? Those were the days when there were two Brandons walking around. Their job has always been the same. They all say the same thing: "We're interested in shows with long-term value, but we have to stay on budget and meet economic goals." The reality is, quality is not their problem. Their problem is putting up shows that get a big number the first time they're on the network. That's their job.

Does it matter that today NBC is part of Comcast, that it has gotten bigger and bigger? At one time it was a network, and now it's part of a big conglomerate. Does that matter at all?

Yes, economically. There are huge differences, but they're invisible in the present. Anything I'm doing right now to put a show on, it's exactly the same. You have to get the director and the cast. You have to get the script in shape. It's exactly the same. But the problem for us right now is that we have no way of telling what revenue streams are going to be rivers or rivulets in ten years.

A perfect example: USA is paying more than a million dollars an episode for every episode of *SVU*. That has been going on for a long time and has been very rewarding. Going forward, I'm not so sure. Every episode we make, we're on the hook for seven figures, but I don't know if USA is even going to be buying shows three years down the road, because in a few years each episode could be available for free on NBC.com, the day after on Hulu, maybe Netflix, and all of a sudden, that potential rerun audience has been cannibalized before USA even has a shot at it. I don't know. I have no idea what's going to happen.

Who would have believed that anybody was going to get over a million dollars an hour from Netflix? Of course, it could be argued that they have already bankrupted themselves. Maybe the streaming deals aren't worth that much and they're overpaying. Who knows? The one thing that's still true about entertainment is nobody knows nothing.

How does that affect the way your contracts are put together? How do you deal with these changing revenue streams?

It's all part of a pool. In my situation, it's just revenue—okay, this much came in.

You don't have any input on how the pie is divided?

I don't have control of that. I think I have consultation rights, which means absolutely nothing. They are going to do what they consider to be in the best interest of Comcast, but luckily whatever they do, it's just part of a revenue pool.

For many writers there's a lot of anxiety about getting their share of new revenue streams.

Of course, there always has been. It goes back to the beginning of time, but my favorite profit story was when Dick Zanuck and I were doing a project twenty-five years ago and Orion wanted to move the video revenues to the fourth quarter rather than the first quarter of the next year. They called it "video burn." Anyway, all this stuff is going on, and Dick says, "Well, you go on the assumption that you know they're lying, they know they're lying, and therefore you send in auditors." It's not contentious. It's just, oh well we should just check this. Dick pointed out that *Jaws* was the highest-grossing picture in the history of France and he only got a check for $250,000. He thought, gee, that doesn't seem right. It turned out that UIP [the international distributor of *Jaws*] had released it with a French short they had made and credited 50 percent of the revenue to the French short.

Sounds like what they do in China these days.

This has been going on forever. Nothing changes. I've been through six owners and God knows how many administrations at NBC. People have different ideas about how things get counted. That's why there are lawyers.

This seems to be a particularly tumultuous time. A lot of the issues that came up during the Writers' Strike in 2007–8 are still unresolved in the minds of many. It has been going on for some time, but the speed of change seems to be increasing. First it was videotape, then DVD, then EST, and now it's SVOD. And, at each turn, people get anxious about how the pie is shared. Do you think we're going to see more labor unrest?

I hope not. It's so self-defeating. The business hasn't come back from the strike. It never comes back to the people that go on strike. It's the same in professional sports. I think that the WGA was so misguided in the way they went about the strike, the way they mounted it, and what they thought they could possibly get. I mean, what planet were they living on? The work that was lost will never come back. After the strike, the producers cut back, and now the writing staffs are smaller. The WGA leaders wanted a knife fight, but they were stabbing themselves in the neck. It was unprofessional and ill-considered for the Guild leadership to take people out on these issues.

What would have been the best way to handle things? As I understand it, when video was negotiated, the writers didn't get a very good deal, and they wanted to make sure that history wouldn't repeat itself in the digital era. As for the television companies, they are saying, "It's not a business yet, so why should we give you anything?" But they said the same thing during the videotape era, and pretty soon they were making buckets of money, but they refused to share much of it with the writers. So wouldn't you, as a writer, want to negotiate something that protects you going forward?

Do you know what the dollar value of digital rights would be to individual writers?

No, I don't.

Miniscule. I don't know how to describe it, maybe the size of one of those pizzas in the airports. You're only going to get 2 percent of that. It should have been a spreadsheet conversation. If we go out for six months and lose six months of income, how much would it take to make that money back if we got everything we wanted? Decades.

One script is worth more than they'd make on the digital payout on a huge hit. What can I say? It was stupid. And on top of it, jobs were lost that are not coming back. After the strike, studio executives started to say, "Oh, hey. We don't need six people on a writing staff. We only need three." And they filled their schedules with a lot of reality shows, which took away scripted programming time.

What do you think would have been the better way to approach it?

I think they should have gone after a benefits package, and they should have steered away from the strike, but Verrone wanted to go on strike.

It just didn't make sense. The payback for success would have been minimal for the average writer. They were sold a bill of goods. The minimum, whatever it is now, on an hour script, is around $40,000, and if it's a network show that's going to rerun, you get a 70 percent residual. Each hour of a network show is worth a minimum of $75,000. Now I would say during that strike most working writers lost at least one television script. Not only that, but they got killed. It's one thing to have a Pyrrhic victory, but they got nothing! That's what was irresponsible. If you go after big game, you have to take it down with one shot.

They brought in David Young [as executive director of the WGAW], and he and Verrone thought, we're going to nail the AMPTP to the wall. The problem was that David came from outside the entertainment industry and doesn't know the business.

And it didn't just affect the writers, it brought everybody down: the makeup artists, the guys that run the food wagon. Ask Mr. Verrone what he thought about the IATSE [International Alliance of Theatrical Stage Employees] reaction to the strike. They were throwing things at people on the picket line. WGAW was taking bread out of their mouths for amounts of money that were statistically unimportant, and even if they become important ten or fifteen years from now, I assure you, it's not going to be anything like the money made on network reruns. That's just the reality.

But you're also somebody who's not very comfortable with the way in which the networks are strategizing about the digital environment. We had an earlier conversation about Hulu where you were telling me you didn't appreciate Jeff Zucker's decision to support Hulu.

It was very ill-considered to cannibalize your own product. I read about NBC's deal with Hulu and said, "This can't be true." Why would he do that? You're taking money out of your own pocket. You're giving it away for free?

Do you think TV networks have gotten smarter about the way they are dealing with the digital environment?

It's not just Hulu. When Disney made the deal with iTunes, it was also a mess. I saw Bob Iger at NATPE [National Association of Television Program Executives] right after that, and we got into a fight that literally cleared out one end of the room. We had known each other for thirty-five years, and I just couldn't understand it. I said, "What were you thinking making this deal? You're paying Steve Jobs 30 percent off the top so that he can sell his little machines? He should be paying you! What are you doing?" I said, "Look, I understand there are economic forces at work inside Disney, and I understand the Pixar thing, but this is just too much. Hasn't he stolen enough?" It was an insane deal. The logic behind it was to distribute our content in a way that we really don't need it distributed, because if we don't, audiences are going to steal it.

But the pressure to pursue digital opportunities is inevitable for most people. You, on the other hand, are among the few still making a very nice living off of syndication.

Not only have USA and TNT been amazing for us, but *CI*, *SVU*, and *Law & Order* are number one, two, and three in free syndication. The three shows are still on an average of 109 times a week.

You're in such a different universe.

I know. I'm not claiming I have the same problems as writers, but I hate seeing writers get screwed. And the strike screwed them. Most of them probably lost two scripts—$150,000. How are you going to make that back?

But they're not playing in the same ballpark you're playing in. They're playing in a ballpark where digital deals are being made that don't include them.

I understand that, but what I'm saying is there was a reason to go out on strike in the 1950s—to get residuals for syndication reruns. Those were real. Today we still don't know where the money is going to be made on digital.

Appendix
Interview Schedule

Gary Newman, 20th Century Fox Studios, Century City, June 2012

Richard Berger, Sony Pictures Entertainment, Culver City, March 2012

Kelly Summers, Carsey-Wolf Center, Santa Barbara, November 2012

Thomas Gewecke, Warner Bros. Studios, Burbank, April 2013

Mitch Singer, Sony Pictures Home Entertainment, Culver City, June 2012

Gail Berman, BermanBraun, Santa Monica, October 2012

Jordan Levin, Generate, Santa Monica, January 2012

Betsy Scolnik, Paley Center for Media, Beverly Hills, November 2011

Christian Mann, Evil Angel Video, Van Nuys, May 2012

Ted Sarandos, Netflix, Beverly Hills, June 2012

Anders Sjöman, Teleconference, Voddler, Stockholm, October 2012

Scott Frank, Carsey-Wolf Center, Santa Barbara, December 2010

Paris Barclay, *Sons of Anarchy* Production Offices, North Hollywood, May 2012

Felicia D. Henderson, Personal residence, Pasadena, May 2012

Stanton "Larry" Stein, Liner Law, Westwood, June 2012

Patric Verrone, *Futurama* Writers Room, 20th Century Fox Studios, Century City, April 2012

Dick Wolf, Carsey-Wolf Center, Santa Barbara, February 2013

Glossary

À La Carte A pricing model that allows customers to pay cable and satellite companies only for the channels or programs they want to watch. This is opposed to the bundling model, where customers are forced to pay for channel packages designed by cable and satellite providers.

Ancillary Value Revenue derived for media content beyond its initial exhibition. Examples of ancillary value for films include earnings from home video, TV rights, on demand, airlines, and streaming through Internet services.

Back-End Deal A contractual agreement in which eligible parties (often, but not exclusively, above-the-line talent) are entitled to a percentage of a film's or a television show's earnings, usually in lieu of a larger up-front payment.

Bundling A strategy cable providers use that forces audiences to pay for hundreds of channels in order to get access to the handful of channels they actually want. This means having to pay for the most expensive channels, such as ESPN, even if the particular customer is not interested in sports. Bundling can also refer to the packaging of TV, Internet, and mobile phone services by telecommunications companies in order to keep and attract subscribers with the convenience of a single bill and provider.

Cannibalization The erosion of earnings in one window (e.g., domestic theatrical exhibition) when media content is released in other windows (e.g., DVD, digital home video) too quickly. This is a major fear for content companies in the digital era as platforms proliferate.

Cloud Computing The use of remote storage of data and applications over the Internet, allowing consumers to access their content "in the cloud" from any connected computer.

Connected TVs Sometimes referred to as Smart TVs, connected TVs represent a convergence between computers, television technologies, and set-top boxes that allows users to access online content and video streams via their televisions without additional set-top boxes.

Connected Viewing   While specifically referring to multiscreen and multitasking entertainment experiences, this also relates to a larger trend across the media industries to integrate digital technology and socially networked communication with traditional entertainment practices.

Content Distribution Networks/Content Delivery Networks (CDNs)   These are the middlemen between content providers and consumers, and they provide the infrastructure to expedite the delivery of large amounts of data.

Digital Entertainment Content Ecosystem (DECE)   Formed in 2008, this is a consortium of major Hollywood studios, consumer electronics manufacturers and retailers, and digital rights management vendors devoted to establishing standards for the digital distribution of Hollywood content across platforms, vendors, and devices. This coalition is behind UltraViolet, a digital content ownership and management system.

Digital Rights Management (DRM)   A term for access-control technologies that are used by hardware manufacturers, publishers, copyright holders, and individuals to limit the use and sharing of digital content and devices.

Domain Name System (DNS) Blocking   This allows the blocking of specific websites by Internet service providers or by individual users.

Electronic Sell-Through (EST)   A method of distribution whereby consumers pay a one-time fee to download and own a digital media file.

First-Sale Doctrine   A court ruling that limits copyright protection for cultural artifacts to the initial sale. Originally applied to books, it meant that once a book was purchased, the owner could lend, lease, or resell the book at their discretion. The ruling was later extended to music albums and video DVDs. It therefore paved the way for the creation of secondary markets for the resale of media products.

Internet Protocol Television (IPTV)   The distribution of television signals over the Internet rather than through more traditional methods such as cable or satellite.

Internet Service Provider (ISP)   A company (e.g., Comcast or Cox) that owns and manages the wires and cables that deliver broadband into the home or workplace.

License Fee   The cost of acquiring the rights to distribute media content through various windows and platforms. Content owners license film and television shows to multiple services simultaneously but strategize in order to avoid cannibalization.

Linear Television   The daily flow of television programming as scheduled by the broadcast or cable network. VCRs, DVRs, and now connected viewing practices have disrupted this model.

Metrics   Standards of measurement used most often in relation to audience analytics, or the collection of deep and detailed audience data that can illustrate how audiences engage with, respond to, and use media content and services.

Multichannel Video Programming Distributor (MVPD)   A cable, a satellite, or an IPTV service provider offering video programming services, often with a subscription fee.

Multiple Systems Operators (MSOs)   These are companies that own and manage many cable or satellite systems across different communities, such as Time Warner Cable or Comcast. Over 90 percent of the cable business in the United States is controlled by the top-ten MSOs.

Net Neutrality   The principle that ISPs may not discriminate between different kinds of content and applications online, or privilege some over others. Currently the United States does not have net neutrality standards as part of its regulatory policies for broadband Internet.

NetRatings   Nielsen's online audience and consumer-generated media measurement and analysis solutions.

Over-the-Top (OTT)   Delivery of media content or services over an infrastructure that is not under the administrative control of the content or service provider. It often refers to any content service available to consumers on the Internet, allowing them to bypass traditional cable TV or satellite providers. Examples of OTT video services include Netflix, iTunes, Amazon, and Hulu.

Platform   Either a hardware- or software-based infrastructure used to access, save, engage with, and/or manage entertainment content. Examples include iTunes, Netflix, Google, and Hulu, among many others.

Pod Deals   Studio deals with renowned executive producers that are given financial and/or administrative support to develop new TV series. These deals take many forms.

Profit Participation   A contract deal that gives certain individuals (most often above-the-line labor) the rights to a percentage of profits made from the sales of a film or TV program.

Proprietary Service   In contrast to an open-source service, this service cannot be changed or customized by a user outside of the options the service owner makes available. These services (e.g., iTunes) tend to be more reliable but less flexible.

Protect Intellectual Property Act (PIPA)   This was a 2011 bill proposed in the Senate that would have given the U.S. government and copyright holders power to go after and shut down websites that illegally distribute copyrighted material, even those outside of the United States. While the Hollywood studios backed the bill, the tech industry, led by giants like Google, opposed it. Massive online and offline protests in January 2012 forced the bill to be tabled.

Residuals   Payments to directors, writers, and others as contracted when feature films or TV shows are distributed in various windows after their initial release/run.

Secondary Market   The sale of used media products, such as DVDs, CDs, and video games. See *First-Sale Doctrine.*

Stop Online Piracy Act (SOPA)   Similar to the PIPA bill proposed in the Senate, the SOPA was a failed 2011 bill proposed in the U.S. House of Representatives with similar aims of giving the U.S. government and copyright holders tools to block funding to and ultimately shut down websites that illegally host or distribute copyrighted media content. Proponents of the bill, such as the Hollywood studios, argued that it would help fight piracy and protect revenue and jobs in the industry. Information technology (IT) companies like Google opposed the bill, arguing that it threatened free speech and innovation in the IT industry.

Strong Identity   Related to authentication, this involves linking users to a social network, credit card information, or a subscription service that provides a direct connection to their actual identity and demographic information.

Synergy   The development, production, promotion, and sale of a product throughout the various subsidiaries of a media conglomerate so that content can be cross-promoted in various holdings owned by the same conglomerate.

TouchPoints   An audience measurement method tested in the United Kingdom and adopted in the United States in 2010 as USA TouchPoints by the Media Behavior Institute. The method uses a multimedia survey and the integration of multiple data sets to measure cross-channel media consumption, simultaneous non-media daily life activities, the environment of media use, and a user's mood and attitude.

TV Everywhere   A verification system announced in 2009 that allows television service providers to authenticate those who wish to use their IPTV video-on-demand Internet television services as being paying customers of satellite or cable television; it also allows viewers to access some of their subscription services and content on computers or mobile devices.

UltraViolet   A digital rights authentication and cloud-based distribution system that allows consumers of digital home entertainment content to store their material online and then stream and download the purchased content via multiple platforms and devices. UltraViolet was created through the DECE, an alliance that, notably, does not include Disney, Apple, and Amazon.

Unbundling (Channels)   See *À La Carte.*

Upfronts   Convened by television networks each May to sell commercial time to advertisers "up front," or before the season gets under way and before advertising rates are set by actual viewing measurements. This is an opportunity for advertisers to get cheaper rates on surprise hits and for broadcasters to sell inventory based on attractive pilots.

Video on Demand (VOD)   A business model allowing consumers to purchase film and television content from an online or a cable service that they can then stream or download.

Whitelisted   Content that has been deemed safe by security firewalls and allowed to pass through their safeguards.

Windows   Periods of exclusivity for the release of movies and television properties in order to maximize sales and revenue. For example, major feature films are released first to theaters and then distributed sequentially through other venues, such as DVD, VOD, and pay TV.

About the Editors

MICHAEL CURTIN is the Duncan and Suzanne Mellichamp Professor of Global Studies in the Department of Film and Media Studies and Director of the Carsey-Wolf Center's Media Industries Project at University of California, Santa Barbara. His books include *The American Television Industry* (2009); *Reorienting Global Communication: Indian and Chinese Media beyond Borders* (2010); and *Playing to the World's Biggest Audience: The Globalization of Chinese Film and TV* (2007). He is currently at work on *Media Capital: The Cultural Geography of Globalization*. He is co-editor of the *Chinese Journal of Communication* and the British Film Institute's *International Screen Industries* book series.

JENNIFER HOLT is Associate Professor of Film and Media Studies at the University of California, Santa Barbara, and Director of the Carsey-Wolf Center's Media Industries Project. She is the author of *Empires of Entertainment* (2011) and co-editor of *Media Industries: History, Theory, and Method* (2009) and *Connected Viewing: Selling, Streaming, & Sharing Media in the Digital Era* (2014). Her work has appeared in journals and anthologies including *Cinema Journal, Jump Cut, Moving Data,* and *How to Watch Television.* She is also a founding editorial collective member of the *Media Industries* journal.

KEVIN SANSON is the Research Director of the Carsey-Wolf Center's Media Industries Project at the University of California, Santa Barbara, where he also teaches in the Department of Film and Media Studies. His current book project focuses on the spatial dynamics of media production and examines issues of location, labor, and creative identity in emergent media hubs. He is co-editor of *Connected Viewing: Selling, Streaming, & Sharing Media in the Digital Era* (2014). Other writing appears in *In Media Res, Popular Communication, Creative Industries Journal, Sage Television Studies Handbook,* and on the MIP website. Dr. Sanson is also a founding editorial collective member of the *Media Industries* journal.

ABOUT KURT SUTTER

Raised in the suburbs of Central New Jersey, Kurt Sutter spent most of his childhood indoors, avoiding people, three feet from a TV screen. That's where he learned the essentials of storytelling and that extreme violence, if performed by animated, brightly colored characters, could be fun and educational. After graduating from Rutgers University with a BA in Mass Media & Film, Kurt spent several years as an actor in New York City before earning an MFA from Northern Illinois University in Chicago. In 2001, he landed a gig on FX's *The Shield* where he started as a staff writer on the first episode and finished the last two seasons as an executive producer. In 2008, Kurt created the critically acclaimed FX drama series *Sons of Anarchy*. Now entering its seventh and final season, *SOA* is the most successful show in the history of the network. Sutter and his wife, Katey Sagal, live in Los Angeles with their three children, Sarah, Jackson, and Esme.

Index